RACE AND SPORT IN CANADA

RACE AND SPORT IN CANADA

Intersecting Inequalities

Edited by
Janelle Joseph, Simon Darnell, and Yuka Nakamura

Canadian Scholars' Press Inc.
Toronto

Race and Sport in Canada: Intersecting Inequalities
edited by Janelle Joseph, Simon Darnell, and Yuka Nakamura

First published in 2012 by
Canadian Scholars' Press Inc.
180 Bloor Street West, Suite 801
Toronto, Ontario
M5S 2V6

www.cspi.org

Copyright © 2012 Janelle Joseph, Simon Darnell, and Yuka Nakamura, the contributing authors, and Canadian Scholars' Press Inc. All rights reserved. No part of this publication may be photocopied, reproduced, stored in a retrieval system, or transmitted, in any form or by any means, electronic, mechanical, or otherwise, without the written permission of Canadian Scholars' Press Inc., except for brief passages quoted for review purposes. In the case of photocopying, a licence may be obtained from Access Copyright: One Yonge Street, Suite 1900, Toronto, Ontario, M5E 1E5, (416) 868-1620, fax (416) 868-1621, toll-free 1-800-893-5777, www.accesscopyright.ca.

Every reasonable effort has been made to identify copyright holders. CSPI would be pleased to have any errors or omissions brought to its attention.

Canadian Scholars' Press Inc. gratefully acknowledges financial support for our publishing activities from the Government of Canada through the Canada Book Fund (CBF).

Library and Archives Canada Cataloguing in Publication

Race and sport in Canada : intersecting inequalities / edited by
Janelle Joseph, Simon Darnell, and Yuka Nakamura.

Includes bibliographical references and index.
Issued also in electronic formats.
ISBN 978-1-55130-414-4

1. Racism in sports--Canada. 2. Minorities in sports--Canada. 3. Sports--Social aspects--Canada. I. Joseph, Janelle, 1978- II. Darnell, Simon C III. Nakamura, Yuka, 1976-

GV706.32.R33 2012   796.089   C2012-904468-7

Text design by Colleen Wormald
Cover design by Em Dash Design
Cover image © iStockphoto/Chris Bulzacki

12 13 14 15 16   5 4 3 2 1

Printed and bound in Canada by Webcom.

Canadä

For Sussex

Table of Contents

Preface
Thinking Race in Canada: What the Critique of Race and Racism in Sport Brings to Anti-racism Studies
Rinaldo Walcott ix

Introduction
The Intractability of Race in Canadian Sport
Janelle Joseph, Simon Darnell, and Yuka Nakamura 1

PART ONE: HISTORICAL APPROACHES TO THE STUDY OF RACE AND SPORT IN CANADA

Chapter 1
Sport and the Canadian Immigrant: Physical Expressions of Cultural Identity within a Dominant Culture, 1896–1945
Russell Field 29

Chapter 2
Football and "Tolerance": Black Football Players in 20th-Century Canada
John Valentine and Simon C. Darnell 57

Chapter 3
Hockey and the Reproduction of Colonialism in Canada
Andreas Krebs 81

Chapter 4
New Racism and Old Stereotypes in the National Hockey League: The "Stacking" of Aboriginal Players into the Role of Enforcer
John Valentine 107

PART TWO: CANADIAN IMMIGRATION AND THE STUDY OF RACE AND SPORT

Chapter 5
Gender, Immigration, and Physical Activity: The Experiences of Chinese Immigrant Women
Xin Huang, Wendy Frisby, and Lucie Thibault 139

Chapter 6
Understanding Structural Barriers in Amateur Sport and the Participation of Immigrants in Atlantic Canada
Lori A. Livingston and Susan Tirone 165

PART THREE: THE STUDY OF RACE AND SPORT BEYOND CANADA'S BORDERS

Chapter 7
Managing Whiteness in Sport for Development and Peace Internships
Simon C. Darnell 187

Chapter 8
Playing in Chinatown: A Critical Discussion of the Nation/Sport/Citizen Triad
Yuka Nakamura 213

Chapter 9
An Intersectional Analysis of Black Sporting Masculinities
Janelle Joseph 237

Chapter 10
Athletic Aspirations: NCAA Scholarships and Canadian Athletes
Sandy Wells 265

Contributors 291

Index 295

PREFACE

Thinking Race in Canada: What the Critique of Race and Racism in Sport Brings to Anti-racism Studies

RINALDO WALCOTT

Ontario Institute for Studies in Education, University of Toronto

As I write this preface, Canada's most decorated figure skater has recently been in the news for claiming a lack of support for the sport. Most importantly, Patrick Chan suggests a lack of personal support, which he claims he would receive in China, where figure skaters are respected. Thus, he reclaims or asserts his Chinese heritage while maintaining that the sacrifices necessary to be at the top in world figure skating were too much for him and his family in Canada.[1] Chan's critique clearly stung. The response was swift and suggestions that he was ungrateful were quickly forthcoming from sporting corners. What further infuriated hegemonic Canada was that Patrick Chan suggested that skating for China might have been a better and more sensible option in the long run. What was also curious about the response to Chan's remarks was Skate Canada's suggestion that Chan was only honouring his Chinese heritage. Chan later recanted some of his comments, explaining that he was "merely daydreaming" about a way to minimize his parents' burdens.[2]

From my vantage point, it seems clear that Chan—who has yet to become a household name despite his feats on the podia and, more particularly, his skill and athleticism at landing quadruple toe loops and triple axles—was launching a profound critique of race, racism, and who can ultimately be a national hero in Canada. It is clear that Chan's talents make him one of the best Canadian, if not global, figure skaters of all time. That Skate Canada chose to interpret Chan's remarks as concerned only with heritage was, in part, their attempt to use a recognizable Canadian discourse that might be understood as embedded in Canadian multiculturalism to deny the more profound elements of Chan's critique.

Race and Sport in Canada: Intersecting Inequalities is an ambitious project that helps to understand why Chan might daydream of a sporting career in another nation. The objectives of the book have been more than achieved by the editors and contributors, and readers will able to use this text to develop anti-racist research and praxis. To question race and racism in Canada, Canadian public discourse, and Canadian studies (broadly defined) remains a difficult project of both theory and empiricism. Race and racism are slippery signifiers and practices everywhere, but in the Canadian realm, race and racism, at least in discourse, refuse to bend to sustained, ongoing, and thorough critique. It often seems as if each intervention claims newness. This collection does not. Rather, it builds and extends the established conversations in far-reaching ways.

This book is about much more than sport, which is not an attempt to undermine the profound impact this book should have on the sociology of sport. Instead it means that the authors' contributions in this work deploy a significant and important conceptual and decidedly political shift in thinking about race beyond the Black/White paradigm in sport studies in Canada. Also, this collection of chapters exceeds the limits of race studies in Canada by opening the field to the challenges, complexities, and far-reaching implications of national sporting cultures.

If a scholarly critique of sport in Canada might mean anything for how we think about our collective lives in Canada, it must begin with a critique of colonialism. These chapters astutely point to the ways in which such a critique is urgently necessary and makes more present, and sustained, the critique of claims to have moved beyond racism to multicultural contentment. That the editors turn to Himani Bannerji and Sunera Thobani and their ideas of exaltation and intersectional analyses is crucially important for understanding the ways in which the multiculturalism of the Canadian state, Whiteness, and patriarchy, or, put more crudely, Eurocentrism, remain handmaidens of the Canadian nation-state formation. But what is truly impressive and important about these chapters is that they do not stop there. Instead they further explore the discourse of "Whiteness" and provide both a critique and the evidence of how sporting institutions work in tandem with other state institutions and wider public discourses to reproduce the violent fiction of the White nation-state, a fiction fully conceived in recent announcements to ban women from taking the oath of citizenship while wearing the veil.[3] Some European countries have already made their ban more encompassing, but the creep of contemporary Canadian racism and Islamaphobia is now apparent. These chapters can help us make sense of such actions in Canada through the ways in which sport both highlights and conceals Canada's continuing Eurocentric, violent, and exclusionary origins.

In this regard Canada is not very different from France, and Britain where, to differing degrees, statesmen and stateswomen have declared multiculturalism a failure. Zidane's head butt embarrassed France, Ben Johnson's positive drug test shamed Canada, and Luis Suarez's on-field racial abuse complicates the meaning of the Liverpool team and English soccer more generally for spectators. In each instance sport compels us to think about the ways in which race, nation, and citizenship conjoin to produce forms of prejudice and violence to which non-White bodies must be constantly alert, and yet the rhetoric of sport also calls for thinking about the body that exceeds the national limits. As the chapters in this book more than amply demonstrate, sport is deeply implicated, not just in the national story, but also in producing the nation itself. Thus, sport represents significant ground for studying how nation, race, citizenship, and belonging are put together to make lives (un)livable in our times.

In multicultural Canada, sport stories are used to recall the halcyon days of Jackie Robinson's time in Montreal as the fiction of Canada's anti-racist past and to reveal this nation as radically different from the U.S. Yet, to use the Jackie Robinson story as a fiction simultaneously denies how Black-Canadian boxers, runners, and Black Canadians in general in Montreal, in Quebec, and across the country remained effectively non-citizens during Robinson's sojourn and asks a different set of questions about the work the Robinson story does for Canada. *Race and Sport in Canada* answers those questions for us and demonstrates how the fiction of that moment continues to shape sporting life in Canada. The chapters not only engage state multiculturalism but also spill over into vernacular multiculturalism, finding communities, leagues, and tournaments operating both within and beyond the contemporary arrangements of the borders of the nation-state of Canada. Such vernacular multiculturalism draws on state multiculturalism to make life livable in the context of increasing new racisms.

Finally, this book is not merely a critique of race and racism in sport in Canada. This book also offers a profound critique of anti-racism studies in Canada. The critique is not hostile, however. The authors all draw on some of the most progressive and indeed challenging anti-racism scholarship to provide some of the most important analyses of the work of sport, race, and racism in Canada. But what these authors also provide are the blind spots of anti-racism scholarship (when sport is not considered). Until this intervention, the critiques of nation, race, racism, and colonialism have not taken up sport, but clearly need to take seriously how sport, sporting lives, and sporting cultures contribute to a very specific racialization of Canada. Indeed, as the discourse of settler colonialism gathers steam in the academy and in non-Native activist circles, alongside the ways in which many a "race study" has used hockey as a trope for Whiteness in Canada, this book asks us to think clearly and sustainably about how hockey, baseball, football, cricket, and even Chinese nine-man volleyball and Brazilian *capoeira* can provide a deep critique of the production of the Canadian nation-state as an ongoing project of racial injustice and ultimately genocide. Sport, then, has something to say about the Truth and Reconciliation Commission and its outcomes. It also has something to say about how we might imagine organizing our futures while living together differently.

Toronto, 2011

Notes

1. CTV News.ca Staff (December 8, 2011). "Canadians Not Supporting Figure Skaters, Patrick Chan Says." Retrieved from http://edmonton.ctv.ca/servlet/an/local/CTVNews/20111208/canada-skater-patrick-chan-feels-unappreciated-111208/20111208/?hub=Edmonton Home
2. P.J. Kwong (December 8, 2011). "Exclusive: Patrick Chan Explains Canada Comments." Retrieved from http://www.cbc.ca/sports/figureskating/opinion/2011/12/exclusive-patrick-chan-explains-his-comments-about-canada.html
3. David Ljunggren (December 12, 2011). "Government Bans Veils during Citizenship Ceremonies." Retrieved from http://ca.reuters.com/article/domesticNews/idCATRE7BB1XY20111212

INTRODUCTION
The Intractability of Race in Canadian Sport
JANELLE JOSEPH, SIMON DARNELL, AND YUKA NAKAMURA

Race, nationality, and social inequality in Canada are materially and discursively connected. Despite claims of idyllic multiculturalism, tensions and inconsistencies remain between the benign, tolerant, and celebratory approach to difference in Canada and the privileging, centring, and "exalting" (Thobani, 2007) of dominant groups through race and its intersections with gender, class, sexuality, and ability. While these relations of power are clearly socially constructed, together they organize and constitute opportunities, life chances, and claims to citizenship in Canada.

For the purposes of this collection, we employ the term "race" to reference how particular people, bodies, and skin colours are constitutive and revelatory of relations of power, privilege, and conflict (Hylton, 2009; Omi & Winant, 2002). This theoretical conception of race is purposefully broad and inclusive of many social dimensions of identity and power precisely because the organization and mobilization of race in Canadian culture is political and arbitrary. Indeed, to invoke the term "race" is to include or make reference to ethnicity, skin colour, religion, language, customs, indigeneity, and cultural habits. Given this complexity, the term "race" is useful to us not for its ability to definitively ascertain behaviour or identity in relation to skin colour or ethnicity, but rather as a means to draw attention to privilege and inequality as constituted through intersecting social hierarchies. We submit that from this point of view, race remains a central element of the Canadian cultural experience even though Canada is regularly presumed to be a place where racism and racial stereotypes no longer exist.

Despite the centrality of race in Canadian life, to date, and with significant exceptions, little research has explicitly attended to the role and place of sport and physical cultures within Canadian racial politics. Likewise, despite the rigorous exploration of the connections between race, racism, and sport in the United States and the United Kingdom, studies of sport in Canada remain largely devoid of conversations about race, leaving scholars to "import" analyses from other national and cultural terrains. In response to these gaps, the goal of *Race and Sport in Canada: Intersecting Inequalities* is to describe, historicize, critique, and ultimately challenge dominant articulations of race within a variety of Canadian sport and physical activity settings, and to confront the ways in which race and its intersections within Canadian sport construct and sustain hierarchies and inequalities more broadly. Bannerji's (2000) imperative to engage strategically with the racialized, classed, and patriarchal foundations of Canadian culture guides this text. We argue for the critical study of race within Canadian sport and physical cultures as a way to refute notions of Canada as "colour-blind" or "race-less."

This approach is based on two foundations. First, we view sport cultures as sites where race, racism, and racial hierarchies are constructed and maintained, yet simultaneously obscured and normalized. This culturally political dimension of sport was made evident in C.L.R. James's (1963) foundational text, *Beyond a Boundary*, in which he illustrated how efforts to name a Black captain of the West Indian cricket team paralleled the pursuit of political independence for the territories of the West Indies. We agree with

INTRODUCTION: THE INTRACTABILITY OF RACE IN CANADIAN SPORT

James's (1963) general observation that "[sport] reflects tendencies in the national life" (1963, p. 214), and that sport plays a key role in constructing the nation and determining national belonging. In Canada, for example, at a time when the "War on Terror" and Canadian racial politics have denied Muslims legitimate claims to rights and citizenship (see Razack, 2008) and constructed Canadian identity as that which "confronts" or "saves" Islam (Thobani, 2010), Toronto Maple Leaf hockey player Nazem Kadri has stated that he has never been confronted about his Lebanese ethnicity and Muslim religion (*Globe and Mail*, 2010). It is reasonable to assert that hockey has offered Kadri entrée into Canadian national belonging, but in ways that obscure broader forms of racism, position Canadian sport as "race-less," and perpetuate myths of Canada's egalitarian racial past and present. We situate this collection against such narratives.

Second, the study of sport offers an opportunity to resist, rethink, and reimagine notions of race in Canada and what it means to be Canadian. There are many instances in which athletes have used sport as a site to resist racism and draw attention to racial inequities. The story of U.S. sprinters Tommie Smith and John Carlos raising closed fists on the medal podium at the 1968 Olympics is one oft-cited example. While few Canadian examples hold such iconic resonance as Smith and Carlos, Canadian athletes of colour have asserted their identity, spoken out against racism, and engaged in political activism and resistance. In 1984, kayaker Alwyn Morris became the first (and still the only) Canadian Aboriginal athlete to win an Olympic gold medal. He held aloft an eagle feather during the medal ceremony. Given the relative invisibility of Aboriginal peoples in Canada, Morris explained, "I am a Mohawk person, and I'm aboriginal in Canada and it was important for me to be self identified [as Mohawk and Aboriginal] in order to share that with the other part of who I am" (Meissner, 2009). More pointedly, Georges Laraque, one of the first Black hockey players from French Canada to play in the National Hockey League, has spoken out about racism in Canada, recounting stories of his youth hockey career when opposing players called him "nigger" and told him hockey was not his sport (Laraque, 2011). Laraque's descriptions of hockey show the game to be a site where racism can be experienced and where resistance may be mobilized. In this way, it is not enough for scholars of sport to focus only on how race is constructed in sport, but there is also a need to propose alternative visions. While not all of the chapters in this text explicitly offer examples of resistance, they all highlight and deconstruct the normativity of racial privilege, and therefore contribute to resistance.

Based on these foundations, the following chapters employ intersectional analyses of race and social relations of power to investigate and deconstruct racial privilege. In turn, the text explores the historical production of the nation-space, the barriers that racial minorities face in accessing mainstream resources, and the importance of race to inter-, trans-, and supranationalisms. Sport and physical cultures in Canada, from recreation and grassroots through to elite and professional levels, are all considered. The chapters illustrate the trauma and systemic injustices of racism in sport and physical cultures, both historical and contemporary, and connect these experiences to the broader social construction of life in Canada.

The remainder of this introductory chapter, then, is divided into four sections. First, we provide an overview of studies of race in Canada, paying specific attention to critical multiculturalism and studies of Whiteness. We then explore the study of race in sport, drawing on relevant insights from U.S. and U.K. national contexts. This organization of the literature is not intended to create a false division between "race scholars" and "sport scholars who study race" but rather to offer a heuristic device that illustrates the need for the ongoing sociological study of race *and* sport in Canada. The third section attends directly to this topic, paying close attention to the few studies that have taken up the issue of race and racism in Canadian sport settings directly, and highlighting the considerable gaps that remain. The chapter concludes with an overview of subsequent chapters and thoughts on the importance of studying race and sport in Canada.

Race in Canada

While the notion of race as an essential or foundational biological construct has been largely debunked, race continues to define social relations in Canada. In response, a critical mass of scholarship has illustrated the simultaneous centrality and contestability of race in the organization and maintenance of Canadian society and culture. In general, there are two approaches to the study of race in Canada: one that celebrates and/or critiques multiculturalism, and another that examines Whiteness and relations of racial dominance. These categories overlap in that Whiteness can be understood as the norm against which multiculturalism operates; still, for the purposes of this discussion, we explore them each in turn.

Those who study multiculturalism primarily use demographic, geographic, and socio-psychological approaches to document the experiences of ethnic, racial, linguistic, and religious minorities; to explore the extent to which groups thrive, retain their identities and meaningful practices and integrate into the dominant culture; and to identify the difficulties of, and strategies for, coping with and resisting economic, political, and social discrimination and inequities (e.g., Abu Laban, 1983; Dei, Mazzuca, McIsaac & Zine, 1997; Dallaire, 2003; Driedger & Halli, 2000; Fleras & Elliott, 2002; Fong & Ooka, 2006; Halli & Driedger, 1999; Henry, 1994; Henry & Tator, 2002; James, 2001, 2003, 2005; Lee & Boyd, 2007; Li, 2003a, 2003b, 2005; Mackey, 2002; Magee, Fong & Wilkes 2007; Martynowich, 1991; Mensah, 2010; Reitz, 2001a, 2001b; Reitz & Breton, 1994; Salaff, Greve & Xu, 2002; Teo, 2007; Walcott, 2003; Wallis & Fleras, 2009, among others).

Walcott's (2000, 2003) analysis of Canadian recording artist Maestro Fresh Wes is a good example of this approach. Walcott shows how musical Blackness is often relegated to the exterior of Canadian national narratives and understood to be something Other than fundamentally or quintessentially Canadian. By illustrating how Black Canadians are forced to affiliate "outernationally" (e.g.,

Wes had to relocate to the U.S. to build and garner support for his career in rap music, yet continually attempted to reclaim the nation as exemplified by his album *Naaah, Dis Kid* Can't *Be from Canada?!!*), Walcott shows that understandings of race in Canada must take into account domestic relationships as well as diasporic and transnational affiliations (Walcott, 2003, p. 42). His analysis also holds purchase for studies of sport as it mirrors the expulsion of sporting Blackness from Canada as seen in the media discourses regarding Ben Johnson and his fall from celebrated *Canadian* sprinter to disgraced *Jamaican* immigrant after testing positive for anabolic steroid use at the 1988 Olympic Games in Seoul (Jackson, 1998; Jackson & Ponic, 2001). These analyses challenge the legitimacy of the discourse of multiculturalism.

Canada enjoys a reputation for creating a "cultural mosaic" that recognizes "the importance of preserving and enhancing the multicultural heritage of Canadians ... [and] the diversity of Canadians as regards race, national or ethnic origin, color and religion as a fundamental characteristic of Canadian society" (Canadian Multiculturalism Act, 1988). While multiculturalism ostensibly celebrates difference, it also constructs racialized Canadians as "'Other' Canadians—people with a 'heritage' from elsewhere and whose 'foreign' cultural values and practices remain static and based on their past experiences in other countries" (James, 2001, p. 171). Thus, multiculturalism remains complex in practice, able to serve both equitable and racist purposes. Multiculturalism can drive programs and initiatives in ways that support equity (Fleras & Kunz, 2001) by promoting language, dance, clothing, and the foods of various ethnic communities, and offering an "entry point into an oppositional, or at least alternative way of contesting the dominant culture and making participatory space for the nation's others" (Bannerji, 2000, p. 18). However, this celebratory multiculturalism can also be co-optive and pacifying (San Juan Jr., 2000) as it "accommodates" and "tolerates" difference, but depoliticizes privilege and inequality (Fleras & Kunz, 2001). Furthermore, as Bannerji states, "it is forgotten that these officially multicultural ethnicities, so embraced or rejected, are themselves the constructs of colonial—Orientalist and racist—discourses" (2000, p. 9).

For many Canadians, "acceptance" of racial minorities is bound by the rules of established institutions (i.e., legal, economic, political, etc.) that tend to represent the views of the dominant cultural group (James, 2003). Multiculturalism as an ideology can be understood to provide a platform to secure the position of dominant groups; in response, critical scholarship seeks "to prod, embarrass, and provoke central policy structures by holding them accountable" (Fleras & Kunz, 2001, p. 19).

The second group of scholars concerned with race in Canada takes Whiteness as its point of entry, particularly the material and discursive intersections between racism and White supremacy, and the antecedents and impact of racial violence and other forms of discrimination in Canadian society (e.g., Bannerji, 2000; Fusco, 2005; Heron, 2007; Mackey, 2002; Razack, 1998, 2001, 2002, 2004, 2008; Razack, Smith & Thobani, 2010; Thobani, 2007). Whiteness does not refer directly to White people but rather to the myriad social and political processes by which hierarchies and privileges are codified and normalized along lines of race (Frankenberg, 1993). In countries such as Canada, these hierarchies secure White bodies and cultures as the standard against which Others are measured. The concept of Whiteness is useful because it allows for the politicization of race and the description of hierarchies. The theoretical and material focus can be broadened from analyses of explicit racisms (such as the use of racial epithets or unapologetic anti-immigrant, White supremacy movements) to include the more mundane and opaque effects of racialization and racial privileging. Identifying and deconstructing these processes of White privilege is particularly important for this collection of chapters, given continued denials of racism in sport (Hylton, 2009).

Studies of Whiteness also explore the reasons why many (White) Canadians feel threatened by racial diversity, and the concomitant processes of racialization that maintain the dominant and Eurocentric Canadian national imaginary. Thobani's (2007) notion of "exaltation" is particularly useful here, in which the "story of Canada" describes a nation built by noble settlers and founded upon modern values of fairness and tolerance. The colonization of Aboriginal populations and stewardship of the Canadian territory—both historical and contemporary—construct Whiteness as naturally dominant and responsible over Others (Mackey, 2002). This colonization-as-exaltation is an ongoing project, given that both the foundations of the exalted subject *and* the Canadian nation are unstable and require constant (re)disciplining (Thobani, 2007).

Key to theorizing Whiteness, then, and of central importance in this text, is the ways in which race is (only) intelligible through its co-constitution with other social hierarchies, such as gender, class, sexuality, and ability (Bannerji, 2000; Jiwani, 2010; Razack, 1998; Thobani, 2007). Systems of domination mutually constitute one another and must be traced in historically and contextually specific ways. For example, Jiwani (2010) has illustrated that the construction and political mobilization of Islam and Muslims as a threat to Canadian culture rely upon notions of gender and sexuality as they *interlock* with race. The veiled Muslim woman, deemed repressed by her culture through the lens of liberal feminism while simultaneously fetishized by dominant masculinity, comes to stand as evidence of the normality and superiority of Whiteness in Canada. This knowledge, in turn, justifies political tools of dominance, notably the 2007 Hérouxville Code of Behaviour (*Les Normes de Vie*) in Hérouxville, Quebec, which declared, among other things, that residents could not cover their faces, except on Halloween. Such proclamations of dominance and responses to the "threat" posed by racialized people can *only* be constructed and secured through processes by which race interlocks with other markers of dominance.

In sum, the dominant Canadian culture normalizes, naturalizes, and privileges the experiences and understandings of the White majority while constructing racial difference itself as problematic, if not pathological. We suggest that sport and physical culture offers an important site at which to understand and challenge White privilege and supremacy, and its effects on cultural Others. For example, Razack's (2002, p. 137) investigation of the murder of Pamela George, an Aboriginal mother of two, by two middle-class, White male athletes in Saskatchewan, exposed sporting cultures that valorize "violence and sexual aggression, and a hatred of the softness that is female, [as] positive signs of masculinity." While she acknowledges that the sport activities of the two men helped to "cement white settler identity" (2002, p. 139), Razack refers readers to a footnote in which she points to the limited work that considers race in the making of contemporary White male athletes in Canada. This book is designed to contribute toward filling these gaps in the study of race and racism in Canada.

Race in Sport

Constructions of race are co-constitutive with modern sport. As foundational sport sociologist Harry Edwards (1969) argued, sport actively produces and reproduces racism by institutionalizing and normalizing hierarchies and the inequitable distribution of resources. In a similar vein, Carrington (2010, p. 3) has noted the role of sport, both historical and contemporary, in the shaping of racial discourse:

> [S]port, as a highly regulated and embodied cultural practice, has, from its manifestation as a modern social institution during the high-period of European imperialist expansionism, played a central role in popularizing notions of absolute biological difference while also providing an important arena for forms of cultural resistance against white racism.

In response to "sport's assumed innocence" as an apolitical space, "removed from everyday concerns of power, inequality, struggle and ideology" (Carrington, 2010, p. 4), it is crucial to expand our understandings of, and learn to resist, the racist assumptions that are grounded in, and affirmed through, sport. Carrington and McDonald (2001) and, more recently, Hylton (2005, 2009, 2010) have examined the opaque and ubiquitous salience of race for ethnic minority, as well as majority groups, within sport and leisure. While their work focuses on the post-colonial U.K. context, and particularly British rugby, cricket, and football, we recognize their critique of sport-focused research in which issues of race and racism have been doggedly peripheral.

There are, of course, important exceptions to this marginal status of race in sport research. Since the early 1990s a growing body of sport scholarship has moved toward the type of intersectional analyses argued for in this collection in ways that reveal the multiplicities of how race is lived through sport culture (see Birrell & Cole, 1994; Douglas, 2005; Jamieson, 1998; McDonald, 2002). A notable example is Thangaraj's (2010) ethnography of North American Indo-Pak basketball leagues in which he elucidates the intersections of South Asian identity and nationalism via prisms of masculinity and heteronormativity. Thangaraj argues that the "South Asian American-ness" performed by Americans and Canadians on basketball courts in Atlanta and Chicago "contains the paradox of featuring subversive elements as it concurrently reinforces other racial, gendered, classed and sexual hierarchies" (p. 373). South Asian players' gestures, styles, and bodily movements signal Black masculine aesthetics and thereby assert a "politics of difference" from mainstream U.S. culture. Yet, the religious iconography they ink on their bodies is significant in its representation of an anti-Black, anti-secular, and therefore anti-American identity. At the same time, American assimilation is celebrated through adoption of basketball in opposition to their cricket-playing South-Asian peers. This work shows the complexities of intersecting identities and the impossibility of understanding race without attending to gender, religion, and nationality among other social categories.

Sport studies have also taken up the analysis of Whiteness in recent years to analyze the role of sport in the construction of White normativity and privilege, although King (2005) reminds us that critical sport studies has been concerned with and challenged Whiteness in sport for at least 40 years. This kind of scholarship has highlighted the complicity, or even political utility, of sport in (re)centring White ethnicity as normative within settler societies (e.g., Cosgrove & Bruce, 2005; Millington et al., 2008). In turn, violence (physical and symbolic) directed at athletes of colour has been shown to assert sport as the dominion of Whiteness or, at the least, to construct a measure of "symbolic inclusion" for racialized athletes that masks the institutional discrimination and reproduction through sport of racism and racial hierarchies (Douglas, 2005). Sport, therefore, offers an opportunity to reassert and reclaim the prestige and dominance of White masculinity that, while undeniably still intact in places such as corporate boardrooms, has purportedly declined in comparison to the success of Black athletes (Brayton, 2005; Cooley, 2010; Kusz, 2001). In this way, sport cultures can denigrate the life experiences of people of colour or Aboriginal populations by privileging Whiteness and reifying or justifying its position in contemporary racial hierarchies.

Race in Sport in Canada

For those interested in the issues discussed above, but in the context of Canadian sport cultures, sources from the U.K. and the U.S. have proved invaluable, though always less than satisfying. Indeed, in our efforts to teach courses on issues of race and multiculturalism in Canadian sport, we have had to rely on a limited number of resources. Texts such as *Who da man?* (Abdel-Shehid, 2005), *Race in Play* (James, 2005), *Black Ice* (Fosty & Fosty, 2004), and *A Fly in a Pail of Milk* (Carnegie, 1997) are definitive but devoted primarily to Black male athletes as the archetype for sport and race relations in Canada. Several book chapters and articles (Abdel-Shehid, 2000, 2003; Harris, 2003; Jackson, 1998, 2004; Wilson, 1997, 1999) have also discussed Black-Canadian men in sprinting, hockey, and basketball. Wilson (1997), for example, forcefully argued that media coverage of Black NBA basketball players in Canada tends to relegate these athletes into a binary of "Good Blacks" or "Bad Blacks," ostensibly based on choices they make, but in ways that eschew the broader political and institutional operations of race and racism. Studies like this expose the omnipresence and invisibility of White supremacy in Canada; at the same time, the novelty of this research and the overemphasis on Black athletes in the literature generally potentially conflate Blackness with race.

There is also important literature addressing Aboriginal-Canadian sporting cultures and experiences. Paraschak (1990, 1991, 1997, 1998, 2007), Forsyth (2007a, 2007b), Heine and Forsyth (2008), and Forsyth and Wamsley (2006) have been in the vanguard of studying the intersections among gender, race, Aboriginal communities, and sport. They have connected Aboriginal sporting practices, traditional games, and cultural events to heritage reclamation, assertions of self-determination, and resistance against (but also reinforcement of) sexism, racism, colonialism, class oppression, and cultural suppression. This work shows that mobilizing, organizing, and structuring sport and physical activity by and for Aboriginal Canadians are intimately connected to identity and a "practical consciousness" within the dominant White settler society (Paraschak, 1997, p. 16).

While the insights of these studies are crucial, a paucity of research on sport and other ethnic minority populations in Canada remains; only a few studies provide a counter-story of sport and athletes within minority cultural groups, such as Chinese Canadians (Millington et al., 2008), Muslim Canadians (Nakamura, 2002), Caribbean Canadians (Joseph, 2011), and French Canadians (Dallaire, 2003). Therefore, the subject of race and sport in Canada continues to be under-addressed and under-analyzed. This book addresses these gaps by grappling with issues of value and power over Others, exploring intersections of race with other social and geographical axes of identity, decentring and exposing Whiteness, and attending to issues of social justice in sport in Canada.

An Overview of the Book

The collection of chapters is divided into three sections, with the first taking an historical approach to the study of race and sport. In Chapter 1, Russell Field makes an intervention into Canadian sport history, which has been slow to fully elucidate the experiences of Canadians other than the colonizing English and French groups. Through an historical survey of 20th-century Canadian sport, he explores the clubs and teams that emerged out of vibrant ethnic enclaves and social organizations as immigrants struggled to retain their own sporting practices. At times, these immigrant groups managed to introduce new sports to the Canadian context that have since become mainstream. Field balances this discussion with an analysis of how some immigrants succumbed to pressures to assimilate, particularly within Canadian public and religious sport institutions.

In Chapter 2, John Valentine and Simon Darnell examine 20th-century Canadian football and the media narratives surrounding Black-American players in the Canadian game. This period is of particular importance given the popular notion of Canadian football as a bastion of racial tolerance in comparison to the racial segregation of the United States. Using a variety of primary and secondary sources, Valentine and Darnell suggest that there were greater opportunities in Canada than in the U.S. for Black men to play football. However, many of these players spoke out about racism in Canada in ways that challenged the normativity of Whiteness. Given these accounts, it would be a mistake to suggest that Blackness was seen as legitimately "Canadian" in and through the game of football, or to characterize Canada and

Canadian sport culture in the 20th century as essentially enlightened or colour-blind.

In a similar vein, Andreas Krebs employs an historical analysis of colonialism, as well as contemporary processes of social, political, and spatial colonization, to examine the ways in which the organization, marketing, media coverage, commercialization, and consumption practices of hockey in Canada privilege the dominant racial group. Using an eclectic mix of methods and sources, Krebs explores how nationalism, masculinity, sexual dominance, and codes of race regularly coalesce in and through hockey to perpetuate the notion of Canada as a quintessentially White country. Krebs's analysis of this "Whitestream" draws critical attention to the paradoxical relationships of power at the intersection of race, sport, and nation that "bind" the country through hockey by excluding people of colour and those who do not conform to dominant masculinity. His chapter shows hockey to be inextricably linked to how Canada is defined in racialized terms.

In the fourth chapter, John Valentine explores the notion of stacking, or the influence of race on an athlete's position within team sports, to examine the place of Aboriginal hockey players throughout the history of the National Hockey League (NHL). Tracing the roles played by Aboriginal hockey players in the NHL from the mid-1970s to 2010, Valentine offers some theories to explain the stacking of Aboriginals into the role of enforcer (a one-dimensional player who does little more than fight), including race-based assumptions of hockey coaches, racial discrimination, self-selection, acts of resistance among Aboriginal players themselves, as well as the enduring racist stereotypes they faced, such as that of the *noble savage*. Valentine shows the culture of professional hockey to be far from egalitarian—and even fundamentally racist—in its treatment of Aboriginal players.

The second section of the text focuses specifically on Canadian immigration and experiences of sport and physical activity on Canada's West and East coasts, respectively. In Chapter 5, Xin Huang, Wendy Frisby, and Lucie Thibault situate Chinese immigrants to

British Columbia within the broader history of Chinese immigration to Canada through a discussion of gender, multiculturalism, and physical activity. They compare political, cultural, and gendered systems in China and Canada in order to highlight: (1) the important role of physical activity in the lives of Chinese immigrant women in adjusting to a "Canadian way of life" and reducing social isolation, and (2) the structural barriers women face, including language, social mobility, changes in family structure, and differential access. Their analysis reveals that issues faced by middle-aged women with child-care responsibilities are specific, and that race, social class, and culture compound barriers to participation in physical activity in ways rarely understood by policy-makers.

In the sixth chapter, Susan Tirone and Lori Livingston examine the structural barriers to sport participation that immigrants arriving in Atlantic Canada face. The authors argue that although administrators of local sport are interested in facilitating the involvement of new Canadians, they often do not know how to ensure access for those who identify with minority ethnic cultures, and/or those who lack racial and class privileges. The authors conceptualize this as a "wicked" problem, one that is difficult or impossible to solve because of incomplete, contradictory, and changing requirements. Both chapters in this section attest to the role that sport policy-makers can play in enhancing and expanding sport participation for immigrants and racial minorities and in challenging the racial privilege that structures opportunities for participation in sport and physical activity in Canada.

The third and final section builds on the previous two, but recognizes that race and racism in Canada cannot be isolated from global processes and acknowledges inter-, trans-, and supranational dimensions of racialized sporting experiences. In Chapter 7, Simon Darnell explores the mobilization of sport to meet international development goals, which is often referred to as sport for development and peace (SDP). He focuses on the volunteer experiences of Canadians who travelled to the Global South to work as interns with Commonwealth Games Canada's International

Development through Sport program. Darnell illustrates that the construction and experiences of race, racial hierarchies, and intersecting inequalities amidst the discourses and spaces of SDP were central to volunteer experiences, but that interns tended to "manage" Whiteness as part of their work, more so than to challenge racism. As a result, the transnational dominance of Whiteness, as an international and domestic norm, was retained and even further secured through SDP.

Yuka Nakamura provides a critical discussion of the nation/sport/citizen triad in Chapter 8 by considering the meanings of Chinatowns and a case study of the 65th North American Chinese Invitational Volleyball Tournament (NACIVT). By exploring Chinatowns in Canada and the U.S. where the NACIVT is played, she demonstrates how Chinatown is a construct that reproduces the effects of Canada as a White settler society, and of Chinese people and Chinatown as outside of the nation. At the same time, Chinatown is claimed as home in a way that provides a resistive counter-story to the assumption that home is the place from where one immigrated. As a result, sport participation in these spaces simultaneously destabilizes racialized understandings of the nation/sport/citizen triad, while reinscribing gendered definitions of who may claim citizenship in Canada.

In Chapter 9, Janelle Joseph provides an exploration of supranational and diasporic connections among Black male athletes in Canada. Drawing on ethnographic research with young Afro-Caribbean *capoeira* (Brazilian martial arts) players and with older Afro-Caribbean cricket players, Joseph uses theories of diaspora to locate Blacks in Canada who identify with Canadian nationalist discourses but also turn to supranational racial communities given their exclusion from Canadian national representation. Joseph demonstrates how performances of Black masculinities are influenced by gender, age, nationality, and diaspora through non-dominant Canadian sports. Black athletes use their sports to affirm and challenge hegemonic masculinity and to share narratives of the (in)tolerance of the multicultural nation-state.

Sandy Wells examines the race and class dimensions of Canadians seeking athletic scholarship in the U.S. in the final chapter. The prestige and economic benefits of an athletic scholarship within the highly commercial, highly competitive environment of U.S. college sport make scholarships desirable to Canadian high school athletes for both their real (monetary) and symbolic value. Using theories of Pierre Bourdieu, Wells examines who is drawn into this system of athletic work and reward, and for what reasons. She argues that Canadian high school athletes derive meanings from their U.S. athletic scholarships, but do so in ways that contribute to, normalize, and sanctify the classed, raced, and gendered positions of track and field athletes in (and through) Canadian society.

The Importance of Race and Sport in Canada

In any discussion of race, it is important to recognize the risks of invoking, and therefore reifying, race as a category. To use Hylton's words, "the irony of race is that talking about it is still problematic even after the customary caveats have been expressed and parentheses denoting dissonance around it ... have been elucidated" (2009, p. 2). Furthermore, as King has argued, studies of race must avoid suggesting that "power is limited to privilege, and that it is all about whites—at the expense of people of color" (2005, p. 402) or reducing the study of Whiteness to the assuaging of White guilt. Recognizing these challenges, we maintain that race (in Canadian sport) has been, and continues to serve as, a structuring category both socially and politically. In turn, the study of race and sport in Canada remains important at this moment for at least two principal reasons.

First, the interlocking workings of power that secure the enduring myth of Canada's benign racial history and contemporary racial equality contribute to a Canadian (sporting) culture in which discussions of race are deemed unnecessary. Yet this stance is problematic amidst Canada's changing social landscape.

According to the 2006 Canadian census, visible minorities constituted at least 16 percent of the total Canadian population and 1.2 million Canadians were of South Asian descent alone. By 2017, Canada's major cities—Toronto, Vancouver, and Montreal— will be comprised of more than 50 percent of ethnic minorities, many of whom will be Canadian-born and of mixed-race status (Bélanger & Caron Malenfant, 2005). These ethnic minorities potentially increase the visibility and significance of diverse cultural practices, including sports such as *kabbadi*, dragon-boat racing, and *capoeira*, but also highlight issues of access and quality in sport and physical activity for Canadians. For example, in an analysis of students recently arrived in Canada, affiliation with a cultural group other than the dominant White majority increased the likelihood of social exclusion within the structures and culture of physical education (Taylor & Doherty, 2005). Given that participation in sport and physical activity offers an important means of positively shaping and expressing cultural identity in Canada, analyzing and challenging racism and the dominance of Whiteness in physical culture is more important than ever (Paraschak & Tirone, 2007).

Second, representations of race and/in sport continue to affect the social world of Canadians and their understandings of race and racism. In a study of the consumption and interpretation of media representations of Black athletes, Wilson and Sparks (1999, p. 615) argued that the (sport) media "constitute an important component in the racial context and racial socialization of youth." Canadians, particularly young Canadians, learn about race and racism, as well as their own racial identity and position within Canada's social hierarchies, through engagements with the culture of sport. Likewise, notions of Canadian nationalism, and the politics and crises of the nation, continue to connect to sport in Canada. As Scherer and Koch (2010) have illustrated, the cultural production of sports like hockey plays an active role in constructing and normalizing narratives of militarism and national citizenship in Canada. Indeed, if both nation and sport can be repressive normalizing structures, and both "by virtue of their over-determining and repressive demand for sameness are troubled or 'haunted' by the reality and complexity of social difference" (Abdel-Shehid, 2005, p. 3), then the ways that these differences are constructed, "managed," and resisted within Canadian sport demand examination. It is our hope and intention that *Race and Sport in Canada: Intersecting Inequalities* will contribute to this enduring project and aid in establishing the importance of ongoing, critical analyses of race and sport amidst the cultural diversity of Canadian social and political life.

References

Abdel-Shehid, G. (2000). Writing hockey thru race: Rethinking Black hockey in Canada. In R. Walcott (Ed.), *Rude: Contemporary Black Canadian cultural criticism* (pp. 69–86). Toronto: Insomniac.

Abdel-Shehid, G. (2003). In place of "race," space: "Basketball in Canada" and the absence of racism. In R.C. Wilcox, D.L. Andrews, R. Pitter & R.L. Irwin (Eds.), *Sporting dystopias: The making and meanings of urban sport cultures* (pp. 265–281). Albany: SUNY Press.

Abdel-Shehid, G. (2005). *Who da man?: Black masculinities and sporting cultures.* Toronto: Canadian Scholars' Press Inc.

Abu-Laban, B. (1983). The Canadian Muslim community: The need for a new survival strategy. In E.H. Waugh, B. Abu-Laban & R.B. Qureshi (Eds.), *The Muslim community in North America.* Edmonton: University of Alberta Press.

Bannerji, H. (2000). *The dark side of the nation: Essays on multiculturalism, nationalism, and gender.* Toronto: Canadian Scholars' Press Inc.

Bélanger, A. & Caron Malenfant, É. (2005). Ethnocultural diversity in Canada: Prospects for 2017. Retrieved from http://www.statcan.gc.ca/cgi-bin/af-fdr.cgi?l=eng&loc=http://www.statcan.gc.ca/pub/11-008-x/2005003/article/8968-eng.pdf&t=Ethnocultural%20diversity%20in%20Canada:%20Prospects%20for%202017

Birrell, S. & Cole, C.L. (Eds.). (1994). *Women, sport, and culture.* Urbana-Champaign: Human Kinetics.

Brayton, S. (2005). "Black-lash": Revisiting the "White Negro" through skateboarding. *Sociology of Sport Journal*, 22(3), 356–372.

Canadian Multiculturalism Act, Revised Statutes of Canada (1988, c 31). Retrieved from the Department of Justice Canada website: http://laws-lois.justice.gc.ca/eng/acts/c-18.7/page-1.html#docCont

Carnegie, H. (1997). *A fly in a pail of milk: The Herb Carnegie story.* Oakville: Mosaic Press.

Carrington, B. (2010). *Race, sport, and politics: The sporting Black Atlantic.* Thousand Oaks: Sage.

Carrington, B. & McDonald, I. (Eds.). (2001). *"Race," sport, and British society.* London: Routledge.

Cooley, W. (2010). 'Vanilla Thrillas': Modern Boxing and White-Ethnic Masculinity. *Journal of Sport and Social Issues*, 34(4), 418–437.

Cosgrove, A. & Bruce, T. (2005). "The Way New Zealanders would like to see themselves": Reading white masculinity via media coverage of the death of Sir Peter Blake. *Sociology of Sport Journal*, 22(3), 236–255.

Dallaire, C. (2003). Sport's impact on the francophoneness of the Alberta Francophone Games (AFG). *Ethnologies*, 25(2), 33–58.

Dei, G.J.S., Mazzuca, J., McIsaac, E. & Zine, J. (Eds.). (1997). *Reconstructing "drop-out": A critical ethnography of the dynamics of Black students' disengagement from school.* Toronto: University of Toronto Press.

Douglas, D. (2005). Venus, Serena, and the Women's Tennis Association (WTA): When and where 'race' enters. *Sociology of Sport Journal*, 2(3), 256–282.

Driedger, L. & Halli, S.S. (Eds.). (2000). *Race and racism: Canada's challenge.* Montreal: McGill-Queen's University Press.

Edwards, H. (1969). *The revolt of the Black athlete.* New York: The Free Press.

Fleras, A. & Elliott, J.L. (2002). *Engaging diversity: Multiculturalism in Canada.* Toronto: Nelson Thompson Learning.

Fleras, A. & Kunz, J.L. (2001). *Media and minorities: Representing diversity in a multicultural Canada.* Toronto: Thompson Educational Publishing Inc.

Fong, E. & Ooka, E. (2006). Patterns of participation in informal social activities among Chinese immigrants in Toronto. *The International Migration Review,* 40(2), 348–374.

Forsyth, J. (2007a). The Indian Act and the (re)shaping of Canadian Aboriginal sport practices. *International Journal of Canadian Studies,* 35, 95–111.

Forsyth, J. (2007b). To my sisters in the field. *Pimatisiwin: A Journal of Aboriginal & Indigenous Community Health,* 5(1), 155–168.

Forsyth, J. & Heine, M. (2008). "A Higher degree of social organization": Jan Eisenhardt and Canadian Aboriginal Sport Policy in the 1950s. *Journal of Sport History,* 35(2), 261–277.

Forsyth, J. & Wamsley, K.B. (2006). "Native to Native ... we'll recapture our spirits": The world indigenous nations games and North American indigenous games as cultural resistance. *International Journal of the History of Sport,* 23(2), 294–314.

Fosty, G. & Fosty, D. (2004). *Black ice: The lost history of the Coloured Hockey League of the Maritimes, 1895–1925.* New York: Stryker-Indigo.

Frankenberg, R. (1993). *White woman, race matters: The social construction of Whiteness.* London: Routledge.

Fusco, C. (2005). Cultural landscapes of purification: Sports spaces and discourses of Whiteness. *Sociology of Sport Journal,* 22(3), 283–310.

Halli, S.S. & Driedger, L. (1999). *Immigrant Canada: Demographic, economic, and social challenges.* Toronto: University of Toronto Press.

Harris, C. (2003). *Breaking the ice: The Black experience in professional hockey.* Toronto: Insomniac Press.

Hartmann, D. (2000). Rethinking the relationships between sport and race in American culture: Golden ghettoes and contested terrain. *Sociology of Sport Journal,* 17(3), 229–253.

Heine, M. & Forsyth, J. (2008). Sites of meaning, meaningful sites? Sport and recreation for Aboriginal youth in inner city Winnipeg, Manitoba. *Native Studies Review,* 17(2), 99–113.

Henry, F. (1994). *The Caribbean diaspora in Toronto: Learning to live with racism.* Toronto: University of Toronto Press.

Henry, F. & Tator, C. (2002). *Discourses of domination: Racial bias in the Canadian English-language press.* Toronto: University of Toronto Press.

Heron, B. (2007). *Desire for development: Whiteness, gender, and the helping imperative.* Waterloo: Wilfrid Laurier University Press.

Hylton, K. (2005). "Race," sport, and leisure: Lessons from critical race theory. *Leisure Studies, 24*(1), 81–98.

Hylton, K. (2009). *Race and sport: Critical race theory.* London: Routledge.

Hylton, K. (2010). How a turn to critical race theory can contribute to our understanding of "race," racism, and anti-racism in sport. *International Review for the Sociology of Sport, 45*(3), 335–354.

Jackson, S.J. (1998). A twist of race: Ben Johnson and the Canadian crisis of racial and national identity. *Sociology of Sport Journal, 15*(1), 21–40.

Jackson, S.J. (2004). Exorcizing the ghost: Donovan Bailey, Ben Johnson, and the politics of Canadian identity. *Media Culture Society, 26*(1), 121–141.

Jackson, S. & Ponic, P. (2001). Pride and prejudice: Reflecting on sport heroes, national identity, and crisis in Canada. *Culture, Sport, Society, 4*(2), 43–62.

James, C. (2005). *Race in play: Understanding the socio-cultural worlds of student athletes.* Toronto: Canadian Scholars' Press Inc.

James, C.E. (2001). Multiculturalism, diversity, and education in the Canadian context: The search for an inclusive pedagogy. In C.A. Grant & J.L. Lei (Eds.), *Global constructions of multicultural education: Theories and realities* (pp. 169–200). Mahwah: Lawrence Erlbaum.

James, C.E. (2003). *Seeing ourselves: Exploring ethnicity, race, and culture.* Toronto: Thompson Educational.

James, C.L.R. (1963). *Beyond a boundary.* London: Stanley Paul.

Jamieson, K.M. (1998). Reading Nancy Lopez: Decoding representations of race, class, and sexuality. *Sociology of Sport Journal, 15*(4), 343–358.

Jiwani, Y. (2010). Doubling discourses and the veiled Other: Mediations of race and gender in Canadian media. In S. Razack, M. Smith & S. Thobani, (Eds.), *States of race: critical race feminism for the 21st century* (pp. 59–86). Toronto: Between the Lines Press.

Joseph, J. (2011). A diaspora approach to sport tourism. *Journal of Sport and Social Issues, 35*(2), 146–167.

King, C.R. (2005). Cautionary notes on whiteness and sport studies. *Sociology of Sport Journal, 22*, 397–408.

Kusz, K.W. (2001). "I want to be the minority": The politics of youthful White masculinities in sport and popular culture in 1990s America. *Journal of Sport and Social Issues, 25*(4), 390–416.

Laraque, G. (2011). *Georges Laraque: The story of the NHL's unlikeliest tough guy.* Toronto: Penguin Group.

Lee, S.M. & Boyd, M. (2007). Marrying out: Comparing the marital and social integration of Asians in the U.S. and Canada. *Social Science Research, 37*, 311–329.

Li, P.S. (2003a). Initial earnings and catch-up capacity of immigrants. *Canadian Public Policy, 29*(3), 319–337.

Li, P.S. (2003b). The place of immigrants: The politics of difference in territorial and social space. *Canadian Ethnic Studies, 35*(2), 1–13.

Li, P.S. (2005). The rise and fall of Chinese immigration to Canada: Newcomers from Hong Kong Special Administrative Region of China and Mainland China, 1980–2000. *International Migration, 43*(3), 9–34.

Mackey, E. (2002). *House of difference: Cultural politics and national identity in Canada.* Toronto: University of Toronto Press.

Magee, W., Fong, E. & Wilkes, M. (2007). Neighbourhood ethnic concentration and discrimination. *Journal of Social Policy, 37*(1), 37–61.

Martynowich, O. (1991). *Ukrainians in Canada: The formative years 1891–1924.* Edmonton: University of Alberta Press.

McDonald, M.G. (2002). Queering Whiteness: The particular case of the Women's National Basketball Association. *Sociological Perspectives, 45*(4), 379–396.

Meissner, D. (2009, December 27). From a single feather to a top-flight program. *Toronto Star.* Retrieved March 5, 2012 from http://www.thestar.com/sports/olympics/article/743005—from-a-single-feather-to-a-top-flight-program

Mensah, J. (2010). *Black Canadians: History, experience, social conditions* (2nd ed.). Halifax: Fernwood Publishing.

Millington, B., Vertinsky, P., Boyle, E. & Wilson, B. (2008). Making

Chinese-Canadian masculinities in Vancouver's physical education curriculum. *Sport, Education, and Society, 13*(2), 195–214.

Nakamura, Y. (2002). Beyond the hijab: Female Muslims and physical activity. *Women in Sport and Physical Activity Journal, 11*(2), 21–48.

Omi, M. & Winant, H. (2002). Racial formation. In P. Essed & D. Goldberg (Eds.), *Race critical theories* (pp. 123–145). Oxford: Blackwell.

Paraschak, V. (1990). Organized sport for Native females on the Six Nation Reserve, Ontario from 1968–1980. A comparison of dominant and emergent sport systems. *Canadian Journal of History of Sport, 21*(2), 70–80.

Paraschak, V. (1991). Sport festivals and race relations in the Northwest Territories of Canada. In G. Jarvie (Ed.), *Sport racism and ethnicity* (pp. 74–93). London: Falmer Press.

Paraschak, V. (1997). Variations in race relations: Sporting events for Native peoples in Canada. *Sociology of Sport Journal, 14*(1), 1–21.

Paraschak, V. (1998). Reasonable amusements: Connecting the strands of physical culture in Native lives. *Sport History Review, 29*(1), 121–131.

Paraschak, V. (2007). Doing race, doing gender: First Nations, sport, and gender relations. In K. Young & P. White (Eds), *Sport and gender in Canada* (2nd ed., pp. 137–154). New York: Oxford University Press.

Paraschak, V. & Tirone, S. (2007). Race and ethnicity in Canadian sport. In J. Crossman (Ed.), *Canadian sport sociology* (2nd ed., pp. 79–98). Toronto: Thomson Nelson.

Razack, S. (1998). *Looking White people in the eye: Gender, race, and culture in courtrooms and classrooms*. Toronto: University of Toronto Press.

Razack, S. (2001). Racialized immigrant women as Native informants in the academy. In R. Luther, B. Whitmore & B. Moreau (Eds.), *Seen but not heard: Aboriginal women and women of color in the academy* (pp. 51–60). Ottawa: Canadian Research Institute for the Advancement of Women.

Razack, S. (2002). Gendered racial violence and spatialized justice: The murder of Pamela George. In S. Razack (Ed.), *Race, space, and the law: Unmapping a White settler society* (pp. 125–147). Toronto: Between the Lines.

Razack, S. (2004). *Dark threats and white knights: The Somalia affair, peacekeeping, and the new imperialism*. Toronto: University of Toronto Press.

Razack, S. (2008). *Casting Out: The eviction of Muslims from western law and politics*. Toronto: University of Toronto Press.

Razack, S., Smith, M. & Thobani, S. (2010). *States of race: Critical race feminism for the 21st century*. Toronto: Between the Lines.

Reitz, J.G. (2001a). Immigrant success in the knowledge economy: Institutional change and the immigrant experience in Canada, 1970–1995. *Journal of Social Issues*, 57(3), 579–613.

Reitz, J.G. (2001b). Immigrant skill utilization in the Canadian labour market: Implications of human capital research. *Journal of International Migration and Integration*, 2(3), 347–378.

Reitz, J.G. & Breton, R. (1994). *The illusion of difference: Realities of ethnicity in Canada and the United States*. Ottawa: CD. Howe Institute.

Salaff, J.W., Greve, A. & Xu, L. (2002). Paths in to the economy: Structural barriers and the job hunt for skilled PRC Migrants in Canada. *The International Journal of Human Resource Management*, 13(3), 450–464.

San Juan Jr., E. (2000). The multiculturalism problematic in the age of globalized capitalism. *Social Justice*, 27(1), 61–75.

Scherer, J. & Koch, J. (2010). Living with war: Sport, citizenship, and the cultural politics of post-9/11 Canadian identity. *Sociology of Sport Journal*, 27(1), 1–29.

Sekeres, M. (2010, January 4). Kadri Regrets Reactions to Swiss. The Globe and Mail, retrieved March 5, 2012 from http://www.theglobeandmail.com/sports/hockey/world-juniors/kadri-regrets-reactions-to-trash-talking-swiss/article1418983

Taylor, T. & Doherty, A. (2005). Adolescent sport, recreation, and physical education: Experiences of recent arrivals to Canada. *Sport, Education, and Society*, 10(2), 211–222.

Teo, S.Y. (2007). Vancouver's newest Chinese diaspora: Settlers or 'immigrant prisoners'. *Geo Journal*, 68, 211–222.

Thangaraj, S. (2010). Ballin' Indo-Pak style: Pleasures, desires, and expressive practices of "South Asian American" masculinity. *International Review for the Sociology of Sport, 45*(3), 372–389.

Thobani, S. (2007). *Exalted subjects: Studies in the making of race and nation in Canada.* Toronto: University of Toronto Press.

Thobani, S. (2010). White innocence, Western supremacy: The role of Western feminism in the "War on Terror." In S. Razack, M. Smith & S. Thobani (Eds.), *States of race: Critical race feminism for the 21st century* (pp. 127–146). Toronto: Between the Lines.

Walcott, R. (Ed.). (2000). *Rude: Contemporary Black Canadian cultural criticism.* Toronto: Insomniac Press.

Walcott, R. (2003). *Black like who?: Writing Black Canada* (2nd ed.). Toronto: Insomniac Press.

Wallis, M. & Fleras, A. (2009). *Readings in historical perspectives, contemporary realities, and future possibilities.* Don Mills: Oxford University Press.

Wilson, B. (1997). "Good Blacks" and "Bad Blacks": Media constructions of African-American athletes in Canadian basketball. *International Review for the Sociology of Sport, 32*(2), 177–189.

Wilson, B. (1999). "Cool pose" incorporated: The marketing of Black masculinity in Canadian NBA coverage. In P. White & K. Young (Eds.), *Sport and gender in Canada* (pp. 232–253). Toronto: Oxford University Press.

Wilson, B. & Sparks, R. (1999). Impacts of Black Athlete media portrayals on Canadian youth. *Canadian Journal of Communication, 24*(4), 589–627.

PART ONE
Historical Approaches to the Study of Race and Sport in Canada

CHAPTER 1

Sport and the Canadian Immigrant: Physical Expressions of Cultural Identity within a Dominant Culture, 1896–1945

RUSSELL FIELD

A dominant historical narrative of sport and the immigrant experience in North America holds that popular New World sports—such as baseball in the U.S. and ice hockey in Canada—offered immigrants an opportunity to "fit in" their new adopted homes. Richard Gruneau and David Whitson (1993, p. 101) note that "although millions of immigrants from other European countries had brought their own popular recreations with them when they moved to Canada, it wasn't long before their children and grandchildren were watching and playing hockey."[1] While possibly part of the story, immigrants did not only assimilate. Their sporting preferences may have extended further, and in Canadian cities today international soccer victories set off celebrations in Greektowns and Little Italies, Portugals, and Koreas across the country. Bruce Kidd (1985, p. 80) contends that "ethnic sport studies [are] necessary for a full understanding of the immigrant experience in Canada." Yet, a recent text on the history of sport in Canada has little to say on the subject of sport and immigrant communities beyond noting that "people participated in patterns of physical activity as a strategy for separating themselves by class and race, or they invoked social meanings to distinguish themselves through ethnic or religious solidarity" (Morrow & Wamsley, 2010, p. 165).

Sport, while by no means a central feature in the lives of all newcomers, was an important cultural practice for immigrants trying to preserve or create a sense of ethnocultural identity or solidarity. Alternatively, sport was also a tool of acculturation, and it was on the playgrounds and sport fields that some "immigrants encountered the agencies and officials who would try to assimilate and control them" (Harney & Troper, 1975, pp. v–vi). These efforts had mixed success, so that, notes Danny Rosenberg (2003, p. 138), "sport and leisure activities expressed cultural values that could both co-exist and challenge or even undermine Old World attitudes and values." Yet immigrant sporting experiences cannot be reduced to a choice between accepting New World practices or rejecting them in an effort to preserve something of the Old World. In avoiding a single, general description of immigrant sport experiences, it is worth borrowing from S.W. Pope's (2006, p. 149) encouragement not to essentialize racialized sporting practices, but rather to see these as "contested, melding, merging, converging, borrowing processes constituting the creation of a culturally distinctive style without linking it to race." This chapter is an examination of the varied "strategies" pursued by immigrants to Canada in the first half of the 20th century in an effort to be physically active. It compiles the extensive secondary literature on this topic and highlights the voices of the historians from whose research conclusions are drawn.

Canada's Changing Face? Immigration in the First Half of the 20th Century

The first half of the 20th century, specifically 1896 to 1914 and part of the 1920s, witnessed a massive increase in immigration to Canada. Between 1901 and 1911, 39 percent of the increase in Canada's population was attributable to immigration, most of it from the British Isles and the U.S., with large numbers also flowing from central and eastern Europe. From a low of 16,835 in 1896, immigration peaked at 400,870 in the year before World War One. These migrants began to change the face of the Dominion of Canada. Most of the Asian newcomers ended up in British Columbia, while Jewish immigrants made their way to major urban centres such as Montreal, Toronto, and Winnipeg. The xenophobia of the first "red scare" and the *Chinese Immigration Act* of 1923 limited immigration. Nevertheless, between 1919 and 1930, Canada welcomed 53,000 Jews, 76,000 from the U.S.S.R. and 52,000 from Poland (both of which would have included Ukrainians and perhaps Jews as well); 30,000 Italians; 7,000 from other southern European nations; 13,000 from China and Japan; and 7,000 from the rest of Asia, Africa, the Caribbean, and Latin America (Bothwell, Drummond & English, 1987, pp. 60, 212–213).

Still, Canada remained composed primarily of its "two great racial stocks." The 1921 census recorded 27.9 percent of the country's population as French Canadian and another 55.4 percent as having "British Isles ancestry" (Thompson with Seager, 1985, p. 7). Indeed, despite the immigration from eastern and southern Europe, and the limited flow of East Asian migrants, the Canadian borders were most open for anglophones. This particular ethnogeographic distribution was intentional. When Clifford Sifton, minister of the interior in the early 20th century, spoke of attracting "Galicians in sheepskin coats," he was targeting agricultural migrants from the Russian and Austro-Hungarian empires who "could be trusted to settle on the land and to stay there" (Bothwell et al., 1987, p. 61). The desire to populate western Canada and develop the breadbasket that would feed the industrial cities and towns of central Canada continued after World War One.

The Depression ended both the incentives and opportunities for work, while a blind eye was turned to other migrant needs, specifically those of refugees fleeing Nazism and fascism in Europe (Tulchinsky, 2008). World War Two "brought overseas immigration almost to an end," with immigration limited essentially to women and children of British descent (Bothwell et al., 1987, p. 350). After 50 years of unprecedented immigration, one assessment of the impact on the face of Canada's major centres noted:

> Winnipeg was a genuinely multicultural, diverse society, even if the cultures existed side by side rather than mixed together. Both in Toronto and Montreal there were small Italian communities, and rather larger communities of Jews. But Toronto was still what the poet Earle Birney had called it: "Anglo-Saxon Town." Vancouver was even more so. Indeed, because of the wartime expulsion of its Japanese residents, it was more Anglo-Saxon than ever. (Bothwell et al., 1987, p. 397)

The Ethnic Enclave: Choosing Sides?

Despite planners' intentions, "most of those migrants went to the cities" (Bothwell et al., 1987, p. 398). In urban settings, immigrants often congregated in what historians have labelled ethnic "enclaves." Established, northern European ethnic groups, such as Scots or Germans, were often widely dispersed throughout cities, while other more "visible" groups—e.g., Jews, Italians, Chinese, Ukrainians, and Macedonians—were instead heavily concentrated in enclaves. Although such neighbourhoods were often defined by ethnic difference, they were also socio-economic concentrations of some of the poorest labourers in Canadian cities. Their existence was, in part, "a response to the prejudice of the receiving society" (Harney & Troper, 1975, p. 182). But they were also neighbourhoods defined by residents as much as by outsiders, and the former acted, as John Zucchi (2007) argues, both to protect immigrants from, and perhaps begin the process of integrating them within, Canadian society.

As immigrants sought to preserve and protect their ethnoculture while at the same time working to integrate themselves and their families into Canadian society, what role did sport play in negotiating this tension? In the article, "Homo Ludens and Ethnicity," Harney (1985b) tries to make sense of the significance of sport in ethnic enclaves. He borrows the title of Cary Goodman's examination of the playground movement, *Choosing Sides*, to portray what he argues is a traditional binary. Immigrants, especially parents making decisions for their children, had to choose between economic survival and the preservation of their ethnoculture on the one hand, and the Euro-Canadian sport that were offered to children in a variety of educational settings and voluntary associations on the other. Many immigrant parents, so the argument goes, opted for preservation, seeing organized sport as "a threat to group solidarity, a process of deprivation, which meant the loss of ethnoculture, parental control, [and] esteem between generations" (Harney, 1985b, p. 2). This binary was based upon the "assumption that newcomers generally wished to maintain old-world ways and ethnic group coherence rather than seek well-being and integration through rapid acculturation" (Harney, 1985a, p. 2). Some historical accounts have assumed that immigrant parents "viewed sports if not as an unnecessary luxury at least as a wasteful activity," writes K.W. Sokolyk (1991, p. 133) of Ukrainian Canadians. "Economic stability and security were foremost on their minds."

Yet in cities across Canada, throughout the 20th century, immigrant children were offered organized sport opportunities. Their participation, Robert Harney and Harold Troper (1975, p. 198) contend, relied upon parents making "a transition from seeing the kid on the sandlot as a good-for-nothing who should have been helping his father in the shop or practising on his violin to acknowledging the importance of sports to their children." The other "side" in choosing sides was a liberal assimilationist perspective whose proponents sought to "emphasize athletics as a ladder of social and economic mobility" (Harney, 1985b, p. 1). These efforts were not unique to Canada. Indeed, Eisen (1994, p. xi) notes that sport played a "role of uniting, integrating, and socializing these newcomers into mainstream America." And it is from the U.S. that the most stereotypical images of immigrant assimilation through sport have emerged, both on the playing field and as spectators. "Italians who turned out to cheer the New York Yankees' first Italian star, Tony Lazzeri," for example, "were acculturating as they sat in the stands" (Harney, 1985b, p. 2). But it was in more organized settings that the advocates of rational recreation (sport for health improvement and social control) viewed participating in sport as a "window of opportunity" for immigrant children.

The Power of Institutions: Sport, Acculturation, and Immigrant Children

In 1918, a researcher at the University of Toronto, examining attempts to assimilate immigrants, concluded of newcomers to Canada that "[t]heir hearts will remain, to a very great extent, bound up with the scenes of their childhood" (cited in Harney & Troper, 1975, p. 110). Efforts to Canadianize immigrants were not futile, however, the researcher noted, if the "teacher, social worker and settlement house volunteer" turned their attention to second-generation Canadians as these children were "more malleable material" (Harney & Troper, 1975, p. 110). To these institutional leaders fell the "official task of Canadianizing the foreigner" (Harney & Troper, 1975, p. 109). And their ranks included sport organizers and physical educators—who worked within the institutional settings of school, settlement house, and voluntary association—many of whom held fast to the liberal assimilationist promise of sport as an entry point to Anglo-Canadian society for the children of immigrant parents.

For educators, schooling was envisioned "not just as the process of learning but, perhaps more importantly, as the process of *becoming*" (Harney & Troper, 1975, p. 110; emphasis original). It was in schools that "new Canadians encountered ... the 'four cornerstones' of British-Canadian citizenship: Imperial patriotism, Protestantism, the English language, and cleanliness" (Axelrod,

1997, p. 85). The elements of a physical education curriculum, as well as school-based games and sport programs, were enmeshed in this delivery of both educational and citizenship outcomes. It was not only the children of Anglo-Canadians who would benefit from the ways in which "athletics could teach many of the lessons about the 'Canadian way': fair play, team effort, and of course, healthy bodies as the temples of the Almighty" (Harney & Troper, 1975, p. 183). Indeed, "British and Canadian games could serve as agents of cultural socialization" (Axelrod, 1997, p. 117). D.S. Woods, the first dean of education at the University of Manitoba, argued in 1913 that play "leads to the heart of the foreign child as readily as [to that of] the British born" (cited in Axelrod, 1997, p. 117). He was not alone among Winnipeggers in holding such opinions. W.J. Sisler, principal of Strathcona School in Winnipeg, contended in his memoir, *Peaceful Invasion*, that the school soccer program he instituted was "a potent factor in creating good-will among children of many racial groups and differing religious beliefs" (cited in Loewen & Friesen, 2009, p. 45).[2]

Beyond the schoolyard, immigrant parents had to confront the athletic choices available to their children in the many settlement houses in Canada's major urban centres, at institutions such as the YMCA and YWCA, and through recreational organizations such as the Boy Scouts, Girl Guides, and Canadian Girls in Training. "Baseball and basketball were the games of the public schools, the playgrounds, and the settlement houses" (Harney & Troper, 1975, p. 198). Dora Nipp (1985, p. 166) recalls that some boys in Toronto's Chinese immigrant community joined scouting troops: "one became an excellent gymnast at the Central Y where the rest were taking swimming, calisthenics and playing basketball." Indeed, in 1935 one Chinese boys' basketball team won a city championship.

Outdoor recreational organizations such as the Boy Scouts shared many similarities with contemporary physical education programs. Exposure to "nature," away from the industrial city, offered the added benefit of (organized) play in the outdoors. These organizations sought to administer the benefits of what Leila Mitchell

McKee (1982, p. 3) has called "nature's medicine": through "hiking, camping and other forms of outdoor recreation ... youth organizations adopted the back to nature movement as particularly relevant to their work of citizenship training and character formation." The antimodernist sentiment that informed such programs often utilized programming based upon essentialized notions of First Nations culture, both in Ernest Thompson Seton's Woodcraft Indians, as well as in the early Ontario camps created by Taylor Statten and others (Wall, 2005; see also Wall, 2009).[3]

If it is ironic that attempts to assimilate ethnocultural groups new to Canada would make use of another culture supposedly frozen in time by its encounter with Euro-Canadian society, outdoor recreational programs also sought to buttress middle-class gender ideologies. Immigrant boys and girls were prescribed the benefits of recreation in a natural environment, although the accompanying programming was highly gendered. Boys were "encouraged to indulge their 'savage' impulses in games of 'scalping' and 'pioneers and Indians,'" while for girls "the emphasis on Native activities was on the development of artistic abilities ... with weaving and painting of 'Indian themes' being popular" (Wall, 2005, p. 522). Even in organizations that did not advocate "Indian" activities, there was a "tendency to emphasize domestic skills over physical training and outdoor recreation" (Mitchell McKee, 1982, p. 6). One such organization was Canadian Girls in Training (CGIT), which was founded in 1915 and had ties to the YMCA, Sunday school associations, and various Christian denominations.

Children in the Chinese community in Toronto during the interwar years pursued "Canadianized activities and interests as scout troops, hockey teams and Canadian Girls in Training" and "girls often joined Brownies at the Bay Street Mission and/or the CGIT" (Nipp, 1985, pp. 160, 166). At the same time, Margaret Prang (1985, p. 172) disputes that CGIT efforts were solely about the "assimilation of immigrants to a 'Canadian way of life.'" Instead she argues the organization "was generally a 'mosaic' and members were urged to study sympathetically the backgrounds and customs of ethnic minorities, especially those represented in CGIT and in their own communities."

Thus, there are limits to understanding the residents of ethnic enclaves as passive actors waiting to receive the assimilative programming of Anglo-Canadian society. Immigrants were neither "people on the threshold of acculturation" nor "potential fossils, living in colonies of an old country, maintaining cultural baggage which changed little" (Harney, 1985a, p. 8). Instead, the ethnic neighbourhoods where immigrants congregated revealed the physical spaces and spatial geographies of the "places where men and women had to negotiate their ethnicity" (Harney, 1985a, p. 13). Ethnic enclaves were vibrant, organic, and constantly changing communities that provided, according to Lowen and Friesen (2009, p. 13), "the vocabulary, symbols, and understandings by which life made sense and social action was ordered." The authors argue that: "The host society may have offered an array of institutions—public schools, theatres, sports halls, and political parties—but the immigrants reached into their own cultural repertoire to build their own responses to this new world." What Harney (1985a, p. 20) calls "responses to this new world" are best understood by considering all the institutions, both formal and informal, that immigrants accessed, modified, and created, be they, in Harney's (1985a, p. 7) formulation, "the classroom, the corner restaurant, the factory or at leisure on street corners." Indeed, to this list could be added the baseball diamond and ice rink, the running track and the gymnasium.

Beyond "Choosing Sides": Baseball as Acculturation and Assertion

If baseball is the quintessential (North) American sport, then the popularity of the game among immigrant communities may have been an example of what many scholars (e.g., Anderson, 2006) have labelled using the masters' tools, if not to resist the masters, then at least to play alongside them. Steven Riess (1999) notes that baseball was most popular among the earliest immigrants—the

Anglo, Irish, and German émigrés—to urban North America.[4] As part of a process that Eisen (1999, p. xiii) calls "ethnic succession," in the early 20th century, baseball soon became the game of eastern and southern European immigrants, specifically the Jewish and Italian communities. Peter Levine (1992, p. 17) asserts of Jewish newcomers that "[A]spiring immigrants eagerly embraced obvious and accessible avenues that permitted immediate identification as Americans." One such avenue was supporting the local baseball team from the stands, while recreating similar sport in neighbourhood games of stickball. Eric Solomon (1994, p. 78) goes on to claim that "baseball gave a focal point to the Jewish immigrant come to America." A similar assimilationist tale is told of Italian-American immigrants whose children "learned to play baseball before they could speak more than a few words of English" (Bazzano, 1994, p. 110). The game "provided the only bridge between the Italians and the surrounding population." Riess (1999, p. 47) argues that "[n]ew immigrants from eastern and southern Europe generally did not become baseball fans," but immigrant children who lived in inner cities were ardent fans. Baseball in the early 20th century was an instrument of acculturation primarily for second-generation North Americans, the children of immigrants.[5]

The widespread popularity of baseball among immigrant children gives lie to the basic premise of "choosing sides," which Harney (1985b, p. 4) notes "could not have been the simple issue of opting for or against sports and organized play." The ethnic diversity of baseball teams throughout Canada suggests that the game's popularity cannot be distilled simply to the assimilating influence of settlement houses and voluntary agencies. Immigrant communities (if one can generalize) played North American sports both to assert their community identity and to acculturate to Canadian society because through sport, "newly arriving immigrant or migrant communities could nurture, alongside a quest for assimilation, their cultural and religious differences until it did not interfere with mainstream values" (Eisen, 1994, p. xii).

Sport clubs, including baseball teams, were, as Eisen (1994, p. xii) continues, "one of the chief social institutions in which individual and communal energies could be marshalled in the newly established ethnic communities." Indeed, Harney and Troper (1975, p. 183) assert that "[t]eams represented more than neighbourhoods. There were Macedonian, Jewish and Italian teams."

Joseph Reaves (2002, p. 3) argues that baseball was both "an important tool of cultural hegemony and a powerful weapon to fight that hegemony."[6] This was certainly true among those in Canada's Japanese immigrant community in the first half of the 20th century who supported Vancouver's Asahi baseball club. By 1941, the Japanese-Canadian population had grown to 23,450, about 95 percent of whom lived in British Columbia, primarily Vancouver. The Asahi baseball team was an important institution in a Japanese community that faced widespread racism and was denied the right to vote in an era of expansionist Japanese foreign policy and accompanying xenophobic fears.[7] Formed in 1914 and playing out of the Powell Street Grounds, in the heart of Vancouver's Japanese enclave known as Little Tokyo, the Asahi included both *nisei* (Canadian-born Japanese) and *issei* (Japanese-born immigrants), and entered local league play after World War One. The Asahi won city championships in 1926, 1930, and 1933, five straight Pacific Northwest Japanese championships (1937–1941), and other local titles in the late 1930s. The club was disbanded with the forced internment of Japanese Canadians in 1941 into labour camps and ghost towns in the interior of B.C.[8]

Anne Dore (2002, p. 448) notes that for many *nisei*, "embracing baseball was symbolic of embracing Canadian citizenship." While this was true of the Asahi to a degree, it is important not to lose sight of sport's (in this case, baseball's) dual utility; it "can promote acculturation and assimilation, or it can encourage defiance and self-assertion" (Reaves, 2002, p. 3). Assessments of the Asahi point to the team's ability to foster a sense of pride in Vancouver's Japanese community. Shannon Jette (2007, p. 6) notes that "the Asahi were able to symbolically resist or challenge the hegemony of the white community and foster a sense of pride and self-respect within their own." Beyond this, the Asahi's success and their acceptance by the Anglo sporting community suggests that the team "symbolized Japanese-Canadians' successful integration into Canadian society" (Jette, 2007, p. 7).[9] In this way, playing a North American sport was not evidence solely of a desire to assimilate, and the Asahi reflected Japanese immigrants' desire to participate in the institutions of their new country, while at the same time offering symbols to which community members, in the face of widespread racism, could turn for comfort and identification. Or, as Dore (2002, p. 440) suggests more broadly, baseball was valuable in preserving "Japanese culture and traditions within the supportive structure of the transnational communities," while at the same time "securing full acceptance and opportunity within mainstream Canadian society."

Nevertheless, immigrants took the field or diamond at the margins of a society that often treated them with disdain, if not overt racism. As one late 19th century Slavic immigrant to the U.S. observed, "My people do not live in America. They live underneath America. America goes on over their heads" (cited in Regalado, 2003, p. 301). Yet, contemporary accounts argued for the egalitarian nature of the playing field. On August 17, 1933, the *Toronto Star* proudly proclaimed that "[A]mateur sport puts up no racial barriers if the personnel of many of Toronto's most successful baseball and basketball teams—with Jews, Gentiles, Italians and other central Europeans playing together—is any criterion" (cited in Levitt & Shaffir, 1985, p. 68). This message was taken up by Jewish immigrants to Toronto, where sport became "a significant social domain, both in practice and in symbol, for immigrants and their children to define themselves as Canadians and as Jews" (Rosenberg, 2003, p. 138).

The date of this *Toronto Star* editorial is not insignificant, published as it was immediately after one of the worst race riots in the history of Canadian sport as Jewish baseball players and their followers clashed with swastika-toting toughs at Christie Pits, a large park in Toronto. Between 1921 and 1931, non-British inhabitants grew from 5 percent to 19 percent of Toronto's population, and Jews were the largest group at more than 7 percent of the population (Speisman, 1979). The majority of Jewish immigrants were from eastern Europe and they settled in Toronto in a poor, central slum, known as the Ward, which also included Polish, Ukrainian, and Irish Catholic immigrant communities. Jews faced "social and occupational resistance from a smug Anglo-Saxon elite and a xenophobic Orange middle and working class" (Levitt & Shaffir, 1985, p. 70; see also Levitt & Shaffir, 1987). One way in which they encountered these communities was on the baseball diamond, often at Christie Pits, where, as Gerald Tulchinsky (2008, p. 325) notes, "Jewish and Italian players dominated several teams and earned reputations for excellent play." Nevertheless, "these games often degenerated into epithets, insults, and fisticuffs between members of competing teams."

The 1933 Toronto city baseball season in particular unfolded against a backdrop of widespread unemployment due to the Depression and the ascendancy of European fascism and Nazism, with its overt anti-Semitism (Levitt & Shaffir, 1987). On August 16, following a game at Christie Pits between teams from St. Peter's and Harbord Playground (the latter predominantly Jewish), some members of the Anglo-Canadian Pit Gang displayed black shirts with swastikas. The teams met again two days later. A large crowd showed up with rumours of more trouble circulating. Jewish youth in the crowd, including some amateur boxers, expected trouble, and when the Pit Gang "unfurled a large banner bearing a swastika to well-orchestrated shouts of 'Hail Hitler,'" a riot broke out and moved throughout the city, lasting four hours, and resulting in the arrest of four Pit Gang members (Tulchinsky, 2008, p. 325). This was not an isolated incident as "swastika clubs flourished, and more ugly antisemitic incidents occurred" in Toronto throughout the 1930s as "Jewish resentment smouldered" (Tulchinsky, 2008, p. 326). The baseball diamonds were a key site for race conflicts.

Athletic Baggage: Transplanting Old World Sport to Canada

As described, sport was clearly more than just a tool of acculturation. Immigrants engaged in physical activity in their countries of emigration, and indeed introduced new sporting practices to North America. Nordic sports, including cross-country skiing and ski jumping, are a prime example. Roland Huntford (2008, p. 298) observes that, in 1879, "a Norwegian had skied from Montreal to Quebec" while at the same time "Norwegians were skiing in Rossland, a mining town in British Columbia." While skiing "did not really take hold in Canada until the first decades of the twentieth century" (Huntford, 2008, p. 298), Alberta's Fram Ski Club was founded in 1911 by "three Engebretson brothers, P. Mikkleson, A. Maland, [and] Lars Maland" (Camrose Ski Club History, 2011). Further east, another pioneer was promoting the Nordic sport. Herman "Jackrabbit" Smith-Johannsen emigrated from Norway to Canada (via the United States) after World War One. He skied while employed in northern Ontario's resource industries before settling in Montreal, where "he helped popularize the sport across Canada and the U.S. In the 1920s and 30s, he cut the first cross-country ski trails in the Laurentians, including the famous Maple Leaf Trail" (Farfan, n.d.).

Jackrabbit, a legend within the skiing community, skied until after age 100. His is only one story that challenges the image of the hard-working peasant with no time or interest in frivolities such as sport and recreation, an image that does a disservice to both the rich cultural lives of immigrants and to the importance that sport and body movement practices could have in their lives. In ethnic enclaves, community leaders understood the value of sport in preserving a sense of identity in a new country. It was especially "[t]he presence of these autonomous immigrant sports traditions," argues Harney (1985b, p. 7), that "provided ethnic leaders, lay and clerical, with an answer to 'choosing sides.'" These neighbourhood figures, "[i]n the face of the secularized weekend, professional sports, movie houses and the Anglo-Protestant siren call of the YMCA," would look to sport, rather than disparage it, as a means to deliver "ethnocultural values to the Canadian- or American-born generations" (Harney, 1985b, p. 8). A common event was the annual picnic, which often included sport and games, and where participation in physical activity offered an opportunity "to affirm membership in the ethnoculture and loyalty to group language, traditions, or liturgy" (Harney, 1985a, p. 20).

Beyond informal picnic games, sport clubs were organized to perpetuate Old World activities and associations. Loewen and Friesen (2009) note that, despite the socio-economic heterogeneity of German immigrants to the Prairies, sport (as well as music and theatre) was a means to bring German Canadians together and preserve German cultural forms—for example, "the 1906 Turnverein organized the immigrants to play Old Country sports" (p. 32). The influence of gymnastic institutions, such as the Turnverein, was not unique to German immigrants; gymnastics were among the most popular transplanted immigrant sporting practices. Harney and Troper (1975, p. 196) observe that "the *sokol* of the Czechs and the *turnverein* of the Germans were as central to cultural retention as any folk dance or literature." Elsewhere Harney (1985b, p. 7) notes that "varieties of patriotically inspired gymnastic and precision exercise pastimes had long existed among the Poles, Jews, Galicians, Slovaks, Hungarians and others who had reached the New World." But the cultural importance of these groups is that "this tradition inspired almost every self-help and mutual aid organization among the newcomers—Prosvita, Jednota, Arbiter Ring, Mutuo Soccorso—to sponsor teams in Canada as early as the 1920s."

By comparison, soccer "had taken root everywhere by the second and third decades of this century and thus was available as an ethnic emblem and resource for many who emigrated" (Harney, 1985b, p. 7). The German Canadian Soccer Club was a dominant team in Windsor, Ontario's city league in the 1930s (Temelini, 1985). Similarly, Italian immigrants in Hamilton, Ontario, during the interwar years set up informal bocce lanes in their backyards before eventually forming the Hamilton Venetian Club, one of whose primary activities was bocce (Cumbo, 1985). Moreover, in northern Ontario, "[m]ost Finn *haali*," notes Harney (1985b, p. 7), "had exercise, wrestling and Nordic sports as an integral part of their activities."

For many of these Finns, sport was not just an element of ethnic identity, but also a badge of class membership. The Workers' Sport Association of Canada (WSAC), an overtly class-based sport movement inspired by international movements and founded in 1928 at the instigation of the Young Communist League, was dominated by immigrant sport clubs that had experience in politicized sport movements in Europe (see Riordan, 1999). As Bruce Kidd (1996, p. 160) notes, "Finnish Canadians were the best organized and most athletically gifted of the worker sport participants in Canada." The domestic workers' sport organization in Finland, TUL, had been founded in 1919, while the Finnish Workers' Sport Association of Canada was an umbrella organization founded in 1925 with 20 member clubs from across Canada, but which featured prominently in Toronto and the mining and lumber communities of northern Ontario and British Columbia. In Canada, Finns practised Nordic skiing, including a race in northern Ontario between Beaver Lake and South Porcupine, a distance of 240 km each way. Finnish-Canadian WSAC athletes were also dominant in wrestling and track and field. By 1933, Finns held all of the senior men's WSAC athletics records and hosted many WSAC meets (Kidd, 1996).

Varied Approaches: Immigrant Sporting Choices in Winnipeg

Among workers' sport participants, Kidd (1996, p. 163) notes, "[r]adical Ukrainian immigrants and their children made up the second most numerous ethnic group." Ukrainian immigrants, radical and otherwise, were common landholders in rural Manitoba and also formed a community in the province's capital, Winnipeg. The largest city on the Prairies was, thanks to immigration, "the quintessential centre of the Canadian immigration myth. The North End of Winnipeg was to be the Canadian shibboleth to match the Lower East Side of New York" (Harney & Troper, 1975, p. v). Beyond Ukrainians, the city boasted, for example, sizable Jewish and Icelandic communities. These groups "situated themselves in relatively discrete areas of the city, thereby creating a distinct tapestry of neighbourhoods which were primarily ethnic in character" (Hiebert, 1991, p. 80). Nonetheless, the city was still predominantly "British," and "even those who did not see themselves as British still often publicly embraced the identity" (Korneski, 2007, p. 175). Such an environment "encouraged non-British immigrants in the city to develop organizations that expressed both their class standing and their alternate—i.e., non-British—ethnic identity" (Korneski, 2007, p. 175). These organizations included sporting ones, and the experience of some of the city's immigrants demonstrates the varied responses of immigrant groups, even within the same community, in the pursuit of athletic opportunities.

Manitoba is now home to the largest Icelandic population outside of Iceland.[10] It is centred around the town of Gimli, 90 km north of Winnipeg, which was within an Icelandic reserve called New Iceland, granted to settlers by the Government of Canada in 1875. There, they organized their own local government, which, until 1880, was outside the boundaries of Manitoba. Darlington (1998, p. 129) calls the Icelandic immigrant community one of western Canada's "large, ethnically exclusive settlements." Eventually, however, working-class members of this community migrated to Winnipeg, the region's major centre. In the early 20th century, the Icelandic community lived in Winnipeg's working-class west end "in small single-storey houses or overcrowded duplexes and tenements in a poor part of the city" (Square, 2007, p. 2). The area was known as Little Iceland, whose geographic heart was the intersection of Victor Street and Sargent Avenue, the latter known derogatively as Goolie Crescent for the presence of the Icelanders.

The most celebrated instance of Icelandic-Canadian sport is the Winnipeg Falcons hockey club. The team, composed primarily of players of Icelandic descent from Winnipeg's west end, was initially denied the opportunity to participate in one of the city's senior hockey leagues. However, the club eventually captured both the civic championship and the 1919 senior Canadian men's hockey championship. The latter won the Falcons the right to compete at the 1920 Olympic Games in Antwerp, where ice hockey was first appearing on the program and the Winnipeggers captured the inaugural gold medal in the sport. Ryan Eyford (2006) argues that the Icelandic community hoped that the Falcons would be a means to gain acceptance from the host society. Not all immigrant groups were viewed in the same way, and Icelandic Canadians were White, willingly learned English, and their Nordic heritage was not seen as particularly different from Anglo-Saxons. While typical narratives of the Falcons highlight the team overcoming racist attitudes and winning acceptance through sport, Eyford argues that the team's initial exclusion from the Winnipeg city league was not simply racial, but economically and culturally motivated, consistent with the middle-class origins of amateur sport. Following their success in Antwerp, Eyford observes, the Falcons were redeemed in the Canadian press, with characterizations of the team moving away from that of Icelandic, working-class immigrants. Subsequent media reports noted some of the players' military service prior to the Olympics to identify them as proud Canadians, loyal to the Empire, who were symbolic of the kinds of men who could be produced by amateur sport. Sport served in the acceptance of these immigrants as Canadian, but the White majority was still able to dictate the terms of this acceptance.

The case of Ukrainian Canadians in Winnipeg offers a fuller portrait of the ways in which immigrants engaged with Canadian society while preserving (and shedding) older sporting practices.

There was considerable Ukrainian immigration to Canada in the early 20th century, with 170,000 arriving between 1891 and 1914.[11] Many settled in Manitoba and were a key target of the Canadian government's effort to settle the large agricultural tracts of the Canadian Prairies.[12] As a result, in Manitoba, few early Ukrainian immigrants ended up in Winnipeg; only 10 families were reported in Winnipeg in 1895 (Lehr, 1994; see also Darlington, 1998). John Lehr (1994, pp. 190–191) argues that immigrants from the Ukraine steppe had "no experience of living in a large city and so had little incentive to remain in any of the cities or towns through which they travelled en route to the frontier." Furthermore, "immigration officers went to some lengths to discourage them from remaining in Winnipeg even for a short time" (Lehr, 1994, p. 181). Nevertheless, migrants eventually made their way to Winnipeg, forming a community in the city's north end, and it was there, as well as in rural communities, that Ukrainian sporting clubs were formed and flourished.

Ukrainians in Winnipeg faced acculturating influences, and sport often accompanied attempts at assimilation. "In North End Winnipeg, where most Ukrainians in that city lived," notes Sokolyk (1991, p. 136), "the United Church operated a fine sports program, but would-be participants had to agree to attend the church's Sunday Bible school." Some Ukrainian-organized institutions mirrored Anglo institutions. Ukrainian Boy Scouts and the Sporting "Stich" Association of Canada, formed in the early 1920s, featured military-style drill and advocated a "patriotic responsibility to Canada and the British Empire" within "a Ukrainian nationalistic organization whose ultimate goal was an independent Ukraine" (Sokolyk, 1991, p. 134). Similarly, Manoly Mihaychuk, a local dentist, organized annual sport days, featuring softball and track and field events, intentionally held on Dominion Day.[13] While some community leaders felt that "youth could participate in the life of their town or city removed from the confines of the ethnic community," this was not a universal belief (Sokolyk, 1991, p. 136). A contrasting view was offered by "members of the pioneer Ukrainian intelligentsia [who] also believed that sport was beneficial to youth" and who could be "exposed to sport as part of their Ukrainian heritage" (Sokolyk, 1991, p. 133). These participants included Ukrainian immigrants who joined workers' sport clubs (affiliated with the WSAC) and the Ukrainian Labour-Farmer Temple Association (whose name reflected the urban and rural nature of Ukrainian settlement in the Prairies).

Sport opportunities also reflected debates concerning the nature of Ukrainian integration in Canadian society. As Sokolyk (1991, p. 136) notes:

> Ukrainian community activists came to the conclusion that non-Ukrainian clubs could not adequately meet the sporting needs of their young people. While the potential for prejudice and discrimination constituted one concern, the fear that Ukrainian youth in a non-Ukrainian sports environment would be inevitably alienated from the Ukrainian community was equally strong.

It was from such a perspective that the Canadian Ukrainian Athletic Club (CUAC) was formed in 1925 to offer Euro-Canadian sport within a Ukrainian institution. As V.K. Koman, CUAC president, observed in 1928, "To ensure that our youth want to be part of our organizations we must foster all aspects of sport" (cited in Sokolyk, 1991, p. 136). Based in Winnipeg, the CUAC offered opportunities to youth in local leagues who played sport such as baseball, softball, hockey, soccer, basketball, lacrosse, and football. While started primarily for Ukrainian youth only, over time the organization accepted participants from a variety of backgrounds to their successful programs. CUAC teams in senior girls' softball, for example, won 22 Manitoba championships, including 17 straight from 1957 to 1973, and won the national championship in 1965.

Conclusion

The choices made by Icelandic and Ukrainian immigrants in Manitoba reflected the varied responses to "choosing sides" in sport, both between and within immigrant communities. Rarely, though, did these choices involve an outright rejection of sport. Community leaders were "choosing between old-country games—e.g., soccer, field hockey—and various Canadian sports such as football or ice hockey, not simply choosing between sports and the absence of sports" (Harney, 1985b, p. 4). Nevertheless, the physical surroundings and conditions of ethnic enclaves in Canadian cities made the children of immigrants ideal targets for the middle-class reformers of the early 20th century.

At the same time, beyond assimilative efforts and influences, sport was "deeply embedded in the ethnoculture, and ethnic associational life was rarely seen as complete, if space in the form of a gym or picnic site with playing fields was not provided within the group's own ambiance." Indeed for some new Canadians, "far from being a novel North American challenge to the immigrant," sport, continues Harney (1985b, p. 8), was "a natural medium for transmission of many small things of the ethnoculture." This did not necessarily lead to a single-minded focus on Old World sport. Some community leaders came to believe that offering Euro-Canadian sport within an ethnic institution was the wisest side to choose because, for example, "[A]s much national feeling went into fielding a Macedonian hockey team as into the more traditional Balkanski Unak" (Harney & Troper, 1975, p. 196).[14] Regardless of the choices made, it is clear that the sport experiences of immigrants in the first half of the 20th century "raise numerous questions related to acculturation, assimilation, ethnicity, social mobility, generational tensions, and identity formation," as Rosenberg (2003, p. 138) suggests. Various groups faced racial discrimination at different times based on class, gender, and ethnocultural difference, with inclusion ultimately dictated by the middle-class, Anglo-White majority. This chapter has sought to shed light on these issues for, as Colin Howell (2001, p. 145, emphasis original) argues, "Canada is a product of the lived experience of *all* of us," and the sport experiences of "marginalized peoples and ethnic minorities is as important as that of elite groups in the metropolis."

Questions for Critical Thought

1. What does historian Robert Harney mean by "choosing sides"? How does he argue immigrant communities resolved this "choice"?
2. What institutions in Canadian society reflected the liberal assimilationist view of sport?
3. How did the material realities of social class and gender identities figure in the immigrant sport experience?

Notes

1. Mah (1985, p. 122) notes of himself and his friends in Toronto's Chinese community during the 1940s: "Hockey was popular because we used to listen to it on the radio all the time." From 2007 to 2010, various *Hockey Night in Canada* broadcasts were available in Cantonese, Italian, Mandarin, and Punjabi.
2. Sisler recounts how he convinced reluctant parents who "wanted the boys to pile wood, dig the garden or run errands after four o'clock and on Saturdays" and others who were forbidden, because of their faith, to work with their hands on Saturdays. Interventions such as these were not unproblematic, however, and one observer a generation later criticized Sisler on the grounds that "the parents of those children valued the Sabbath and obviously the teachers had no idea of what they were doing to separate the children from their parents" (cited in Loewen & Friesen, 2009, p. 45).
3. Although a consideration of sporting practices among the First

Nations is beyond the scope of a chapter on immigrant Canadians, it is worth noting the similar ways in which both these groups were treated by the programs of Canadianizing institutions, both within and beyond sport (see Iacovetta & Bohaker, 2009).

4. Anderson (1996) confirms a similar pattern in Canadian baseball, specifically in his study of the 1908 Vancouver Beavers, where the local media subscribed to and reproduced ethnocultural stereotypes, so some ballplayers displayed "Irish tenacity," while "players of German origin were invariably 'strong and silent'" (p. 551).

5. Baseball was an equally popular game among other marginalized communities besides immigrants, including the First Nations, Francophones, and Black Canadians. Anderson (1996) notes that racial stereotypes ("weak, dishonest, and unpredictable performers") were also applied to First Nations players, who were usually saddled with the moniker, "Chief" (pp. 551–552). William Humber (1995) outlines the process by which migrant French-Canadian labourers played baseball while working winters in the mills of New England and brought the game back to Quebec in summertime. Finally, Colin Howell (1995), as well as Humber, examines the popular spectacle created by teams of Black ballplayers who barnstormed throughout Canada in the early 20th century.

6. I am grateful to Shannon Jette (2007) for highlighting the work of Anne Dore (2002) and Joseph Reaves (2002).

7. The Chinese community in Vancouver faced similar forms of discrimination and structural barriers (Anderson, 1991).

8. The Asahi club has remained in the public memory, thanks to the work of Pat Adachi (1992) and the National Film Board documentary film *Sleeping Tigers* (Osborne, 2003).

9. The Asahi's success was due, in part, to a distinctive style of play in the face of physically larger Caucasian opponents. Called "smallball" or "brainball," it emphasized teamwork, defence, bunting, and stealing on offence. Reaves (2002) has drawn a connection between Japanese and American styles of play and cultural values of individualism and communal effort. Robert Whiting makes a similar argument in *You Gotta Have Wa* (1989, pp. xxii, 16).

10. According to the Census of Canada, in 2006 there were 30,555 Manitobans of Icelandic descent in a province whose total population was 1,133,510, making Icelandic Canadians 2.7 percent of the population (2006 Community Profiles, 2010).
11. Without the existence of a sovereign Ukraine state, many of these immigrants were likely recorded in immigration documents as either Polish or Russian.
12 According to the Census of Canada, in 2006 nearly 15 percent of Manitobans claimed Ukrainian descent (167,175 out of a total population of 1,133,510) (2006 Community Profiles, 2010).
13. While the Ukrainian July 1 sport day was intended as a patriotic gesture, Nipp (1985, p. 159) argues that, with July 1, 1923, the day that the regressive *Chinese Immigration Act* was officially enacted, Dominion Day was known among the Chinese-Canadian community as "'Humiliation Day.' Understandably, for years afterwards Chinese across the country refused to participate in Dominion Day festivities."
14. Balkanski Unak was a Macedonian gymnastic group.

References

Adachi, P. (1992). *Asahi, a legend in baseball: A legacy from the Japanese Canadian baseball team to its heirs*. Etobicoke: Asahi Baseball Organization.

Anderson, E.D. (2006). Using the master's tools: Resisting colonization through colonial sports. *International Journal of the History of Sport, 23*, 247–266.

Anderson, K. (1991). *Vancouver's Chinatown: Racial discourse in Canada, 1875–1980*. Montreal & Kingston: McGill-Queen's University Press.

Anderson, R.J. (1996). "On the edge of the baseball map" with the 1908 Vancouver Beavers. *Canadian Historical Review, 77*, 534–574.

Axelrod, P. (1997). *The promise of schooling: Education in Canada*. Toronto: University of Toronto Press.

Bazzano, C. (1994). The Italian-American sporting experience. In G.

Eisen & D.K. Wiggins (Eds.), *Ethnicity and sport in North American history and culture* (pp. 103–116). Westport: Greenwood Press.

Bothwell, R., Drummond, I. & English, J. (1987). *Canada, 1900–1945*. Toronto: University of Toronto Press.

Camrose Ski Club History. (2011). Retrieved from www.camroseskiclub.com/history

Cumbo, E. (1985). Recreational activity at the Hamilton Venetian Club. *Polyphony, 7*(1), 59–63.

Darlington, J.W. (1998). The Ukrainian impress on the Canadian West. In F. Iacovetta, P. Draper & R. Ventresca (Eds.), *A nation of immigrants: Women, workers, and communities in Canadian history, 1840s–1960s*. Toronto: University of Toronto Press.

Dore, A. (2002). Japanese-Canadian sport history in the Fraser Valley: Judo and baseball in the interwar years. *Journal of Sport History, 29*, 439–456.

Eisen, G. (1994). Introduction. In G. Eisen & D.K. Wiggins (Eds.), *Ethnicity and sport in North American history and culture* (pp. xi–xvii). Westport: Greenwood Press.

Eyford, R. (2006). From Prairie goolies to Canadian cyclones: The transformation of the 1920 Winnipeg Falcons. *Sport History Review, 37*, 5–18.

Farfan, M. (n.d.). Herman "Jackrabbit" Smith-Johannsen (1875–1987). *Laurentian Heritage*. Retrieved March 15, 2011 from laurentian.quebecheritageweb.com/article/herman-jackrabbit-smith-johannsen-1875-1987

Gruneau, R. & Whitson, D. (1993). *Hockey night in Canada: Sport, identities, and cultural politics*. Toronto: Garamond.

Harney, R.F. (1985a). Ethnicity and neighbourhoods. In R.F. Harney (Ed.), *Gathering place: Peoples and neighbourhoods of Toronto, 1834–1945* (pp. 1–24). Toronto: Multicultural History Society of Ontario.

Harney, R. (1985b). Homo ludens and ethnicity. *Polyphony, 7*(1), 1–12.

Harney, R. & Troper, H. (1975). *Immigrants: A portrait of the urban experience, 1890–1930*. Toronto: Van Nostrand Reinhold.

Harney, R.F. & Troper, H. (1978). Introduction. *Urban History Review, 7*(2), 3–7.

Hiebert, D. (1991). Class, ethnicity, and residential structure: The social geography of Winnipeg, 1901–1921. *Journal of Historical Geography,* 17, 56–86.

Howell, C.D. (1995). *Northern sandlots: A social history of Maritime baseball.* Toronto: University of Toronto Press.

Howell, C.D. (2001). *Blood, sweat, and cheers: Sport and the making of modern Canada.* Toronto: University of Toronto Press.

Humber, W. (1995). *Diamonds of the north: A concise history of baseball in Canada.* Toronto: Oxford University Press.

Huntford, R. (2008). *Two planks and a passion: The dramatic history of skiing.* London: Continuum.

Iacovetta, F. & Bohaker, H. (2009). Making Aboriginal people "immigrants too": A comparison of citizenship programs for newcomers and indigenous peoples in postwar Canada, 1940s–1960s. *Canadian Historical Review,* 90, 427–461.

Jette, S. (2007). Little/big ball: The Vancouver Asahi baseball story. *Sport History Review,* 37, 1–16.

Kidd, B. (1985). The workers' sports movement in Canada, 1924–40: The radical immigrants' alternative. *Polyphony,* 7(1), 80–88.

Kidd, B. (1996). *The struggle for Canadian sport.* Toronto: University of Toronto Press.

Korneski, K. (2007). Britishness, Canadianness, class, and race: Winnipeg and the British world, 1880s–1910s. *Journal of Canadian Studies,* 41, 161–184.

Lehr, J.C. (1994). Peopling the Prairies with Ukrainians. In G. Tulchinsky (Ed.), *Immigration in Canada: Historical perspectives* (pp. 177–202). Toronto: Copp Clark Longman Ltd.

Levine, P. (1992). *Ellis Island to Ebbets Field: Sport and the American Jewish experience.* New York: Oxford University Press.

Levitt, C. & Shaffir, W. (1985). Baseball and ethnic violence in Toronto: The case of the Christie Pits riot, August 16, 1933. *Polyphony,* 7(1), 67–71.

Levitt, C.H. & Shaffir, W. (1987). *The riots at Christie Pits.* Toronto: Lester & Orpen Dennys.

Loewen, R. & Friesen, G. (2009). *Immigrants in prairie cities: Ethnic diversity in twentieth-century Canada*. Toronto: University of Toronto Press.

Mah, D. (1985). Early Chinese sports in Toronto. *Polyphony, 7*(1), 120–123.

Mitchell McKee, L.G. (1982). Nature's medicine: The physical education and outdoor recreation programmes of Toronto's voluntary youth organizations, 1880–1930. In B. Kidd (Ed.), *Proceedings of the 5th Canadian symposium on the history of sport and physical education* (pp. 128–139). Toronto: University of Toronto Press.

Morrow, D. & Wamsley, K.B. (2010). *Sport in Canada: A history* (2nd ed.). Toronto: Oxford University Press.

Nipp, D. (1985). The Chinese in Toronto. In R.F. Harney (Ed.), *Gathering place: Peoples and neighbourhoods of Toronto, 1834–1945* (pp. 147–175). Toronto: Multicultural History Society of Ontario.

Osborne, J. (Dir.). (2003). *Sleeping tigers: The Asahi baseball story* [motion picture]. Canada: National Film Board.

Pope, S.W. (2006). Decentering "race" and (re)presenting "Black" performance in sport history: Basketball and jazz in American culture, 1920–1950. In M.G. Phillips (Ed.), *Deconstructing sport history: A postmodern analysis* (pp. 147–177). Albany: SUNY Press.

Prang, M. (1985). "The girl God would have me be": The Canadian Girls in Training, 1915–39. *Canadian Historical Review, 66*, 154–184.

Reaves, J.A. (2002). *Taking in a game: A history of baseball in Asia*. Lincoln, NE: University of Nebraska Press.

Regalado, S.O. (2003). Base lines and beyond: The national pastime and its meanings. *Reviews in American History, 31*, 298–306.

Riess, S.A. (1999). *Touching base: Professional baseball and American culture in the Progressive Era* (2nd ed.). Urbana & Chicago: University of Illinois Press.

Riordan, J. (1999). The worker sport movement. In J. Riordan & A. Kruger (Eds.), *The international politics of sport in the 20th century* (pp. 105–117). London & New York: E. & F.N. Spon.

Rosenberg, D. (2003). Athletics in the Ward and beyond: Neighbourhoods, Jews, and sport in Toronto, 1900–1939. In R.C. Wilcox, D.L. Andrews, R. Pitter & R.L. Irwin (Eds.), *Sporting dystopias: The making and meaning of urban sport culture* (pp. 137–151). Albany: SUNY Press.

Sokolyk, K.W. (1991). The role of Ukrainian sports teams, clubs, and leagues, 1924–52. *Journal of Ukrainian Studies, 16,* 131–146.

Solomon, E. (1994). Jews and baseball: A cultural love story. In G. Eisen & D.K. Wiggins (Eds.), *Ethnicity and sport in North American history and culture* (pp. 75–101). Westport: Greenwood Press.

Speisman, S.A. (1979). *The Jews of Toronto: A history to 1937.* Toronto: McClelland & Stewart.

Square, D. (2007). *When Falcons fly: The story of the world's first Olympic gold hockey team.* Vancouver: Poppy Productions.

Temelini, W. (1985). The growth of sports involvement in the Windsor area. *Polyphony, 7*(1), 21–26.

Thompson, J.H. with Seager, A. (1985). *Canada, 1922–1939: Decades of discord.* Toronto: McClelland & Stewart.

Tulchinsky, G. (2008). *Canada's Jews: A people's journey.* Toronto: University of Toronto Press.

2006 Community Profiles. (2010). Statistics Canada. Retrieved from http://www12.statcan.ca/census-recensement/2006/dp-pd/prof/92-591/index.cfm

Wall, S. (2005). Totem poles, teepees, and token traditions: "Playing Indian" at Ontario summer camps, 1920–1955. *Canadian Historical Review, 86,* 513–30.

Wall, S. (2009). *The nurture of nature: Childhood, antimodernism, and Ontario summer camps, 1920–55.* Vancouver: UBC Press.

Whiting, R. (1989). *You gotta have wa.* New York: Vintage Books.

Zucchi, J. (2007). *A history of Canada's ethnic enclave.* Canada's Ethnic Group Series, booklet no. 31. Ottawa: The Canadian Historical Association.

CHAPTER 2

Football and "Tolerance": Black Football Players in 20th-Century Canada

JOHN VALENTINE AND SIMON C. DARNELL

Racial "Tolerance" in Canadian Football

This chapter draws on the history of Black football players in 20th-century Canada in order to explore and challenge the notion of Canadian racial tolerance in relation to Blackness. A review of historical accounts suggests that beginning with Canadian senior football in the 1920s and 1930s, through to the integration of African-American players in the 1940s to 1960s, the Canadian game allowed for some measure of racial diversity, particularly when compared to football in the United States. In turn, Canadian football provided an opportunity in the 1970s and 1980s for Black quarterbacks to establish themselves at a time when the position continued to be largely a White preserve in the American game. These experiences of Black football players in Canada tend to support the enduring popular belief that the treatment of racial minorities and immigrants in Canada differs positively from those in the United States and Britain, a belief that has not held up to critical scrutiny (see Reitz & Breton, 1994; Reitz, 1988).

The following analysis uses primary sources, particularly newspaper and magazine accounts, as well as the few secondary sources that examine the experiences of Black football players in Canada (Smith & Grindstaff, 1972; Longley, Crosset & Jefferson, 2008). We suggest that the first Black football players in Canada became successful, model citizens and were generally well received in Canada as they assumed a position that did not challenge the dominance of Whiteness. Yet, as football became more popular and Black players more successful on the field, many began to use their prominence to challenge racism and the notion of Canadian tolerance. The response in Canada to such resistance was a general denial of racism, particularly in comparison to the entrenched racial divides of the United States; such denials served (and continue) to preclude critical awareness of racism in Canadian sport culture.

Race and Football in Canada: Historical Context

Canada has a long and complex history of racism that often tends to be oversimplified through popular myths. The policy of multiculturalism, underpinned by the notion of Canada as fundamentally tolerant of difference, often provides Canadians with a sense of superiority or a belief in Canada as a country free from racism (Reitz & Breton, 1994). These truths can result in what Henry, Tator, Mattis, and Rees (2000) call "historical amnesia" toward racism in Canada, the tendency to forget or deny 300 years of racist laws, policies, practices, and ideologies, including slavery in New France, residential schools for First Nations peoples, and the internment of many Canadians during World War Two. In turn, the history of U.S. racism—typified by slavery, the underground railroad, and legal segregation—have underpinned the belief that Black people have fared better in Canada than in the U.S. (Winks, 1997; Walcott, 2003). Notably for this chapter, such myths have been supported by the popular history of Canadian sport in which trail-blazing Black athletes—like baseball player Jackie Robinson and football player Warren Moon, who began their professional careers in Montreal and Edmonton respectively before breaking through into the United States—have come to stand as further evidence of Canadian tolerance.

Such notions of a history of racial tolerance in Canada are contestable given the ways in which Black people have historically been written out of the official text of the nation (Abdel-Shehid, 2005; McKittrick, 2006; Walcott, 2003, 2004). The game of football is a prime example. Amidst the general dearth of historical analyses of football in Canada (Stebbins, 1987), the involvement and role of Black players have been particularly overlooked. For example, Cosentino (1969, 1995), Stebbins (1987), and O'Brien (2005) published academic works on Canadian football, but none significantly addressed the issue of race and racism or Blackness. There have been some important analyses on the topic showing that Black players faced sustained racism both on and off the field even though the situation may have been better for these players compared to Black players in American football (Smith & Grindstaff, 1972), and that African-American football players in the 1950s attempted to "quit" the racism they faced in the U.S. by accepting opportunities to play in Canada (Longley et al., 2008). Yet neither of these studies explored the question of Blackness within Canadian culture. Our goal in this chapter is to extend the time frame and sources of previous analyses but, more fundamentally, to analyze critically the implications of the experiences of Black football players in Canada in relation to the discourses of acceptance and racism more broadly in Canadian culture and in cultures of sport. To do so, we supplement the traditional historical analysis/methodology with critical sociological understandings of race and racism in Canada, which are explored in the next section.

Histories of Race in Canadian Football: Theory and Method

While this chapter is historical in its focus and methodology, it employs contemporary theorizing to inform the analyses. In particular, cultural understandings of Blackness in Canada, compared to the normativity of Whiteness, are employed that speak to the peripheral positioning of Black football players within the history of the Canadian game. When Black Canadians in the early 1900s, and Black Americans after World War Two, began to play elite football in Canada, there was the expectation that they would integrate and assimilate into Canadian society by assuming an appreciative, non-threatening social and political position. However, as Abdel-Shehid (2005, p. 134) reminds us, it was difficult for Blacks to show their appreciation because "as a result of racism in the United States, [they] came to a place with which many were unfamiliar and that, in many respects, was equally racist." He maintains that because of the unwillingness or inability of the Canadian majority to reconcile and embrace social differences like race, ethnicity, and culture, racial Others have been tolerated in Canadian sport as long as they engaged in the dominant performative element of Canadian nationalism and appeared grateful to be in Canada.

This understanding aligns with the classification of the "Good Black" athlete in Canadian culture as described by Wilson (1997), one portrayed and interpreted in the popular Canadian imagination as modest, hard-working, successful, and a good role model. Wilson contrasts this notion with the characterization of the "Bad Black," the Canadian athlete typified as undisciplined, vocal, and arrogant. Former CFL player Anthony Prior (2006) articulated this as the difference between the "Good Blacks" and the "Niggers" within the pool of football players in Canada. As the following sections demonstrate, the first wave of Black players to Canada largely existed—and succeeded—amidst the racist structures of the culture and, in the process, established roots and contributed to cultural, political, and economic life in Canada. In subsequent years, Black football players in Canada used their status to resist racism, challenge the normativity of Whiteness, and fight for social change. Following Abdel-Shehid (2005), the critical issue for our analysis is not one of confirming racism or its absence, but of interrogating what racism in the history of Canadian football means for understandings of Blackness within the relations of power and dominance that constitute(d) Canadian sport culture.

Race and Racism in Early Canadian Football

Canadian society in the early 20th century was marked by firm segregation along lines of race and ethnicity (Winks, 1997) and as a result, athletes of colour were segregated in both hockey and baseball (Cosentino, 1998). In football, Black men began to play the game, but they were identified first and foremost by the colour of their skin. Russ Gideon, from Nova Scotia, was one of the first Black men to play the Canadian senior game—the highest level of football in Canada at the time—starring in Calgary from 1928 to 1933. He was named the star of the game on several occasions (Penley, 2006) and was referred to as "Calgary's popular, colored athlete and brilliant end performer" (*Calgary Albertan*, 1930). Robert "Stonewall" Jackson signed to play with the Regina Roughriders in 1930 and a headline reading "DUSKY ATHLETE JOINS RIDERS" appeared in the *Leader-Post*. Referred to at the start of the season as the "ebony-hued boy," the same newspaper deemed him a fan favourite by the end of the season (Calder & Andrews, 1984).

Gideon's retirement marked the low point of participation for Black players in Canada as an unofficial ban in the United States extended north. After the successes of Gideon and Jackson, there would not be another Black player in Canadian professional football until 1946. The normativity of Whiteness, pressure to save paying jobs for White people during the Depression and the war, and the largely unwritten racist policies and practices of U.S. football likely contributed to this.

The end of World War Two marked the beginning of changing attitudes in many areas of Canadian society, including attitudes toward racial discrimination. According to Owram (1997, p. 167), notions of racial segregation and other "such formalized prejudice flew in the face of prevailing notions about democracy and freedom." Incremental change could be seen in sport at this time. In 1946, Jackie Robinson became the first Black player in professional baseball when he suited up with the Montreal Royals. His success and perseverance in Montreal helped to facilitate the Montreal Alouettes football club's signing of Herb Trawick and John Moody that same year. In response, both the Toronto and Ottawa football teams threatened to boycott games against Montreal, though the threats were ultimately never acted upon (Humber, 1983).

Change came slowly. In Canadian football in 1946, each team was allowed only five American players so the opportunities for Black Americans to play in Canada were restricted. Despite import restrictions, many Black Americans sought the opportunity to play football north of the border and several enjoyed significant success. In 1947, American Gabe Patterson, of the Saskatchewan Roughriders, led the West in scoring. In 1948, the Calgary Stampeders signed Woody Strode, who had broken the colour barrier just two years previously in the United States before being released by the Los Angeles team, which objected to his interracial marriage (Ross, 2000; Strode & Young, 1990; Wolff, 2009). In 1949, Ottawa signed Ray Skerrett, and Hamilton signed American Tom Casey, who moved to Winnipeg to attend medical school and play for the Winnipeg Blue Bombers. In 1950, the Toronto Argonauts, a team that had resisted using any American players, signed Billy Bass and Ulysses Curtis. The next year Edmonton gave contracts to Rollie Miles and Jim Chambers. By the end of the decade, 13 percent of the American players in Canadian football were Black while only 3 percent of U.S.-based teams were made up of Black players (Longley et al., 2008; Ross, 2000). By 1951, all of the professional football teams in Canada were racially reintegrated, a process that clearly happened much faster in Canada than in the U.S. In 1956, a decade after the colour barrier was broken, 17 percent of the American players in Canada were Black, while only 8 percent of American-based teams were comprised of Black players (Leonard, 1980; Lomax, 1999; Ross, 2000) with many American teams still refusing to reintegrate (Ross, 2000; Smith & Grindstaff, 1972). Indeed, the majority of Black football players in Canada were American, a fact that likely contributed to the tendency to "blame America" when racism emerged in Canada.

It is important to consider why Black football players were playing professional football in Canada at a rate two to four times higher than in the U.S. First, in post-World War Two Canada, top American players were enticed by salaries that were often much higher than they could earn playing at home and paid in a currency that, through the 1950s, was more valuable than the U.S. dollar. In addition, Canadian teams practised less often than in the U.S., allowing opportunities for careers outside of football to be developed. This was an attractive proposition for players planning for a career after football, and many of the first Black football players to arrive in Canada made Canada their home after retiring from football. Third, the influx of American players into Canadian football coincided with the adoption of many rules, strategies, and even terminology that was derived from American football. American coaches familiar with these strategies were hired, and they were interested in signing players experienced with these rules and style of play. Finally, it is reasonable to suggest that Black players were more acceptable in football in Canada not because of anti-racist policies or thinking, but because football in Canada did not carry the same cultural importance as it did in the United States (see Abdel-Shehid, 2005, p. 133).

The Invisibility of Blackness

During the 1950s, many of the Black players in Canadian football were superb players and model citizens, and were honoured by the teams and the cities they represented. These men were outstanding football players yet, compared to Black football players in Canada in subsequent years, they remained largely invisible off the field, rarely challenging the dominant Canadian culture politically or socially at a time when Black people were denied many opportunities in Canadian society.

For example, Bernie Custis, after being denied the opportunity to play quarterback in the United States, was voted most popular player by the fans in 1951 and an all-star, and Tom Casey was named Winnipeg's "Citizen of the Year" in 1956 (Danakas, 2007). Herb Trawick was awarded the Calvert Trophy as the fans' choice for most popular player for two consecutive years; prior to the 1951 season he became the first Black player to be named captain of a professional football team. Trawick became a Canadian citizen in 1953, as did Ulysses Curtis.

The success these players enjoyed on the field resulted in more high-profile players seeking opportunities in Canada. In 1952, Johnny Bright, a top U.S. college player, was selected in the first round of the NFL draft by the Philadelphia Eagles, but chose to play in Canada. Years later he spoke about his reluctance to be the first Black player on the Philadelphia team, and expressed his concern about playing with White teammates who had been raised amidst southern cultures of segregation (Sebring, 1999). By 1954, Bright was playing for Edmonton in a backfield made up of African-American Rollie Miles and Chinese-Canadian Normie Kwong, referred to as the "United Nations team" (Redmond, 1989, p. 12). They went on to win three consecutive Grey Cup championships, and Bright retired as the all-time leading rusher in CFL history. He eventually became a Canadian citizen, football coach, and school principal, and a school in the city of Edmonton was named in his honour.

Clearly, there were opportunities for Black men in Canadian football as compared to the U.S. Yet overt racism in Canada continued. In 1953, Billy Vessels, a White halfback on the Edmonton Eskimos, was named the Most Outstanding Player in Canadian football when many felt that he was not even the best player on his team. In his acceptance speech, Vessels acknowledged that he felt his Black teammate Rollie Miles should have won the award (Brooke, 1953, p. 20). Years later, Normie Kwong stated that "conditions in the country then weren't conducive to a person of colour winning awards" (Kelly, 1999, p. 22).

There were other racist incidents as well, particularly involving Black football players off the field. In the late 1950s, hotels refused to provide services to Black players on the Eskimos, Stampeders, and Blue Bombers teams (Hall, 2006; Kelly, 2001). Star players like George Reed (Sokol & Millson, 1967), Leo Lewis (Kelly, 1999), Ulysses Curtis (Christie, 2004), Willie Fleming (Longley et al, 2008), and Herb Trawick (Frayne, 1956) described discrimination and difficulties in renting apartments or finding work. In 1963, sportswriter John Robertson wrote that three Black players on the Saskatchewan Roughriders were having trouble finding places to live. He asked readers to contact him if they knew of any furnished apartments, adding that "this makes me a little sick inside ... I am embarrassed for a few of my bigoted fellow Reginans" (Robertson, 1963, p. 17). Black players also had to deal with racism perpetuated by teammates. It was reported that Herb Trawick faced more racial hostility from his Canadian teammates than from his American teammates (Bell-Webster, 2009).

While football in Canada may have been more open to Black players than in the United States, the broader Canadian society was less than tolerant. This suggests that the racist discrimination faced by the average (and non-football playing) person of colour in Canada at the time was likely even more violent and abusive. As Rollie Miles stated, "You don't have to be a football hero to avoid discrimination in Canada—but it sure helps" (Rowan, 1960, p. 98). From this perspective, the invisibility of Blackness in Canada connected to the pressure and desire among Black football players to assimilate into the dominant Canadian culture. Football offered an opportunity to do so. Not until the 1960s did challenges to this invisibility begin to emerge.

Black Athletes' Resistance against Racism in Canada

While sport can play an important role in perpetuating existing power relations, it can also provide opportunities for resistance. During the 1960s, while the U.S. civil rights movement expanded, so too did the number of Black professional football players in Canada, as well as their profile and status. Black players in particular became more established in the CFL and in their communities, and increasingly spoke out against long-standing discrimination and oppression. They challenged the relations of power that sustained the dominance of Whiteness.

Rollie Miles worked to expose the forms of discrimination in Canadian society (Rowan, 1960) of which he was a victim (Rowan, 1960). In a game against Calgary, the opposing coach pushed Miles and hurled racial slurs, yet no action was taken by the league (*Edmonton Journal*, 1951, p. 10). In an invited speech delivered in 1957, Miles became one of the first players to speak about racism in Canada, using the Eskimos' United Nations backfield as an example of how prejudice can be overcome (CP, 1957). In 1960, the American Black magazine *Ebony* featured Miles in an article entitled "Negroes in Canada" (Rowan, 1960). Miles acknowledged his privileged position, saying "Just because I get special treatment here and there doesn't mean that I don't know what the situation is. I still see a lot of ignorance and prejudice on the part of people" (Rowan, 1960, p. 98). He also expressed frustration: "Canadians are so damn smug. You can tell them what's going on, where the discriminations are, and they still won't believe you" (p. 104).

In 1961, Miles, along with fellow Edmonton Eskimos Johnny

Bright and Art Walker, wrote a lengthy letter to the *Edmonton Journal* newspaper "protesting against the anti-Negro and anti-Indian attitudes they found in Canada" (Bright, Lorch, Miles, Robinson & Walker, 1961, p. 4). The letter was also signed by Lee Lorch, a professor of mathematics in Edmonton, who had been prevented from teaching in the U.S. due to his civil rights activities. The letter expressed hope that "enough persons will come forward at home to wipe out all forms of discrimination here." While some analysts have argued that Black players on the Eskimos reported "virtually no evidence of discrimination directed against them" (see Winks, 1968, p. 461), clearly the Black players on the Eskimos felt it necessary to speak out against racism in Canadian society.

Similarly, Carlton (Cookie) Gilchrist, who joined the Hamilton Tiger-Cats in 1956 and one year later led them to a Grey Cup victory, railed against "insidious racism," had a near fist fight with his head coach, and was suspended often. Gilchrist also married a White woman, which, he suggested, resulted in both the league administration and media turning against him (Simonich, 2003). In 1983, citing discrimination on the part of former coaches, Gilchrist refused induction into the Canadian Football Hall of Fame (Peters, 2007). Gilchrist stated that most of the problems he encountered were a result of his standing up for principles during a time when Black athletes were expected to remain silent and invisible (Kernaghan, 2003).

In 1967, a feature article in *Canadian Magazine* entitled "The Negro in the CFL" examined the situations Black players faced in playing professional football in Canada (Proudfoot, 1967): "The Negro is a hero on the field, and a bum off it, when it comes to getting work," said superstar Willie Fleming (p. 5). Some players commented that most teams had two or four Black players, usually an even number so that a White player need not be forced to room with a Black player on road trips. Ottawa general manager Red O'Quinn spoke of the importance of set quotas for the number of Black players, claiming that "[p]roblems come in if you have more than four or five colored players" (p. 5). Amidst such practices, Ralph Goldston, a former player and coach, said "it would be the dumbest thing in the world to say there's no prejudice in Canadian football" (p. 8).

Shortly after the publication of the article, several Canadian cities were compared to the southern U.S. for the degree of racism experienced by Black players. Former Ottawa player Ted Watkins was quoted in an interview on the CBC television show *The Public Eye*, stating "I have had many problems in Ottawa which made me feel like I was in Mississippi somewhere" (Sokol & Millson, 1967, p. 25) in reference to the racial violence and segregation of the American South. A feature article in the *Toronto Telegram* followed this, in which Saskatchewan All-Star George Reed was quoted as saying that:

> Regina is like living in the heart of Alabama as far as I'm concerned.... People talk about racial discrimination here and point to the south. Well, I hope what Ted Watkins said makes them open their eyes and realize what's going on in Regina, and do something about it now. (Sokol & Millson, 1967, p. 25)

Dave Raimey, of the Winnipeg Blue Bombers stated: "I want to leave this city [Winnipeg]. In the U.S. at least I knew where I stood as far as discrimination went. Here you never really can tell for sure" (Sokol & Millson, 1967, p. 25). The *Regina Leader-Post*, in a follow-up article, cited Reed as joining "the list of Negro athletes who consider they can no longer be silent about racial discrimination in this country" (Artiss, 1967a, p. 30). In the article, Reed challenged Canadian views on the absence of racism and expressed concern about the plight of Black people living in Canada.

These experiences suggest that the social upheaval of the time period, coupled with success on the football field, provided Black football players in Canada with a venue to speak out against racism in an effort to challenge the dominance of White Canada. The fact that Miles, Reed, Bright, and others held down jobs in their communities may also have afforded them stability from which to speak out against racism and discrimination. Still, their actions produced minimal change. When these prominent Black men spoke out, Canadians were largely surprised because racism was rarely acknowledged in Canada (McKittrick, 2006). As Abdel-Shehid (2005) and Walcott (2003) argue, resistance to racism—of the sort mobilized by Miles, Reed, and Bright—tends to do little more than cause a minor stir in the broader Canadian culture and even more radical performances of Blackness tend to be depoliticized within the popular Canadian imagination in which Black people are positioned as passive and unlikely to participate in political activism (Sealy, 2000).

An Era of Black Quarterbacks

Longley et al. (2008) concluded their analysis of Black-American football players in Canada by calling for further research into the era of the late 1960s to the 1980s. While racist stereotypes have traditionally led to limited opportunities for Black quarterbacks in the U.S., this time period was characterized first and foremost by the visible success of Black players at the quarterback position in Canada. According to J.C. Watts, the quarterback for the Orange Bowl champion University of Oklahoma team who also played the position in Canada, "NFL coaches and managers had a tough time seeing Blacks in leadership positions, and they worried that fans would react negatively to putting Blacks in charge of a team" (Watts & Winston, 2002, p. 124). In a 1972 article in *Sports Illustrated*, George Taliaferro, former Black quarterback with the Baltimore Colts, echoed Watts when he stated in reference to the U.S.: "[t]his country is not at a point where it will accept a Black quarterback leading its finest white boys" (Marshall, 1972, p. 93).

Bernie Custis was denied the opportunity to play quarterback in the U.S., so in 1951 he signed with Hamilton, was named to the All-Star team as quarterback, and was voted most popular player on the team by the Hamilton fans (Danakas, 2007). In 1954 Willie Thrower went to Canada for an opportunity to play quarterback. John Henry Jackson followed in 1961, as did Sandy Stephens in 1962 after leading his college team to the national title. In 1968, Marlon Briscoe became the first starting Black quarterback in American football, but was cut after one season and went to Canada to play. Chuck Ealey won 35 straight games, including three Bowl games as a starting quarterback for a top 20 U.S. college team, but was ignored by NFL teams. In 1972, his first year in the CFL, he won rookie of the year honours, led his team to the Grey Cup championship, and was named game MVP. A Black quarterback would not start in a Super Bowl game for another 16 years, but by that time seven Black quarterbacks had played in a Grey Cup. In 1976, there was one Black starting quarterback among the 28 NFL teams, while the next season one-third of the Canadian teams were led by Black quarterbacks, including the quarterbacking pair of Matthew Reed and Chuck Ealey, the highest paid quarterbacking tandem in the league. The proliferation of Black Americans in Canadian football was most prevalent at this position (Maxymuk, 2009).

The player who drew the most attention to the success of the Black quarterback in Canada was Warren Moon. In 1978, Moon was the Pac-10 player of the year in U.S. college football, as well as the Rose Bowl winning quarterback, yet was ignored by American professional teams. Moon found an immediate difference playing in Canada:

> The biggest thing was, for me, you could really feel that I was only being judged by how I played on the field and that was it. I wasn't being judged by the colour of my skin. I never heard any type of racial slurs while I was up there. It was very refreshing to know that I could just prepare for a game, go out there and not have to worry about anything else. (Campbell, 2009, p. 12)

Moon went on to face J.C. Watts in the 1981 Grey Cup game, 20 years before the Super Bowl would see a second Black quarterback. Both Roy DeWalt in 1980 and Watts in 1981 were drafted by NFL teams planning to play them at positions other than quarterback. This was a common practice for Black quarterbacks who, at the time, were thought not to have the requisite leadership skills for the position. Both signed to play quarterback in Canada instead. By 1998, even though the NFL had three times as many teams, more than 40 Black quarterbacks had thrown 25 or more passes in the CFL, but only nine had done so in the U.S. Maxymuk (2009) suggests that the recent increase in Black quarterbacks in the U.S., such as it is, may be due to the success Black quarterbacks demonstrated in Canada. As of 2011, 29 Black players had started at the position of quarterback in Canada's Grey Cup, while only four had played the position in the Super Bowl.

After six years in the CFL, Moon returned to the U.S. and went on to play 17 seasons in the NFL and earn election to the Pro Football Hall of Fame. He once again experienced the racism he had faced in high school and college when he returned to the United States (Moon & Yaeger, 2009). In his NFL Hall of Fame induction speech, Moon went so far as to publicly thank Canada for its racial tolerance and the opportunities he enjoyed. Other recent African-American imports, including Watts (Watts & Winston, 2002) and Pinball Clemons (Fitzgerald, 2007), have similarly claimed that Canada has been, and continues to be, more racially tolerant than the United States. Such accounts should not be dismissed for they surely are true as far as men like Moon, Watts, and Clemons experienced them. Still, it is reasonable to argue that none of these men, despite their class privilege and athletic fame, came to be viewed as quintessentially Canadian, even at a time when athletic Blackness could be moulded to national narratives (see Jackson, 2004). Furthermore, to say that Canada was more racially tolerant than the U.S. is not to say that it was free of racism. It is reasonable to suggest that such accounts from athletes have proven a challenge to anti-racist efforts in Canada to the extent that they have prevented ongoing examination of the racism faced by Black football players, not to mention average Canadians of colour. More recent events bear this out. The 1988 CFL rookie of the year, Orville Lee, stated that racism is clearly evident in the CFL (Spence, 1999). In 1997, two of the top defensive players in the league—K.D. Williams and Lamar McGriggs—complained about racism on the Saskatchewan team and both were quickly traded (York, 1997). In 2004, All-Star receiver Nik Lewis reported to the CFL administration that a referee had used a racial slur against him, but there was no response from the league (Petrie, 2004).

"Blame America" for Racism in Canadian Football

The dominant narrative in Canadian football—perpetuated in the popular press and even by some players—in response to claims and descriptions of racism has been to position Canada as tolerant relative to the United States. Such responses are intelligible in the ways they lay claim to Canadian racial innocence despite its origins as a land of White settlement and entitlement (Razack, 1998). Indeed, many Black players, as well as writers and commentators in Canadian football in the 1950s and 1960s, supported the positive stereotype of the "more hospitable social environment north of the border" (Rowan, 1960, p. 98). In 1959, the American sports magazine *Sports Illustrated* published an article urging American athletes to head north, arguing that Canada was a land without prejudice, and citing examples of American football players working and enjoying Canadian life (Herndon, 1959). In 1960, Rowan argued that Canadians were more tolerant than Americans, resulting in a better life for the Black Americans who had moved north, and explained that Edmonton player Rollie Miles "was in a position that few Negroes enjoy in the United States. He lived in an integrated neighborhood, worshipped in an integrated church, taught in a predominantly white school, and was a full-fledged member of the Lions club" (p. 98). In a feature newspaper article published in 1967, numerous players were adamant that the social climate in Canada for Black people was far superior to what they would have faced in the U.S. George Dixon, Marv Luster, Willie Bethea, and Bill Munsey emphasized that they and their families enjoyed a better life in Canada. Many of this first wave of U.S.-born CFL players decided to stay in Canada and become citizens, including Rollie Miles, who, when asked about his decision, stated, "I don't want to raise my children in a country where they're second-class citizens, where they can't use the same bathrooms and the water fountains" (MacKinnon, 2004, p. C1). It is worth noting that these opinions were provided to Canadian newspapers in cities where these athletes were living, likely providing a relatively stable platform that "allowed" for speaking out about racism.

Others perpetuated this narrative as well. Accompanying the 1967 *Toronto Telegram* feature on racism in the CFL was a smaller article by award-winning sports columnist Bob Pennington, in which he blamed the discrimination against Black football players in Canada on American coaches and administrators. Pennington's message to Watkins was that he should "stifle his criticism" of racism in the CFL and be thankful to be in Canada. Pennington went so far as to argue that "To a U.S. Negro, Canada is almost a haven of tolerance, compared to what he has known in his own country" (Pennington, 1967, p. 25). Similarly, accompanying the *Regina Leader-Post* article on racism was a column by sports editor Laurie Artiss (1967b, p. 30) in which he disparaged Reed's accounts, writing that the player was "over-stating a case" and "being overly-sensitive" about racism in the Canadian game. Artiss also dismissed Reed's concerns about the racism Reed's son endured, arguing that it was just "boys being boys," and implied that Reed's difficulty in renting an apartment and the racist taunts he endured in public stemmed more from him being a recognizable figure than because he was Black.

Any shift on the part of Black football players in the CFL from invisible subjects to outspoken critics of Canadian racism tended to result more in finger pointing at American culture and claims to relative innocence rather than critical reflection on racism in the game or culture of Canada. Importantly, this narrative was available to the Canadian racial majority. White people connected to the game welcomed Black football players. As Sealy (2000, p. 99) argues, most Canadians feel that "there is little if any racism in Canada to protest. Black Canadians, unlike their Black-American counterparts, have little to worry about, since Black people and white people live in harmony in Canada."

It is crucial to remember, then, that such narratives have been, and will continue to be, challenged and resisted. In 1972, after interviewing a number of CFL players, Smith and Grindstaff concluded that:

> [t]he Black players felt that the Canadian racial situation was slightly better than the United States. They still, however, experienced prejudice and discrimination, both on and off the field. . . . They expressed bitterness that white players were able to obtain better jobs while playing football even though they weren't necessarily better qualified. (205)

Even some White players felt that Black players were at a disadvantage in finding jobs on CFL clubs and securing housing because of racism (Smith & Grindstaff, 1972).

Conclusion

Notions of Canadian tolerance, supported by popular notions of "racism-free" sport like football, continue to inform Canadian history and culture. As Walker (1985, p. 18) argues, "the Underground Railroad fostered a myth that the North Star led not just out of slavery, but into freedom, equality and participation in Canadian life." This North Star myth continues to underpin Canadian identity particularly as a feature that positively distinguishes the politics of race in Canada from that of the United States. While many Black football players thrived in Canadian professional football and the CFL, this does not serve as evidence of racial tolerance. These men fought against the racism that constituted an accepted part of Canadian culture and worked for social change amidst racial hierarchies. Given this ambivalence in Canadian racial politics, the experiences of Black football players in Canada show race to be a contested terrain, and Blackness to be precarious, within the cultural norms and relations of power that constitute(d) Canadian football and Canadian culture more broadly.

Questions for Critical Thought

1. Consider the various similarities and differences between the racism experienced by Black football players in Canada versus those in the United States. Discuss the implications of these similarities and differences for understandings of race, tolerance, and Canadian culture.
2. How have cultures of sport in Canada, including football, justified racial oppression? How have they provided opportunities for resistance to racism?
3. Consider how the racism experienced by Black football players in Canada intersected with other social categories of dominance, such as gender and social class. How did notions of gender and class perpetuate racism in Canadian football?
4. How can the North Star myth and a policy like multiculturalism be used for nation-building and for reinforcing the dominant culture and racism in Canada?

References

Abdel-Shehid, G. (2005). *Who da man? Black masculinities and sporting cultures.* Toronto: Canadian Scholars' Press Inc.

Artiss, L. (1967a). George Reed charges discrimination here. *Regina Leader-Post* (December 15), 30.

Artiss, L. (1967b). George Reed. *Regina Leader-Post* (December 15), 30.

Bell-Webster, J. (2009). *Herb Trawick*. Retrieved from www.cfl.ca/page/his_legends_trawick

Bright, J., Lorch, L., Miles, R., Robinson, F.P. & Walker, A. (1961). Racial equality. *Edmonton Journal* (June 16), 4.

Brooke, J. (1953). Sooner Schooner to receive $1,000 cheque at Toronto Granite Club. *Edmonton Journal* (November 27), 20.

Calder, G. & Andrews, B. (1984). *Rider pride: The story of Canada's best-loved football team*. Saskatoon: Western Producer Prairie Books.

Calgary Albertan. (1930). Russ Gideon only player to score try. *Calgary Albertan* (October 2), 7.

Campbell, C. (2009). Interview. *Maclean's*, 122(28) (July 27), 12–13.

Christie, J. (2004). Crazy Legs put a stiff arm on racism. *Globe and Mail* (February 4), S2.

Cosentino, F. (1969). *Canadian football: The Grey Cup years*. Toronto: Musson.

Cosentino, F. (1995). *A passing game: A history of the CFL*. Winnipeg: Bain & Cox.

Cosentino, F. (1998). *Afros, Aboriginals, and amateur sport in pre-World War One Canada*. Ottawa: Canadian Historical Association.

CP. (1957). Rollie's Negro "curfew" speech throws town fathers for loss. *Edmonton Journal* (February 22), 1.

Danakas, J. (2007). *Choice of colours*. Toronto: James Lorimer & Company.

Edmonton Journal. (1951). Eskimos need three wins to finish first. *Edmonton Journal* (September 19), 10.

Fitzgerald, S. (2007). Pinball lauds NFL gains made by Smith, Dungy: Super Bowl race barrier falls. *National Post* (January 23), S8.

Frayne, T. (1956). The gentle bone-crusher of the Alouettes. *Maclean's*, 69(23) (November 10), 26–27, 80–82.

Hall, V. (2006). One of CFL's best ever stood up for teammates. *Edmonton Journal* (November 11), D1.

Henry, F., Tator, C., Mattis, W. & Rees, T. (2000). *The colour of democracy:*

Racism in Canadian society (2nd ed.). Toronto: Harcourt Brace & Company.

Herndon, B. (1959). Young man, go north! *Sports Illustrated, 11*(17) (October 26), 84–96.

Humber, W. (1983). *Cheering for the home team: The story of baseball in Canada.* Erin: The Boston Mills Press.

Jackson, S. (2004). Exorcizing the ghost: Donovan Bailey, Ben Johnson, and the politics of Canadian identity. *Media, Culture & Society, 26*(1), 121–141.

Kelly, G. (1999). *The Grey Cup: A history.* Red Deer: Johnson Gorman.

Kelly, G. (2001). *Green grit: The story of the Saskatchewan Roughriders.* Toronto: HarperCollins.

Kernaghan, J. (2003). Cookie. *London Free Press* (November 15). Retrieved from slam.canoe.ca/Slam/Football/CFL/GreyCup/2004/06/10/493796.html

Leonard, W.M. (1980). *A sociological perspective of sport.* Minneapolis: Burgess Publishing Company.

Lomax, M. (1999). The African American experience in professional football. *Journal of Social History, 33*(1), 165.

Longley, N., Crosset, T. & Jefferson, S. (2008). The migration of African-Americans to the Canadian Football League during the 1950s: An escape from racism? *The International Journal of the History of Sport, 25*(10), 1374–1397.

MacKinnon, J. (2004). The class of '54: Players from first Esks Grey Cup team became Edmonton's future leaders. *The Edmonton Journal* (October 10), C1.

Marshall, J. (1972). Chuck Ealey: Champion and still winner. *Sports Illustrated, 37*(24) (December 11), 90–93.

Maxymuk, J. (2009). The great quarterback migration. *The Coffin Corner, 31*(5), 11–12.

McKittrick, K. (2006). *Demonic ground: Black women and the cartographies of struggle.* Minneapolis: University of Minnesota Press.

Moon, W. & Yaeger, D. (2009). *Never give up on your dream.* Philadelphia: De Capo Press.

O'Brien, S. (2005). *The Canadian Football League: The phoenix of professional sports leagues*. Morrisville, NC: Lulu Press.

Owram, D. (1997). *Born at the right time: A history of the baby boom generation*. Toronto: University of Toronto Press.

Penley, K. (2006). Russ Gideon: Athlete and business leader. *Alberta History* (Spring), 18–20.

Pennington, B. (1967). Discrimination? Yes! But why the surprise? *Toronto Telegram* (December 7), 25.

Peters, K. (2007). Lookie, lookie, here comes Cookie. *Hamilton Spectator* (May 30), A7.

Petrie, M. (2004). Three downs, racism await Black players. *Calgary Herald* (October 27), E6.

Prior, A. (2006). *The slave side of Sunday*. Vancouver: Stonehold Books.

Proudfoot, D. (1967). The Negro in the CFL. *Canadian Magazine* (November 18), 5–8.

Razack, S. (1998). *Looking White people in the eye: Gender, race, and culture in courtrooms and classrooms*. Toronto: University of Toronto Press.

Redmond, G. (1989). *Forty years of tradition: The Edmonton Eskimos 1949 to 1989*. Edmonton: ESP Marketing & Communications.

Reitz, J. (1988). Less racial discrimination in Canada, or simply less racial conflict? Implications of comparisons with Britain. *Canadian Public Policy,* 14(4), 424–441.

Reitz, J. & Breton, R. (1994). *The illusion of difference: Realities of ethnicity in Canada and the United States*. Ottawa: C.D. Howe Institute.

Robertson, J. (1963). *Regina Leader-Post* (August 4), 17.

Ross, C.K. (2000). *Outside the lines: African-Americans and the integration of the National Football League*. New York: NYU Press.

Rowan, C.T. (1960). Negroes in Canada. *Ebony* (August), 98–106.

Sealy, D. (2000). "Canadianising" Blackness: Resisting the political in Rude. In R. Walcott (Ed.), *Contemporary Black Canadian cultural criticism* (pp. 87–108). Toronto: Insomniac Press.

Sebring, B. (1999). Johnny Bright could do it all on the field. *Fort Wayne News-Sentinel* (December 30), 30.

Simonich, M. (2003). Cookie Gilchrist breaks the silence. *Saskatoon Star-Phoenix* (March 22), B3.

Smith, G. & Grindstaff, C.F. (1972). Race and sport in Canada. In A. Taylor (Ed.), *Training: Scientific basis and application* (pp. 197–206). Springfield: Charles C. Tomas.

Sokol, A. & Millson, L. (1967). The Watkins furor picks up steam. *Toronto Telegram* (December 7), 25.

Spence, C. (1999). *The skin I'm in: Racism, sports, and education*. Winnipeg: Fernwood Publishing.

Stebbins, R. (1987). *Canadian football: The view from the helmet*. London: Center for Social and Humanistic Studies, University of Western Ontario.

Strode, W. & Young, S. (1990). *Goal dust*. Lanham: Madison Books.

Walcott, R. (2003). *Black like who? Writing Black Canada* (2nd ed.). London: Insomniac Press.

Walcott, R. (2004). "A tough geography": Towards a poetics of Black space(s) in Canada. In C. Sugars (Ed.), *Unhomely states: Theorizing English-Canadian postcolonialism* (pp. 277–288). Peterborough: Broadview Press.

Walker, J. (1985). *Racial discrimination in Canada: The Black experience*. Ottawa: Canadian Historical Association.

Watts, J.C. & Winston, C. (2002). *What color is a Conservative? My life and my politics*. New York: HarperCollins.

Wilson, B. (1997). "Good Blacks and bad Blacks": Media constructions of African-American athletes in Canadian basketball. *International Review for the Sociology of Sport, 32*(2), 177–189.

Winks, R. (1997). *The Blacks in Canada: A History* (2nd ed.). Montreal & Kingston: McGill-Queen's University Press.

Winks, R.W. (1968). The Canadian Negro: A historical assessment: The Negro in the Canadian American relationship. *The Journal of Negro History, 53*(4), 291–300.

Wolff, A. (2009). The NFL's Jackie Robinson. *Sports Illustrated, 111*(14) (October 12), 60–71.

York, M. (1997). At large: Dissension in the ranks sinking Roughriders. *Globe and Mail* (September 3), C14.

CHAPTER 3
Hockey and the Reproduction of Colonialism in Canada
ANDREAS KREBS

Introduction

Sport has been linked to colonial endeavours throughout its modern history. While physical games are as old as humanity, it was only in the mid-19th century that sport came to be viewed as a means of inculcating social values, particularly in the young men who played them. In England, cricket and football began their lives as disorganized country games, but developed into institutions through the manoeuvring of heads of schools and other organizations, who saw them as means of spreading bourgeois values of work, discipline, and manliness through the young, impressionable members of their own class, and ultimately the entire nation (James, 1993). Starting in the 19th century, organized sport was used by imperial powers to discipline their colonized subjects. I argue in this chapter that hockey continues to produce colonial relationships in Canada by maintaining the hegemony of a White, masculine subjectivity to which all other subject positions must refer. The chapter examines four intersecting sites through which hockey reproduces colonialism in contemporary Canada: nationalism, race, gender, and space.

The notion that sport holds the capacity to mould minds through the body extended beyond the metropole, manifesting itself in the colonial policy of imperial powers. For instance, Gems (1999) discusses the importance of sport for the American colonization of the Philippines. Not only was sport a means of civilizing the so-called "savage" Filipino, they also united Filipinos into a nation through competition, and prepared Filipino students for the capitalist economic system. Similarly, in Africa, as Darby (2000) argues, while football came to be seen as a tool of resistance, it had a long history of being used by colonial powers to discipline their subjects.

In much the same way that cricket, football, and other games were used in various colonies to instil values among native players, hockey was used in Canadian Aboriginal residential schools to shape the students' approach to the world around them. Residential school hockey teams, which competed against each other and rarely with non-Aboriginal teams, led to the highly developed, but mostly separate, Aboriginal hockey leagues and tournaments of today (Library and Archives Canada, 2010; Paraschak, 1997). The very existence of these separate leagues speaks to the racial—and spatial—hierarchies that continue to mark Canadian society as colonial.

While these overt exercises in shaping the subjectivity of the colonized can seem relegated to the past, in this chapter I will argue that Canada's most high-profile sport, hockey, continues to play a role in reproducing colonialism. Rather than being the work of school administrators and colonial officials, in contemporary Canada, hockey reproduces colonial subjectivity by maintaining the dominance of particular narratives. The following five sections of this chapter describe the micro-political techniques through which hockey maintains these colonial narratives, and how these narratives maintain White masculinity as central, and against which all other subject positions must be defined.

First, I outline my theoretical and methodological approach, which analyzes the reproduction of colonialism through the maintenance of White, male, anglophone hegemony using discourse analysis. The remaining sections deal with intersecting forces that reproduce or amplify Whiteness and hypermasculinity in Canada, two trends constitutive of colonial subjectivity. The second section deals with nationalism and multiculturalism; the third with violence, masculinity, and race; the fourth with women and sexuality; and the fifth with space.

I: Theoretical and Methodological Framework

Claude Denis (1997) underscores the colonial character of the Canadian mainstream by referring to it as the *Whitestream*, an amalgam of forces and trajectories that position Whiteness, masculinity, and a liberal-capitalist conception of the individual as central to social, cultural, and political life in Canada. The Whitestream functions as an invisible normative touchstone, with difference defined against it. This concept also allows for subjects not marked as White, or gendered as male, to be incorporated into its flow and for their energies to further augment the Whitestream's force. For the purposes of this chapter, in referring to the reproduction of colonialism, I am referring to the reproduction of the Whitestream.

The Whitestream is ever-shifting, but its link to the colonial past cannot be denied. Racial and gendered hierarchies continue to mark Canadian politics and society. The turning back of the *Komagata Maru*, the prohibition of the potlatch, or the internment of Japanese Canadians may seem distant given the advent of multiculturalism, the *Charter of Rights and Freedoms*, and a new relationship with Aboriginal peoples. However, lower socio-economic standing continues to correlate with non-White ethnicity and newcomer status (Nakhaie, 2006), indicating that a hierarchy of race and immigrant status persists in Canada. Even since 1967, when citizenship and immigration laws began to be liberalized, the Canadian state has retained the right to deport foreign-born citizens; "family-class" immigrants are denied equal access to social programs (Thobani,

2007, pp. 96–99); and what amounts to indentured servitude in exchange for permanent residency exists in the Foreign Domestic Movement program (Cohen, 2000).[1] Combined with the persistence of abject poverty, high rates of suicide and incarceration, poor and overcrowded housing conditions, and a further litany of statistics relating to the often horrific circumstances that Aboriginal peoples face on a daily basis, the persistence of colonialism in Canada cannot be denied (see Allard, Wilkings & Berthelot, 2004; Statistics Canada, 2006b; Statistics Canada, 2006a; Statistics Canada, 2010).

The theory of subjectivity elaborated by Gilles Deleuze and Felix Guattari (1983, 1988) refers to subjectivity as assemblages of "fuzzy aggregates" (1988, p. 507). The imagery here is important: subjectivity can be thought of as being constituted by a number of aggregates, each produced by flows of desire; all are difficult to define because of their capacity to shift shape and trajectory, and to flow into one another, creating new aggregates that emerge from moment to moment. The constitution of these fuzzy aggregates that make up subjectivity is a process that is both natural and social, occurring at all levels of society and of the individual, from visceral responses through to higher reasoning; from intimate interactions between lovers, family members, and friends through to impersonal interactions between state organs, interpellations at work, and by the media. Flows are directed along certain trajectories, with channels gradually wearing into the social fabric where these trajectories are pushed, becoming habitual. These channels exist at the individual, subjective level and at the broader, interpersonal level; the flows follow the same channels, and reinforce each other by resonating together. In Canada, these flows are overwhelmingly colonial.

Given the ubiquity of hockey in Canadian society and culture, I have cast my net wide, analyzing discursive and affective techniques mobilized in the media, in academic and popular literature, and in everyday experience. The principal method utilized for data gathering and analysis was intertextual discourse analysis. The adjective "intertextual" refers to the situatedness of texts, which includes all manner of cultural productions (Shapiro, 1989). Each text within a given cultural milieu does not carry meaning in and of itself, but requires cultural translation through the act of reading in order to have meaning. The positioning of these texts is carried out in the analysis to follow.

II: Nationalism and Multiculturalism

English Canadian nationalism conceives of itself as, perhaps more than anything else, inclusive; diversity has become a matter of self-identity for the Canadian mainstream. Yet, hockey's overwhelming Whiteness and masculinity produce an embodied nationalism that is White and male. Furthermore, the mixing of this desire to be perceived of as inclusive, tolerant—*anything but* racist—with the White, male nature of hockey creates an absorption and minimization of difference.

NATIONAL EMBODIMENT
In her text, *Of Hockey and Hijab*, Sheema Khan relays her experience of playing hockey in Montreal as a youngster:

> I grew up playing street hockey, driveway hockey, and table hockey. I was both Danny Gallivan and Yvon Cournoyer, describing the play-by-play of an electrifying rush leading to a goal with seconds left to play. At the time there was no organized hockey for girls—only ringette. Later in high school I found a recreational league and laced up every week. In one game, I had a breakaway from the blue line. *I was Guy Lafleur*, ready to swoop in on the hapless goalie. (Khan, 2009, pp. 99–100)

As a young *hijabi* girl (one who wears a headscarf) in Montreal, Khan unself-consciously embodies a White, male athlete in her daily recreational activities. This amounts to more than viewing hockey players as role models for Canadian youth; hockey players embody the nation, and the nation embodies them. And those whom we embody in watching and playing hockey have been and, for the most part, continue to be White and male.

The racial and gendered character of these embodiments should not be underestimated. For instance, Varda Burstyn (1999, p. 206) discusses the possibility of racial subversion opened up by the success of Black athletes in the United States through the following example: During a lecture, bell hooks was deconstructing an image of Michael Jordan, critiquing the relationship between athleticism and capitalism. During her lecture, a White student commented that looking at images of Black athletes on cereal boxes as a child was the first time that he wanted to be a Black man. The comment forced hooks to revise her critical deconstruction, given the potential for subversion of racial hierarchies implicit in young White men's desire to embody Blackness.

But this is not the case with hockey.[2] Subjects who are themselves racially constructed as being outside the norm perform their (sporting) identity primarily through embodying White, male hockey players. This is not a matter of lacking the properly racialized role models for non-White, non-male Canadian youth; it is a matter of recognizing the importance that the White male body plays in constructing Canadian national culture. These are the bodies that we emulate as we swim within the current of the Whitestream.

"IT'S THEIR GAME TOO"

Saturday, January 30, 2010, was the 10th annual *Hockey Day in Canada* for the Canada Broadcasting Corporation (CBC), hosted by Ron McLean. The day-long event included interviews with hockey greats, short journalistic pieces on what hockey means to Canadian communities, and segments linking hockey to Canadian military personnel fighting in Afghanistan.

One segment was dedicated to a group of athletes in wheelchairs playing hockey in Stratford, Ontario. The segment told the story of one athlete in particular, and how this opportunity meant so much to him. The player's mother tearfully explained how important hockey was to all of her sons, to which her two able-bodied sons added that they fully supported their brother, and were always excited to see him score a goal. Once the segment was complete, Ron McLean turned to the camera and earnestly proclaimed "It's their game too." And, just like that, disabled players were both absorbed into the nation and distinguished from it: they played the same game as we do, but the "ours/theirs" language maintained a distinction.

Similar notions of extending hockey toward the margins of the Whitestream crop up all over Canadian popular culture. In a recent Tim Hortons commercial titled "Proud Fathers," we see an elderly, Asian man, Charlie, enter a hockey rink carrying a tray of Tim Hortons coffee. "Based on a true story" appears in the top left corner of the screen, and we are instantly aware of a flashback: the colours bleed into sepia; a much younger Charlie approaches a group of children; he chides Jimmy for playing hockey all the time and not studying hard enough, and leads him back home. Twenty years later, we are back in the hockey arena, and Charlie is approaching his grown son, whose attention is fixed on the ice; Jimmy claps and exclaims "Thatta boy" before noticing the approach of his father. "Dad, what are you doing here?" he asks. "See, Tommy, double double," Charlie responds, handing his son a Tim Hortons coffee. There is another flashback, with young Jimmy at the coffee table with his homework and hockey on the television. Charlie enters: "Jimmy-ah, you study, no hockey." The long-standing tension between father and son over hockey is established. But through another series of flashbacks (all involving Tim Hortons coffee) and interrogations by adult Jimmy, it becomes evident that Charlie did support Jimmy's hockey, at least covertly—he secretly came to watch Jimmy's games. The commercial ends with a father–son reconciliation. Jimmy says, "Thanks for coming, Dad."

These examples of hockey-related pathos machines all anchor their narratives to a Canadian national mythology of ever-increasing inclusiveness: we possess this sport, and *we* is universally inclusive of all Canadians, new and old, and of all ethnicities, ages, and abilities. This narrative both reflects and reinforces a certain flow within the Whitestream in contemporary Canada—a desire to be perceived of as open and respectful, and definitely *not* expressing any sort of racism. This narrative is precisely that which denies the persistence of colonialism most overtly. It does not hide its ambition—to absorb all who were heretofore considered different or outside the Whitestream. In the Tim Hortons commercial, we are presented with father–son alienation and rapprochement that seems a pop-psychology cliché, and is an abundant theme in hockey literature. We are allowed to observe this emotionally charged moment, which links to our desire to define ourselves as an open, welcoming society—and to characterize *our game* as a reflection of this openness. And it is the perception of this openness of Canada to difference that intersects with the clichéd father–son reconciliation and puts a lump in our throat (and pours the coffee down it). But, of course, the openness to difference is cut off in this instance in two ways: the commercial relies on a shared understanding that people who look Asian are different, and that this difference is slowly undermined by their integration into Canadian society. It is only through an absorption into this racialized, hypermasculine arena that Jimmy becomes Canadian. And even then, the commercial reproduces stereotypes of overbearing Asian parents, reinforcing the Whitestream's racial imagination.

III: Violence, Masculinity, and Race

Violence plays an important role in hockey. Checking is integral to the game, and, at least in the NHL, fighting is an accepted means of resolving disputes between players, even if it is technically outside the rules. The NHL itself considers violence a "'goods characteristic,' an attribute of the product deliberately fostered by teams to generate revenue in their drive to maximize profits" (Jones, Stewart & Sunderman, 1996, pp. 231–232). Crucially, however, extra-legal violence within the game must be performed in very specific ways. This section examines how the Whitestream pushes alternative violence to the margins through maintaining a code of acceptable violence, which reinforces specific conceptions of masculinity and the racial hierarchy that mark Canadian society as colonial.

According to Atkinson and Young (2008), a set of unwritten rules, *The Code*, governs the use of violence in the NHL and men's hockey in general. These authors argue that *The Code* was acutely visible in the discourse around two highly publicized and brutal hits in the 2000s, both involving the Vancouver Canucks: Marty McSorley's stick-swinging assault on Donald Brashear in 2000, and Todd Bertuzzi's 2004 attack on Steve Moore. The way that the hockey world, including media commentators and league officials, dealt with such incidents made the aggressors into victims, and "publicly frame[d] violence in the game as noncriminal, socially unthreatening and rare—and therefore tolerable" (173). *The Code* effects an embodiment of a violent and dangerous masculinity that normalizes brutality in the guise of protection of a teammate, and justifies illegal hitting and fighting as honourable means of exacting vengeance.

THE CODE AND RACE

Race and violence intersect in hockey, reinforcing colonial flows that privilege White, male anglophones. Francophones in professional hockey are often portrayed as cowardly and unable to take a hit by one of the game's most public personalities, Don Cherry.[3] While many Canadians disagree with Cherry's opinions, he is nevertheless expressing a series of recognizable stereotypes regarding francophone players in the NHL (and, arguably, in the junior leagues). As Dallaire and Denis (2000) argue, Cherry "navigates the same discursive waters as the rest of us: it is the anchoring of his rants in Canadian culture (including the political culture) that makes him so popular on Hockey Night in Canada" (419–420).[4] The stereotypes mobilized in Cherry's polemics maintain themselves through performances on and off the ice.

Bob Sirois (2009), a former NHLer from Quebec, compiled exhaustive statistics comparing francophone players to the rest of the NHL from 1970 to 2009, demonstrating a deep-seated antifrancophone sentiment in the league. Sirois hypothesizes that in order to gain admission to an institution that is contemptuous of their mythical defensive inferiority and wimpiness, francophone players must outperform their anglophone counterparts. His findings reveal the link between the Cherry discourse and the practice of the NHL: a full 42 percent of francophone career players from Quebec (those playing over 200 games) received some award or other from the league, demonstrating that in order for francophones to gain admittance to the league, they must outperform their anglophone competitors. Sirois explains how this anti-French sentiment is reproduced:

> You see, the problem is that so many of those hockey players who referred to us with this primitive language [*fucking frog* or *fucking Frenchman* on the ice] are presently employed by numerous NHL teams. They occupy strategic positions such as scouts, assistant coaches, or trainers in minor professional leagues and even the NHL. Do you think that they have become more civilized with the passing of time? No, by now they've become the perfect Detritus. (260)[5]

It is not only francophones who threaten and potentially challenge the Whitestream. In their analysis of hockey played in the Inuit community of Holman, Collings and Condon (1996) discuss the different ways that Inuit players use violence in the game:

> Many non-Inuit who play hockey in Holman invariably

complain about the style of play.... The game is often violent in a manner unfamiliar to these outsiders.... A former [Euro-Canadian] recreation coordinator once complained that the problem with the way Inuit play hockey was that they "weren't real men." They relied on hitting people from behind and skating away (what Holman players call "bothering") instead of dropping the gloves and fighting it out on the ice.... This infuriates all Euro-Canadians witnessing or experiencing the violent action, but it makes perfect sense in light of traditional Inuit methods of violent expression, which rarely involve face-to-face confrontation. (Collings & Condon, 1996, p. 257)

This view of Inuit not being "real men" is another example of the way *The Code* is mobilized in mainstream Canadian hockey culture. The introduction of any sport to a group will result in a cultural appropriation that redefines how the game is played. This seems particularly true of sport played in relative isolation.[6] Thus, *The Code* works in this example to emasculate a cultural group—it assigns certain negative characteristics to the Inuit in much the same way that it does to francophones. Neither are purported to be manly enough to drop the gloves and fight. Here masculinity and race overlap, with the alternative or non-violence practised by a colonized or francophone culture being associated with a lack of masculinity.

These are deep-seated discourses within Canadian hockey. In the first episode of *Hockey: A People's History*, CBC Television's 10-part documentary that links the development of the game of hockey to the development of Canada's national character, there is a short section that details the origins of the sport. Hockey is linked to the ball-and-stick games of the ancient civilizations of the Middle East and we are told that "as civilization spread westward, so did its games, taking root in Europe and the British Isles." But "it wasn't until the old country games arrived with the immigrants on the shores of Nova Scotia that the last missing pieces were found." A drum is heard beating rhythmically, and we are shown a tableau of hundreds of bronze-coloured, shirtless men carrying curved sticks, obviously competing in a game. "The French called it lacrosse. In the native tongues it had many names, including one that means *'little brother of war'*" (CBC Television, 2006). Michael McKinley, hockey expert and author of the companion coffee table book, then states:

> The Aboriginals considered sport as a rehearsal for battle, and consequently in these games it was winner take all, literally. Sometimes the opposing players might be killed.

While McKinley claims that the new immigrants likely imitated the intensity with which the Aboriginal peoples played, it is clear that this imitation did not go so far as to descend into a battle to the death. And so, in a 2006 documentary by the self-consciously polite and correct CBC, we once again see a nod back to the purported barbarism of Canada's first peoples. As with most popular discourses relating to Aboriginal peoples, McKinley's story homogenizes a wide group of cultures by referring to "the Aboriginals" rather than a specific group that was playing the game in this way.

Still, counter-narratives are available. Michael Robidoux (2002) quotes a conflicting account from an 18th-century English traveller, who claimed that while Chippewa players of lacrosse often wounded each other on the pitch, "there never appears to be any spite or wanton exertion of strength to affect them, nor do any disputes ever happen between the parties" (p. 212). McKinley delights in detailing the savagery that the Aboriginals inflicted on one another, even while ignoring at least some documentary evidence that goes against (undocumented) evidence used for his argument. The point here is not that the Aboriginal peoples who played this game never played it as practice or pretext for war; many did (as documented by other historical accounts in Robidoux, 2002). Rather, the significance of the game (and, indeed, of war) to a culture so far removed from the Whitestream becomes difficult to fathom. This kind of simplistic caricature of Aboriginal culture does little but extend the essentialism so common to constructions of colonized peoples, reinforcing the Whitestream's self-identification as civilized.

IV: Women and Sexuality

VIOLENCE IN WOMEN'S HOCKEY: "TOO ROUGH FOR GALS"

In November 2009, the hockey media lit up briefly after Hayley Wickenheiser, the most celebrated female hockey player in Canada, if not the world, face-washed Dion Phaneuf's younger brother during an exhibition game between Canada's women's team and a junior men's team. Online discussions of the event ranged from questioning why women were playing against teenage boys, to derisive comments about the quality of women's hockey, and to outright misogyny.[7]

When we speak of hockey being integral to Canada, we are generally speaking of men's hockey. One of the reasons that women's hockey may be marginal to the Whitestream is its relative lack of violence—as many hockey fans have opined to me, hockey is an entirely different game without the hitting. Open-ice contact is prohibited in women's hockey; only rubbing along the boards is generally allowed (a rule more or less the same as seniors' hockey).

This was not always the case. During the 1920s and 1930s, women's leagues enjoyed unprecedented popularity, and the rules governing their play (as well as extra-legal violence) were the same that spectators had become accustomed to watching in men's hockey (Norton, 2009). The fact that women are currently prohibited from engaging in the same level of violence that Canadian society *expects* of men points to the postwar resurgence of the ideal of ladylike behaviour and women's expected role as mother and caregiver, just as it points to the importance that violent retribution plays in the crafting of Canadian masculinity.[8] As Nancy Theberge points out, the "modified model" of women's sport that came to prominence in women's athletics after World War Two "came to symbolize and reinforce the myth of female frailty that the growth of women's sport from 1890 through the 1930s had initially challenged" (1989, p. 512). Clarence Campbell neatly summed up the newly normalized perspective on female frailty in the mid-1950s when he claimed that hockey was "too rough for gals" (quoted in Norton, 2009, p. 9). And while starting in the 1970s the modified model was gradually replaced by rule sets compatible with men's games in other sport, violence in women's hockey has been curbed by the prohibition of bodychecking in women's leagues, starting in the 1980s.

After conducting participant observation with a women's hockey team in Ontario, Theberge (2000) concluded that the main obstacle to bodychecking in women's hockey was the social norm against women playing violent games. Prior to 1989, when the rules in Ontario were changed to prohibit open-ice hits, adult women playing in leagues suffered a high number of injuries. The response was to modify the rule set and prohibit bodychecking. This change neglected the problem that lay at the root of these injuries: women were not being trained how to hit and take hits in a sport where hitting was fundamental. Furthermore, the majority of women playing on Theberge's team were in favour of reintegrating hitting, indicating that they enjoyed the physicality of the game when the opportunity presented itself. However, in quoting a marketing executive from the Canadian Hockey Association, Theberge underscores the persistence of the expectation that women's sport should refrain from violence, and that women athletes should be ladylike, demonstrating the Whitestream perspective that views violence in men's hockey as the only acceptable (profitable) style of play:

> It's a lot easier to sell [a game like] women's tennis where the emphasis is on finesse. It's tougher to see women participating in those physical games. It's not a positive in

terms of sales circumstances; it's a hurdle to overcome. (2000, p. 136)

VIOLENCE AGAINST WOMEN

Of course in discussing women, hockey, and violence, the prohibition of hitting in women's hockey is rarely the central concern. As Laura Robinson (1998) argues, a "rape culture" pervades men's minor hockey. Investigating a series of cases from the 1980s and 1990s, Robinson uncovers a pattern: the exceptional treatment afforded to young hockey-playing men in Canada infuses a sense of entitlement to sex, which can and does result in sexual assault. However, as a number of cases detailed by Robinson show, the *victims* of such assaults are often charged with mischief, as charges against their assailants are dropped by a justice system that, from police through to Crown prosecutors, is intimately linked to the junior hockey establishment through ownership, coaching, and billeting of players. In other cases, victims do not bring charges against their assailants. For example, in the case of Jarrett Reid, his girlfriend (the victim of multiple sexual assaults) did not want to charge her boyfriend because she "was concerned that ... if the charges did go through then it would affect his [chances in the NHL] draft" (Robinson, 1998, p. 33).

The men and boys who commit these crimes are also often untroubled by remorse; in the Jarrett Reid case and the case of athlete rapists detailed in Razack (2002) "lost opportunities weighed more heavily" on their minds than the assault of another human being (2002, p. 149). Further, while these horrific instances of sexual assault and cover-up may be marginal to mainstream experience in Canada, the masculinity that allows for women to be treated as sex objects is not. When I watch hockey with friends in a bar, talk often turns to women, and is almost invariably of the sort that reduces women to their body parts. This homosocial environment, where men relate to one another through a fetish or proxy (admiration for a player's finesse with the puck, or expression of sexual desire for an attractive waitress), is a reflection of the same forces that produce the "rape culture" that Robinson points out. As Varda Burstyn (1999, pp. 171–173) argues, organized sport and military service both share an aversion to femininity (softness), which is often expressed through aggression, ranging from disdainful disparagement to outright violence against not only women, but also men who display feminine traits.[9]

V: Colonialism and Space

Discursive and affective techniques mobilized through hockey construct conceptions of space that reproduce colonialism. From early in their childhood, hockey-playing boys learn that they are entitled to the space of the rink, a fixture central to many communities across Canada (Adams, 2006). Racialized teams of Aboriginal players are systematically excluded from the Canadian Whitestream through the production of the reserve as a space of hostility and potential violence (Robidoux, 2004), even while entitlement-bearing young athletes enter the urban reserve to commit horrific violence against the colonized in acts that reinforce the dominance of White masculinity (Razack, 2002).

THE RINK: SPACE OF ENTITLEMENT, EXCLUSION, AND EXCEPTION

As Mary Louise Adams (2006) argues, the rink is constructed as a space of masculinity, and entitlement to that space is ingrained in the mentality of boys; the space itself becomes masculinized. Bruce Kidd (1990) claims that the arena—from the NHL's palatial playing surfaces to the modest community rink in every small town—is a cultural centre for Canadian men. And since arenas are most often constructed with public money, the connection between hockey, masculine entitlement, and the state becomes readily apparent. Consider the numerous arenas that were constructed to mark Canada's centennial; in this instance, we have the nation-state commemorating itself with the construction of space intimately linked to hockey, and thus to men's culture. A sense of entitlement not only to this space, but also to what amounts to privileged citizenship, cannot help but be established within masculine subjectivity.

The space of institutional hockey also effects an exclusion of women and those who would use the ice for pursuits other than hockey. Women who would like to use the ice to play hockey continue to be stonewalled by institutions that allocate ice time based on prior use. While Adams (2006) points to a 1994 study by the City of Toronto that addressed the problem women had in accessing artificial ice, complaints by women denied access to community rinks in the city were again raised in the winter of 2009/2010 (Vincent, 2009). The issue of unequal access to ice persists despite the report prepared over a decade ago.

This space of exclusion extends beyond mere physical exclusion. Professional hockey culture is, like "monasteries, mental institutions, [and] cults," extremely insular (Steven Ortiz, quoted in Robinson, 1998, p. 57). Criticism of certain of hockey's shibboleths, such as illegal violence, automatically marks one as an "outsider." Former NHL start Theoren Fleury demonstrated this in discussing media commentary on the disqualification of the 1987 Canadian world junior team from the tournament due to participation in a bench-clearing brawl:

> Brian Williams ... kept beaking off, calling it an ugly, disgraceful incident. The guy probably never even laced up in his life. The most adversity he ever faced on ice was making it to his car in the winter. Don Cherry was behind us because he played the game, so he understands the game. I don't think it gives him the right to be as critical as he is sometimes, because he was never a big success story in the game, but he knows what goes on in the heat of the moment. It gets out of hand at times. That is the nature of hockey. (Fleury & Day, 2009, pp. 43–44)

Fleury's comments echo an oft-repeated feature of hockey discourse: that Canadians play hockey, and, by implication, those who do not play lack the credentials to discuss, and especially to criticize, the national passion and perhaps even the nation itself.

Furthermore, masculine entitlement to the space of the rink resonates with the entitlement to women's bodies exhibited by many hockey-playing youth. Sherene Razack's (2002) study of two White, middle-class athletes who raped and murdered Pamela George, an Aboriginal woman, is a case in point. The area in Winnipeg where Pamela George, who occasionally worked as a prostitute, was working the night she was murdered is an example of a marginal space, even a space of exception, like the Indian reserve. Razack chillingly demonstrates how the homosocial space of men's sport produces a masculinity that identifies itself in terms of its capacity to inflict violence on women. She also argues that such violence must be seen in terms of the history of colonialism, in which White males have come to see themselves as entitled to the land and the rights and privileges of the state to the exclusion of racialized Aboriginal peoples.

Similarly, in his article detailing race relations in southern Alberta, Robidoux (2004) explores how the Whitestream maintains the spatial segregation of colonialism through hockey. The Kainai Minor Hockey Association, comprised of First Nations players, was ejected from the regional hockey association, not for having broken league rules (which they had), but because the parents of another (non-Aboriginal) association in the league continuously complained that travelling to the reserve put their children and themselves at risk. Robidoux's research on non-Aboriginal minor hockey in the same southern Alberta area found that violence and aggression on and off the ice were commonplace. In analyzing the letters from parents sent to the minor hockey association, he found that First Nations peoples were overwhelmingly characterized as "unruly and dangerous" (p. 293). These parents did not want to play against Kainai teams—not because of the infractions levelled against Kainai, or any other quantifiable reason—but because "they want[ed] nothing to do with Kainai. In other words, it is not desirable for these communities to go to the reserve to play hockey because it is not desirable to go to the reserve in general" (p. 292). It was not desirable because it hooked into general conceptions of Indian reserves as places where there are rusting hulks on front lawns and dilapidated, overcrowded housing that defy the middle-class norm of well-manicured lawns and well-maintained homes, that is, Whitestream civility.

Conclusion

What I have argued through this overlapping, multifarious view of hockey is that the history, organization, and culture of the game produce a subjectivity and a normative complex that valorizes hypermasculine violence, and that puts the White (and, at least in English Canada, anglophone) male in a position of reverence to be emulated, thereby reproducing racial and gender hierarchies. Taken together, these aspects of hockey in Canada are an assemblage that runs in the same trajectory as historical and contemporary colonial, discursive, affective, and material techniques and practices. Gender, sexual orientation, and race of the colonizer are further reproduced as the main normative current within Canada.

As I have related here, Canadian men are supposed to play hockey; masculinity in Canada is defined by the way this single sport is played. While I have never played in a league, I played street hockey with friends and neighbours during my youth. However, the first time I skated onto the frozen surface of a lake in northern B.C. near a family member's house, stick in hand, I was suddenly flooded with a feeling that I have rarely experienced—I felt like a "real man." All of a sudden I could identify with those hearty, bearded, plaid-clad men from the beer commercial as I rushed across the ice on my rusty pawnshop skates. The irony is that those with whom I would be playing later that night were mostly members of my sister's hockey team, and mostly women—and, for the most part, conscious of how masculinity and race operate in Canada. I include this short anecdote here for two reasons: first, even those (such as myself) who attempt to maintain a critical distance from the hegemony of hockey's version of masculinity are susceptible to its allure. How could we not be, considering that we are nourished on a diet of images, sounds, and feelings that constantly reinforce this singular means of accessing manliness? Second, this story also undermines this masculinity—playing Canada's sport with a motley crew of social workers, schoolteachers, painters, and municipal planners, all coached by the former chief of an Indian band, I finally gained access to this masculinity even while its content was being transformed by the circumstances.

Questions for Critical Thought

1. This chapter argues that through space, gender, race, and violence, hockey reproduces colonialism in Canada. Can you think of other sites through which hockey reproduces colonialism?
2. What examples can you think of in contemporary hockey where the reproduction of colonialism is challenged?
3. Can you identify sites other than hockey that reproduce colonialism in contemporary Canada? What are they? How do they function?

Notes

1. In 1967, what was effectively a "Whites only" immigration policy was repealed.
2. The last North American professional sport to integrate Black players; Willie O'Ree began playing for the Boston Bruins in 1958 (McGourty, 2010).

3. This popular rhetoric flies in the face of the reality that there are plenty of francophones among the NHL's enforcers, and that the Ligue Nord-Américaine de Hockey is the most violent in the world (Klein, 2011).
4. And, in fact, beyond; not only did Cherry place 7th in CBC's *Greatest Canadian* program in 2004, but he was voted Canada's leading public intellectual by the readers of the *National Post* a year later (Elcombe, 2010).
5. Translation of: "voyez-vous, maintenant, le problème, c'est que plusieurs des hockeyeurs qui utilisaient ce langage primitif [*fucking frenchman* ou *fucking frog*, sur la glace] pour nous désigner sont présentement employés par plusieurs équipes de la LNH. Ils occupent des postes stratégiques à titre de dépisteurs, d'assistanants-entraîneurs ou d'instructeurs dans les ligues mineures professionelles et même dans la LNH. Alors pensez-vous que leur culture s'est civilisée avec le temps? Non, ils sont aujourd'hui devenus de parfaits Détritus." The last reference is to a comic-strip character from Asterix and Obelix who was sent by Caesar to sow discord among those heroic Gauls, and whom Sirois sarcastically compares to Don Cherry—without actually mentioning his name. It also merits mention that *détritus* means "garbage" in French.
6. The Trobriand Islanders' adaptation of cricket, including ritualistic dances, is an excellent example of such colonial syncretism (Leach & Kildea, 2004). See Paraschak (1997) for a discussion of the differences in Aboriginal sporting cultures in the Arctic and in southern Canada.
7. One user, Odiedodie of 25stanley.com, commented: "When will the novelty act of women's hockey finally go away? This politically correct side-show has gone on way too long. Why are unskilled players still making news headlines because of their gender?" (25stanley.com, 2009). "That was barely a bump, Hayley was probably on the rag." Comments by user Skorka85 of hockeyfights.com (hockeyfights.com, 2009).
8. The negative attention brought by the media to the members of the Canadian women's Olympic hockey team caught smoking cigars

and drinking champagne on the ice is further evidence of the persistence of the expectation of ladylike behaviour in Euro-American societies, particularly when juxtaposed to the way Jon Montgomery became a media darling after parading through the streets of Whistler with a pitcher of beer after winning gold in men's skeleton during the 2010 Winter Olympics.

9. See CBC News (2010) in which the two gay victims of a hate-motivated assault linked their experience to the holding of a mixed martial arts event in their city that night.

References

Adams, M.L. (2006). The game of whose lives? Gender, race, and entitlement in Canada's "national" game. In D. Whitson & R. Gruneau (Eds.), *Artificial ice: Hockey, commerce, and cultural identity* (pp. 71–84). Peterborough: Broadview Press.

Allard, Y.E., Wilkings, R. & Berthelot, J.-M. (2004). Premature mortality in health regions with high Aboriginal populations. *Health Reports*, 15(1), 51–60.

Atkinson, M. & Young, K. (2008). *Deviance and social control in sport.* Champaign: Human Kinetics.

Burstyn, V. (1999). *The rites of men: Manhood, politics, and the culture of sport.* Toronto: University of Toronto Press.

CBC News. (2010). Gay bashing victims blame UFC fight event. Retrieved from http://www.cbc.ca/canada/british-columbia/story/2010/06/14/bc-gay-bashing-vancouver-ufc.html#ixzz0qrIc4jHt

CBC Television. (2006). *Hockey: A people's history.*

Cohen, R. (2000). "Mom is a stranger": The negative impact of immigration policies on the family life of Filipina domestic workers. *Canadian Ethnic Studies*, 32(3), 76–88.

Collings, P. & Condon, R.G. (1996). Blood on the ice: Status, self-esteem, and ritual injury among Inuit hockey players. *Human Organization*, 55(3), 253–262.

Dallaire, C. & Denis, C. (2000). "If you don't speak French, you're out":

Don Cherry, the Alberta francophone games, and the discursive construction of Canada's francophones. *Canadian Journal of Sociology/Cahiers Canadiens de Sociologie,* 25(4), 415–440.

Darby, Paul. (2000). Football, colonial doctrine, and indigenous resistance: Mapping the political persona of FIFA's African constituency. *Culture, Sport, Society,* 2(1), 61–87.

Deleuze, G. & Guattari, F. (1983). *Anti-Oedipus: Capitalism and schizophrenia.* Minneapolis: University of Minnesota Press.

Deleuze, G. & Guattari, F. (1988). *A thousand plateaus: Capitalism and schizophrenia.* London: Continuum.

Denis, C. (1997) *We are not you: First Nations and Canadian modernity.* Peterborough: Broadview Press.

Elcombe, T. (2010). The moral equivalent of "Don Cherry." *Journal of Canadian Studies,* 44(2), 194–218.

Fleury, T. & Day, K.M. (2009). *Playing with fire.* Toronto: HarperCollins.

Gems, G.R. (1999). Sports, war, and ideological imperialism. *Peace Review,* 11(4), 573–578.

Gruneau, R. & Whitson, D. (1993). *Hockey night in Canada: Sport, identities, and cultural politics.* Toronto: Garamond Press.

hockeyfights.com. (2009). Phaneuf's 15-year-old brother vs Hayley Wickenheiser. Retrieved from www.hockeyfights.com

James, C.L.R. (1993). *Beyond a boundary.* Durham: Duke University Press.

Jones, J.C.H., Stewart, K.G. & Sunderman, R. (1996). From the arena into the streets: Hockey violence, economic incentives, and public policy. *American Journal of Economics and Sociology,* 55(2), 231–243.

Khan, S. (2009). *Of hockey and hijab: Reflections of a Canadian Muslim woman.* Toronto: Tsar Books.

Kidd, B. (1990). The men's cultural centre: Sports and the dynamic of women's oppression/men's repression. In M. Messner & D. Sabo (Eds.), *Sport, men, and the gender order* (pp. 31–44). Champaign: Human Kinetics.

Klein, J. (2011). Fighting to stay in the game. *New York Times* (February 28). Retrieved from http://www.nytimes.com/2011/03/01/sports/hockey/01hockey.html?_r=1

Leach, J.W. & Kildea, G. (2004). *Trobriand cricket: An ingenious response to colonialism*. Berkeley: Berkeley Media.

Library and Archives Canada. (2010). Aboriginal hockey. Retrieved from http://www.collectionscanada.gc.ca/hockey/kids/024003-2400-e.html

Mackey, E. (2002). *The house of difference: Cultural politics and national identity in Canada*. Toronto: University of Toronto Press.

McGourty, J. (2010). O'Ree became NHL's first Black player 52 years ago. Retrieved from http://www.nhl.com/ice/news.htm?id=513590

McKinley, M. (2006). *Hockey: a people's history*. Toronto: McClelland and Stewart.

Nakhaie, M.R. (2006). Contemporary realities and future visions: Enhancing multiculturalism in Canada. *Canadian Ethnic Studies*, 38(1), 149–158.

Norton, W. (2009). *Women on ice: The early years of women's hockey in western Canada*. Vancouver: Ronsdale Press.

Paraschak, V. (1997). Variations in race relations: Sporting events for Native peoples in Canada. *Sociology of Sport Journal*, 14, 1–21.

Razack, S. (2002). Gendered racial violence and spatialized justice: The murder of Pamela George. In S. Razack (Ed.), *Race, space, and the law: Unmapping a White settler society* (pp. 122–156). Toronto: Between the Lines.

Robidoux, M. (2002). Imagining a Canadian identity through sport: A historical interpretation of lacrosse and hockey. *Journal of American Folklore*, 115(456), 209–225.

Robidoux, M.A. (2004). Narratives of race relations in southern Alberta: An examination of conflicting practices. *Sociology of Sport Journal*, 21(3), 281–301.

Robinson, L. (1998). *Crossing the line: Violence and sexual assault in Canada's national sport*. Toronto: McClelland & Stewart.

Shapiro, Michael J. (1989). Textualizing global politics. In J. Der Derian and M.J. Shapiro (Eds.), *International/intertextual relations: Postmodern readings of world politics* (pp. 11–22). Lexington: Lexington Books.

Sirois, B. (2009). *Le Québec mis en échec*. Montreal: Les Éditions de l'Homme.

Statistics Canada. (2006a). Aboriginal ancestry (14), area of residence (6), age groups (8), sex (3), and selected demographic, cultural, labour force, educational and income characteristics (227A), for the total population of Canada, provinces, and territories, 2006 census—20% sample data. Retrieved from http://www12.statcan.gc.ca/census-recensement/2006/dp-pd/prof/sip/Rp-eng.cfm?LANG=E&APATH=3&DETAIL=0&DIM=0&FL=A&FREE=0&GC=0&GID=0&GK=0&GRP=1&PID=97445&PRID=0&PTYPE=97154&S=0&SHOWALL=0&SUB=0&Temporal=2006&THEME=73&VID=0&VNAMEE=&VNAMEF=

Statistics Canada. (2006b). Labour force activity (8), Aboriginal identity (8B), age groups (13A), sex (3), and area of residence (6A) for the population 15 years and over of Canada, provinces, and territories, 2001 and 2006 censuses—20% sample data. Retrieved from http://www12.statcan.gc.ca/census-recensement/2006/dp-pd/tbt/Rp-eng.cfm?LANG=E&APATH=3&DETAIL=0&DIM=0&FL=A&FREE=0&GC=0&GID=0&GK=0&GRP=1&PID=92101&PRID=0&PTYPE=88971,97154&S=0&SHOWALL=0&SUB=738&Temporal=2006&THEME=73&VID=0&VNAMEE=&VNAMEF=

Statistics Canada. (2010). Chart 7: Proportion of dwellings in need of major repairs by Aboriginal identity, population aged 15 and over. Retrieved from http://www.statcan.gc.ca/pub/89-645-x/2010001/c-g/c-g007-eng.htm

Theberge, N. (1989). Women's athletics and the myth of female frailty. In J. Freeman (Ed.), *Women: A feminist perspective* (4th ed., pp. 507–522). Mountain View: Mayfield Publishing Company.

Theberge, N. (2000). *Higher goals: Women's ice hockey and the politics of gender.* Albany: State University of New York Press.

Thobani, S. (2007). *Exalted subjects: Studies in the making of race and nation in Canada.* Toronto: University of Toronto Press.

25stanley.com. (2009). Video: Dion Phaneuf's little brother Dane hits Hayley Wickenheiser. Retrieved from www.25stanley.com

Vincent, D. (2009). Female teams get short shift, survey shows. *Toronto Star* (November 18). Retrieved from http://www.thestar.com/sports/hockey/article/727258

CHAPTER 4

New Racism and Old Stereotypes in the National Hockey League: The "Stacking" of Aboriginal Players into the Role of Enforcer

JOHN VALENTINE

Introduction

Tracing the roles played by Aboriginal hockey players in the National Hockey League (NHL) from the mid-1970s to 2010, this chapter takes an historical, longitudinal view to explain the abundance of Aboriginals, that is, Indians, Inuit, and Métis men, in the role of enforcer, a one-dimensional player who does little more than fight. "Stacking" is a term that draws attention to certain social factors that account for the position—or, for the purposes of this chapter, the role—a player is assigned or expected to fulfill as a member of a team. To situate the phenomenon of stacking Aboriginal hockey players as enforcers, the place of Aboriginal peoples within Canada is examined, particularly an historically informed analysis of the concept of *Othering* within democratic racism. To build the case of the stacking of Aboriginal hockey players, quantitative data is analyzed, with penalty minutes, major penalties, and fights examined for each National Hockey League season in which Aboriginal representation made up at least 1 percent of the league's players. The results indicate that Aboriginal NHL players have disproportionately fulfilled the role of enforcer; these results are considered in relation to the history of the culture of racism in Canada.

Racism and Aboriginal Peoples in Canada

Despite resistance and repeated calls for justice, the history of Aboriginal peoples in Canada since colonization is fraught with oppression, racism, exploitation, poverty, violence, stereotyping, dehumanizing objectification, and the denial of justice and self-government (LaRocque, 2007). From a post-colonial perspective, Aboriginal culture in the land that became Canada experienced profound change and damage through colonial oppression and invasion by foreign cultural influences. Much of the evidence of this change is grim, from the beginning of White settlement through to the 21st century. In 2005, unemployment levels and poverty rates remained three times higher in Aboriginal communities than in Canadian society at large (Canadian Heritage, 2005). Native households often experience overcrowded housing and a lack of nutritious food, clean water, and health care (Smylie & Adomako, 2009). Aboriginal peoples' rates of homelessness were 10 times higher than those of the non-Aboriginal population (Hwang, 2001). The average income for on-reserve Aboriginal peoples is half that of the Canadian population and for off-reserve it is two-thirds that of the Canadian population (Canadian Heritage, 2005). While education is important for social mobility, only 40 percent of Aboriginal peoples graduate from high school compared to almost 90 percent in the general population, and slightly more than 5 percent of Aboriginals have a university degree compared to nearly 30 percent among other Canadians (*Globe and Mail*, 2009).

The statistics regarding incarceration and violence are equally bleak. Aboriginals account for only 4 percent of the Canadian population yet make up 24 percent of the prison population. In addition to higher rates of incarceration, Aboriginals are much more likely to be victims of violence and have dramatically elevated rates of infant mortality, sexual violence, injury, and death by homicide. Suicide is the leading cause of death for Native youth, and the hockey community has not been spared; in 2002, Terrence Tootoo, an Inuit professional hockey player, took his own life.

Such facts reflect a history of racism in Canada. The capacity to dehumanize and objectify proceeds from the colonial relationship that understood Aboriginals as the racialized Other who was, and continues to be, deemed a threat to the existing moral fabric of society. Wendell (1996) argues: "When we make people 'Other,' we group them together as the objects of our experience instead of regarding them as subjects of experience with whom we might identify, and we see them primarily as symbolic of something else—usually, but not always, something we reject and fear and project onto them" (p. 60). Somewhat ironically, moral panics about Others are arguably more prevalent than ever in countries like Canada, which have championed the discourse of multiculturalism where tolerance, accommodation, harmony, and diversity are thought to be celebrated (Henry & Tator, 2005).

The Othering of Aboriginal peoples in Canada regularly occurred through the construction and maintenance of the trope of the *noble savage*, spawned when the British Empire sought to civilize and enlighten conquered peoples who were thought to be inferior and violent. By the mid-19th century, colonial thought increasingly constructed Aboriginals as confined to a permanent state of nature, more animal-like, aggressive, and uncivilized than the White establishment. Through what Coakley (2006) refers to as *race logic*, such stereotypes of Aboriginals became hegemonic. The result was a racial hierarchy based on physical characteristics, often related to skin colour, which positioned the Native population as primitive and violent (Gems, 2005).

This process of Othering is clearly connected to racism. Henry and Tator (2002) illustrate that racism includes "the assumptions, attitudes, beliefs, and behaviours of individuals and to the institutional policies, processes, and practices that flow from those understandings" (p. 11). Racist notions of the inherent nature of Aboriginal violence and aggression remain part of contemporary Canadian culture, albeit often in different forms given the social and political malleability of racism. Indeed, beginning in the 1980s, scholars drew attention to more subtle forms of racism, or the *new racism* (Barker, 1982), through which racist views are expressed in relatively neutral language in an attempt to render them more acceptable. Henry and Tator (2002) argue that new racism "manifests itself in more subtle and insidious ways and is largely invisible to those who are part of the dominant culture.... [New racism] rarely demonstrates itself in violence or overt racist behaviour" (p. 23). For example, a 2008 poll found that almost 80 percent of Canadians had favourable opinions of Aboriginal peoples (Jedwab, 2008), yet racism and poor living conditions continue to exist for First Nations peoples in Canada.

Racism and Aboriginal Athletes in Canada

Historically, Aboriginal peoples were excluded from sport organized by the dominant class in North American society (see Cosentino, 1998; Paraschak 1989), and the notion of the racialized Other was used to label Aboriginal leisure practices as inferior, primitive, and immoral (Paraschak, 1998). Lacrosse, for example, was regularly read as an inherently violent game illustrative of Aboriginal savagery, a process that Robidoux (2004) refers to as "villainizing the native" (p. 297). Indeed, traditional Aboriginal physical culture was different from that of the colonizers. Traditional recreational activities associated with First Nations often emphasized physical strength and involved "pain tolerance and self-testing" (Paraschak, 2008, p. 1061). Brown (1989), Robidoux (2006), and Wamsley (2007) illustrate how these Aboriginal notions of masculinity were markedly different from those associated with the upper-class, educated British. The key point is the extent to which the White majority has interpreted Aboriginal physical culture through racist stereotypes of physical aggression. According to Churchill, Hill, and Barlow (1979), "[t]he Native American within non-Indian mythology is (and has always been) an overwhelmingly physical creature. Sport was and is an expedient means of processing this physicality into a 'socially acceptable' package without disrupting mythology" (p. 31). Witnessing the Aboriginal athlete as savage was consistent with the myth held by non-Aboriginals, a myth that has been "updated, but essentially unchanged" (Churchill et al., 1979, p. 31).

Indeed, while some stereotypes seem to be diminishing, the idea of the savage continues to inform contemporary understandings of Aboriginal culture (King, 2005). Waneek Horn-Miller, a Mohawk from the Kahnawake Mohawk Territory, captain of the 2000 Canadian Olympic Women's water polo team, was cut from the team after nine years. She was told that she "terrified" and "intimidated" her teammates, to which she replied "as an Aboriginal Canadian, this sounds very familiar" (Kohler, 2003, p. A3). During the 2008 Summer Olympic Games, Richard Pound, former Olympian and member of the International Olympic Committee, stated: "We must not forget that 400 years ago Canada was a land of savages" (Mason, 2008). Not only did his comments perpetuate the savage stereotype, but they also implied that civilization in Canada originated with the arrival of European settlers.

In North American sport, Aboriginal athletes continue to be underrepresented relative to population, with the possible exception of lacrosse. This underrepresentation may be due to the poverty experienced by many First Nations, as well as the lack of sporting infrastructure, such as access to coaching, travel, and equipment. Further, the segregation of Aboriginal peoples from the dominant White culture results in significant cultural challenges for athletes who leave Aboriginal communities to pursue sport (Canadian Heritage, 2005). Many Aboriginal hockey players from Canada have faced these challenges, including Ted Nolan (Kernaghan, 1993), Gino Odjick (Spector, 1997), Jonathon

Cheechoo (Mason, 2006), and Sheldon Souray (Wiwchar, 2009). As a result, Aboriginals have been underrepresented in the NHL. Figure 4.1 compares the actual number of Aboriginal men playing hockey in the NHL with the number that might reasonably be expected based on the percentage of North Americans in the NHL and the Aboriginal population in North America. Notably, amidst the general absence of racial minorities, and in an attempt to recruit more Black players, the NHL created a diversity task force in 1995, but there has been no such attempt to try and attract more Aboriginal players.

Figure 4.1: Aboriginals in the NHL

While there are multiple reasons that might account for such underrepresentation of Aboriginal players in the NHL, including cultural and political resistance to hockey and the NHL, racism almost certainly plays a role, particularly given that the number of Aboriginal hockey players in the NHL actually increased during the era when the enforcer—a one-dimensional player expected to do little more than fight and intimidate opponents—was most prevalent. Indeed, there are numerous accounts of Aboriginal hockey players facing racism on and off the ice at all levels from children's hockey to the NHL (see Cardinal, 2008; Marks, 2008). Individual players have suffered as well. Everett Sanipass was not allowed to play on off-reserve teams until his father hired a lawyer to help fight this racism (Joyce, 2006). Ted Nolan was a successful coach in the NHL who was subjected to racist taunts from opposing fans when coaching in major junior hockey (Canadian Press, 2005). Despite winning coach-of-the-year honours in the NHL in 1997, it took him nine years to find another head-coaching position in the league. Chris Simon kicked another player and received a 30-game suspension in 2007. Three months after Simon's suspension, Chris Pronger, a non-Aboriginal voted dirtiest player in the league by both players (*Sports Illustrated*, 2009) and hockey writers (thehockeywriters. com, 2009), received only an eight-game suspension for a similar incident. This prompted an editorial in the national newspaper, the *Globe and Mail*, raising questions of racism in hockey.

It is reasonable to argue that new racism gains traction within such a culture of sport that is often purported to be a meritocracy, and where the increase in the number of athletes from visible minority backgrounds—such as Black athletes in the National Football League and National Basketball Association—to majority status is often used to demonstrate the absence or non-existence of racism. In this way, new racism has come to be a seemingly invisible, yet dominant, discourse that operates within the context of competitive sport and both informs and is informed by social and cultural life in Canada.

The "Coach's Corner" episode of December 22, 2007 on *Hockey Night in Canada* effectively illustrates this new racism. Regarding the Chris Simon suspension and Ted Nolan's lack of coaching opportunities, Don Cherry immediately dismissed the possibility of racism and blamed the victims (Najak, 2007). In so doing, Cherry invoked two discourses outlined by Henry and Tator (2002): "the discourse of equal opportunity" and "victim blaming." The former argues that everyone in our democratic society shares the same starting point, while the latter assumes that whenever an individual from a minority group fails to achieve a level of success, some other deficiency or form of deviant behaviour is to blame instead of racism. As a result, indigenous peoples in Canada are often blamed for not taking full advantage of all of their apparent opportunities.

The Concept of Racial "Stacking" in Sport

Stacking, a concept that Nixon and Frey (1996) attributed to foundational sport sociologist Harry Edwards, emerged in the 1960s and refers to the process by which players of a certain race or ethnicity are over- or underrepresented in specific positions or roles on a sport team. Stacking has been used to illustrate that members of the dominant culture tend to be funnelled into more important and supposedly cerebral roles (such as the quarterback in football), while racialized Others are found in roles that are stereotypically viewed as more intrinsically athletic (such as the football running back). In effect, stacking refers to the process and the result of including/excluding players from certain positions, often based on race. Stacking studies have looked at a range of team sports, including Australian rules football (Hallinan, Bruce & Coram, 1999), baseball (Sack, Singh & Thiel, 2005), cricket (Malcolm, 1997), rugby league (Hallinan, 1991), and netball (Melnick, 1996). Most stacking studies concluded that racialized athletes are overrepresented in positions that are stereotyped as requiring above-average athleticism or in positions not commonly associated with leadership.

The concept of stacking generally fell out of favour in the sociology of sport as it was deemed problematically positivist; stacking provides examples of racism in sport, but offers little in terms of explanation or causation. Melnick (1996) argues that racial stacking in sport is a complex process involving multiple social and political dynamics. For example, socio-economic realities are such that members of lower economic classes may not have access to equipment, coaching, or facilities, and therefore may assume positions on the field that require less skill or development. Self-selection or role-modelling theory (Castine & Roberts, 1974) proposes that high-profile athletes who receive a disproportionate amount of media coverage serve as role models to youth, in particular to those of similar ethnic or racial backgrounds. A third theory, and the one supported in this chapter given the history and culture of racialized Othering of First Nations peoples in Canada, argues that people in positions of authority in sport, like coaches or scouts, ascribe racist stereotypes to athletes (McPherson, Curtis & Loy, 1989; Hallinan, 1991, Malcolm, 1997) that are often based on presumed abilities (Johnson et al., 1999; Hallinan et al., 1999) in ways that funnel them toward certain positions. These stereotypes support a belief in biologically distinct racial categories that are allegedly genetically linked not only to particular strengths but also weaknesses, and are often equated with dubious notions of the physical superiority and intellectual inferiority of racial minorities. That is, while White athletes are often considered to be harder workers, superior leaders, and more mentally astute, non-White athletes continue to be represented or understood through physical prowess, quickness, or aggression, and their success is attributed to innate gifts. Clearly, racial stereotypes can be reified amidst such processes and ideas.

It is important to note that as early as 1978, Curtis and Loy reported that there had "been something of an 'industry' in stacking studies" (p. 286), while in 1996 Melnick described the field as a "swollen corpus" (p. 271). However, more recently Hallinan et al. (1999) argued that it would be ironic to discontinue studies on the structures of racial inequality simply because so many have been completed, particularly with the shortage of research examining opportunities for Aboriginal athletes.

> [I]t would be ironic if researchers were dissuaded from studies of this form of inequality because authors of previous studies have concluded that the numerical count had

reached its zenith. In countries ... where little research has been completed, studies like this are particularly needed for questioning beliefs about the alleged improvement of opportunities for Aboriginal athletes. (p. 374)

More recently, Woodward (2004) argued that stacking still exists and therefore is an important concept to be explored. Lavoie's (1989) work on stacking among French-Canadian hockey players remains the only study to explore stacking in hockey, while four academic works have examined stacking among Aboriginal peoples. Melnick and Thomson (1996) and Melnick (1996) did not find evidence of stacking based on stereotyping among Aboriginals in New Zealand. However, Hallinan (1991) and Hallinan et al. (1999) document evidence of the stacking of Aboriginal players in rugby league and Australian rules football. Racial stacking among North American or Canadian Aboriginal peoples has not been explored at all, even though Aboriginal peoples are the largest minority group in Canadian society.

This study takes several different approaches to the traditional approach to racial stacking in sport. First, this work does not explore a formalized position in the sport of hockey but rather a cultural role, that of the fighter or enforcer. Another way that this study differs is that instead of examining visible minorities who are overrepresented, this study examines those who are underrepresented within elite levels of sport and considers the roles filled by this minority. This work also places a greater emphasis on connecting these roles to the culture and history of racism in Canada. A final but important difference is the relatively longitudinal approach taken in this study. Despite the call from Leonard and Phillips (1997) for more longitudinal studies on stacking, very few studies examining stacking have used this approach to look at changes over time for racial minorities. Since this study analyzed data from over 35 years of NHL hockey, it can be considered longitudinal in comparison.

It is important to note that examining the role of Aboriginal players in the NHL is especially important because hockey continues to be the sport most often associated with Canada and, as such, holds important connotations for national identity (Earle, 1995; Gruneau & Whitson, 1993) and because Aboriginal peoples continue to feel the ravages of colonialism. Further, while hockey has arguably become more racially diverse in recent years, it nevertheless remains a sport that attracts primarily a homogeneous group of participants, particularly in the professional ranks. Even though Aboriginal peoples have a strong historical connection to the game (see Robidoux, 2006), the national identity constructed through hockey excludes Canadians who are classified as Other, a group that continues to include Aboriginal peoples. The idea of hockey as a universal Canadian practice that builds unity across Canada's multicultural population is common to the dominant culture, but not to Aboriginal peoples. In addition, since the NHL is regarded as the dominant hockey league in the world, these messages can be disseminated to Canadian hockey fans and fans around the world through the league. For these reasons, critical analysis of the role of Aboriginal hockey players in the NHL is called for.

History of the Enforcer

The hockey enforcer evolved as a player designed to protect the talented players, as well as sell tickets and entertain fans (Morra & Smith, 2002; Fitz-Gerald, 2001). From its inception, hockey has been played at high speeds that result in body contact. Violent altercations and fights were not uncommon even in the early days of the game, but it was not until after the NHL expanded that the role of the enforcer emerged within the league. Between 1967 and 1974 the NHL expanded from six to 18 teams, adding franchises in non-traditional hockey markets like California, Missouri, and Georgia. In addition to its utility as strategy, fighting offered an easily understood entertainment form that served to sell hockey in markets where the game was viewed as foreign. In addition, the fact that the league tripled in size depleted the talent levels and resulted in the addition of many new players of relatively marginal skill. This served to make the best NHL players more valuable. Gordie Howe and Bobby Orr were among the superstars of this era. A CTV poll in the mid-1960s found that Gordie Howe was one of the most famous men in Canada, better known than the governor general (Rutherford, 1990). In 1971, Orr signed the first $1 million contract in the NHL, signalling a new celebrity era in professional hockey and demonstrating his importance as a superstar not only to his team, but also to the league.

Gradually, changes in the NHL meant that superstars were deemed to need protection from mediocre players, who might take physical liberties against them. As a result, the more specialized and formal role of enforcer began to emerge and the role was taken over by a player who could do little more than fight. Many subsequent star players had personal enforcers, notably Wayne Gretzky, who was protected by players like Dave Semenko and Marty McSorley.[1] As Andrews and Jackson (2001) argue, personalities are central to the institution of televised sport, and celebrity players like Gretzky and Mario Lemieux, featured in magazines, paid to promote and sell products, and seen on television across North America, were increasingly understood as valuable commodities to be protected. To have these players injured or in the penalty box would not only harm their respective teams, but the entire league. As the following analysis suggests, Aboriginal hockey players have been disproportionately asked to fulfill this role throughout the history of the league.

Methodology

The peak era of the NHL enforcer can be demonstrated using normalized or adjusted statistics that allow for cross-era comparison. By dividing a player's per-game statistic, such as penalty minutes, by the historical per-game penalty minute average, normalized statistics are achieved and comparisons can be made among players of different eras. These adjusted statistics are common and appear in *Total NHL* (Diamond, 2003) and *The Hockey Compendium* (Klein & Reif, 2001). Hockey statistician Daryl Shilling developed a system to rate enforcers using normalized points scored and normalized penalty minutes. A player with few (normalized) points and many (normalized) penalty minutes has a high enforcer rating. Separating the 100 players with the highest enforcer ratings by year yields a breakdown of the years with the greatest number of enforcers. Figure 4.2 displays a comparison of high-ranking enforcers per year from 1960 to 2005.

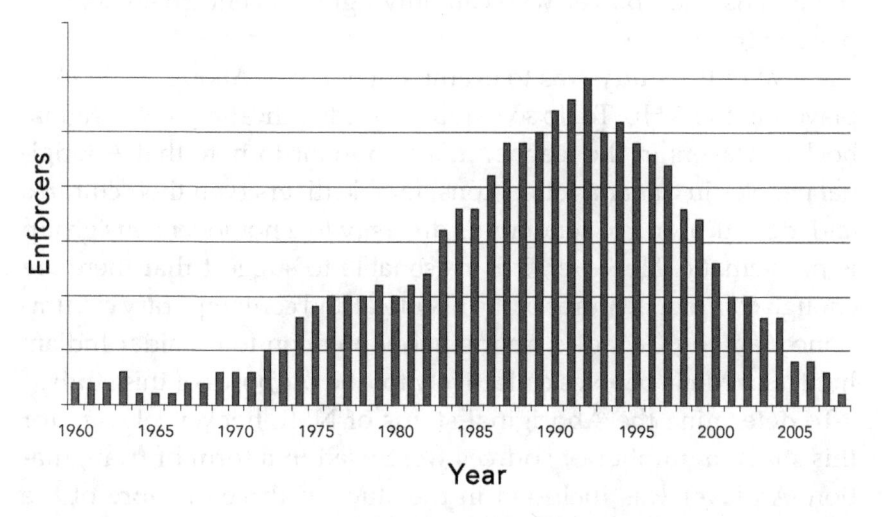

Figure 4.2: Number of Enforcers Per Year

The data suggests that the pure enforcer began to emerge in the 1974–75 season, the final year of rapid NHL expansion, and the number of pure enforcers remained relatively stable until the mid-1980s, at which point the numbers increased and remained high until the lockout of 2004–05.[2] After the lockout, the numbers declined to roughly pre-expansion levels. In the season prior to the start of expansion in 1967, no player had more than eight fights, and the three players with the most fights were all among the top third of the scorers in the league.[3] By the 1986–87 season, the player with the most fights had been in 30, and two of the three players with the most fights were not even in the top half of scorers in the league. The rise of the enforcer was due to expansion and the rise of the culture of the celebrity athlete, and the general decline of the enforcer after the lockout coincided with the shrinking of the NHL rosters, the rise in player salaries, the influx of European players, and rule changes designed to reduce brawls (Hruby, 2002; Murphy, 2011). While most teams still employ at least one tough player, many authors (Cardinal, 2008; Gatehouse, 2009; Gordon, 2010; Kennedy, 1999; Murphy, 2011) argue that the enforcer, the one-dimensional, unskilled player who can only fight, has effectively lost his place in the league.

A goal of the study was to examine the role of Aboriginal hockey players in the NHL. To do so requires the identification of Aboriginal hockey players in the league. It is important to note that Aboriginal peoples in Canada reflect considerable diversity in their cultures and identities, and to render this diversity to a homogeneous group is problematic. However, it is reasonable to suggest that there are enough common features of the historical and contemporary circumstances among Canada's Aboriginal population to consider Indian, Inuit, and Métis peoples collectively for the purposes of this study.

To determine the Aboriginal status of NHL hockey players for this study, a number of sources were used in a form of triangulation. A player was included in the study if three or more of the following sources cited the player as being Aboriginal:

- http://www.virtualmuseum.ca/Exhibitions/Hockey/English/Amateur/everyone.html, a Canadian federal government website on Native hockey players
- Nativehockey.com, a non-profit corporation that assists in the promotion and development of young Native players throughout North America
- *They Call Me Chief: Warriors on Ice* by Marks (2008)

- *First Nations Hockey Players* by Cardinal (2008)
- magazines/newspapers devoted to Aboriginal issues (for example, *Windtalker Hockey News*, *Windspeaker*, and *Indian Country Today*)
- newspaper accounts

This method was deemed superior to other methods that have been used in some previous stacking studies, like visual classification from pictures or player cards.

Based on these sources, a total of 66 Aboriginal players were identified who have played in the NHL since 1918.[4] Five players were goaltenders and were therefore excluded from the final sample as goaltenders rarely play the role of enforcer. Players who appeared in fewer than four games during a single season were also not included, leaving a total of 57 Aboriginal players in the NHL since 1918. For the longitudinal analysis, any year in which Aboriginal players made up at least 1 percent of league players was included. A total of 31 years of longitudinal data were analyzed, including all years from 1974–75 to 2009–10, with the exception of 1983–84, 1984–85, 1985–86, and 1987–88, when Aboriginal participation was below 1 percent in the league. Data analyzed included penalty minutes per game, major penalties per game, and fights per game for all Aboriginal players who played more than four games in each of those years.

Results

There are three different statistics that can be used to evaluate enforcers: (1) penalty minutes, (2) the number of major penalties assessed, and (3) the number of fights.[5] An enforcer is not only a fighter but, even more importantly within the culture of the NHL game, the enforcer intimidates opponents. In effect, a successful enforcer can be intimidating to the point that he does not need to fight in order to protect his teammates. Given this, assessing enforcers requires considering not only the number of fights but also the penalty minutes and major penalties as these are other forms of agitation and intimidation.

PENALTY MINUTES

Examining Figure 4.3, it is evident that while Aboriginal players were assessed more penalties than their non-Aboriginal counterparts, there was a dramatic escalation starting in 1981–82 that increased for the next 15 years. Between 1986 and 2004, when examining penalty minutes per game, Aboriginal players were overrepresented in the top 20 percent of penalized players at almost three and a half times the rate of non-Aboriginal players. During the 1995–96 season, 85 percent of the Aboriginal players in the league were in the top 20 percent of players in penalty minutes per game.

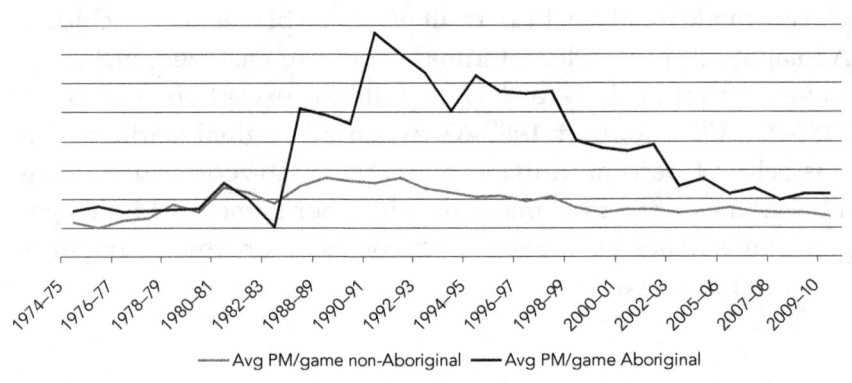

Figure 4.3: Penalty Minutes Per Game

MAJOR PENALTIES

Major penalties are more serious infractions, such as fighting, spearing, butt-ending, charging, and boarding. These penalties are clearly associated with fighting and intimidation and are also much less common than minor penalties. Data, displayed in Figure 4.4, have been available only since 1997, which limits examination to the latter half of the enforcer era. In the first year for which results are available, Aboriginal players were assessed five times more major penalties than non-Aboriginals, but that declined steadily until the NHL lockout in 2004. During the era of the enforcer, Aboriginals players took almost three times the number of major penalties as non-Aboriginal players. Since 1997, close to 85 percent of Aboriginal players have taken a major penalty, almost twice the percentage of non-Aboriginals. Since the lockout, Aboriginal players still earn major penalties at twice the rate of non-Aboriginal players.

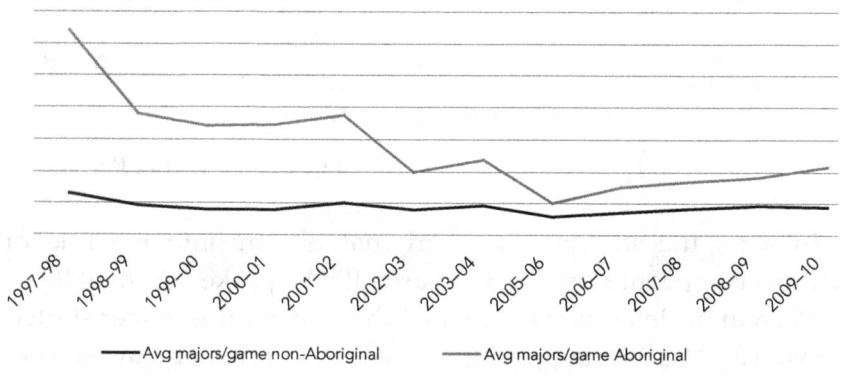

Figure 4.4: Major Penalties Per Game

FIGHTS

Fights have historically been the benchmark of the enforcer and this is also where there is the greatest difference between Aboriginal and non-Aboriginal players. As Figure 4.5 demonstrates, prior to the 1982–83 season, there was no difference in the average number of fights per game between Aboriginal and non-Aboriginal players, but by 1986–87, Aboriginal players fought at four times the rate of non-Aboriginal players and this number remained high until the lockout season. During the 1994–95 season, Aboriginal players had more than seven times the number of fights per game as non-Aboriginal players. During the next season, 92 percent of Aboriginal players were among the top-fifth in fights per game. From 1986 through to the lockout season, more than 80 percent of Aboriginal NHLers had been in a fight, twice the rate of non-Aboriginals. Since the 2004 lockout, while fights per game have dropped for Aboriginals, the rate is still twice as high as for non-Aboriginal players.

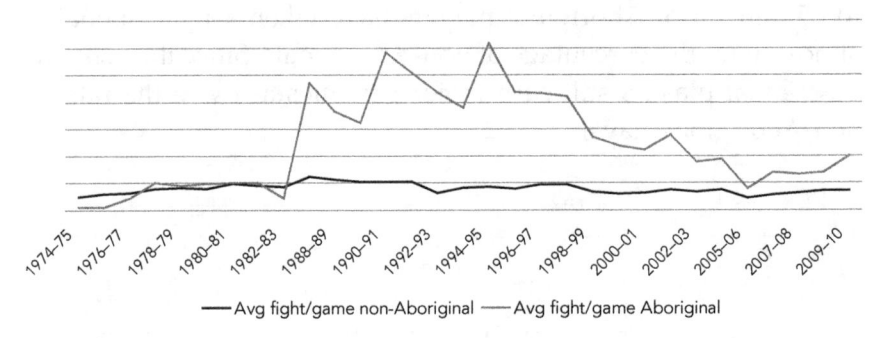

Figure 4.5: Fights Per Game

In sum, the stacking of Aboriginal players into the role of enforcer appeared during the early 1980s, peaked from 1990 to 2000, and declined precisely when the role of the enforcer started to vanish. The data support the idea that Aboriginal players were used to fill roles as enforcers when the enforcers' era was at its peak. Most damning is that since 2000, as this era of the enforcer has declined, so too has the number of Aboriginal men playing in the NHL, suggesting that the reduction in enforcers reduced the opportunities for Aboriginal players in the NHL overall. In other words, the NHL saw an increase in the number of players of Aboriginal descent when the enforcer was most prevalent in the league. Of the enforcers in the NHL at that time, many were Aboriginal even though Aboriginal players constituted a small percentage of the league's players. Theories to account for these results are discussed in the next section.

Discussion

This section considers the reasons why Aboriginal hockey players have traditionally been stacked into the enforcer position. Four factors are considered: the coach, discrimination, self-selection, and stereotypes.

THE COACH

A coach could decide to have a player perform the role of enforcer at some level of player development. In the 1970s, Eitzen and Sanford (1975) found that coaches often converted players into positions they deemed to be more acceptable for that player. Scott Taylor, sport editor for an Aboriginal newspaper, contends that coaches still play a role in stacking. Bristow (2008, para. 11) argues that coaches will mistreat, belittle, and bench Aboriginal players who are not the toughest players on their team:

> As sports editor of *Grassroots News*, the country's largest Aboriginal newspaper, I've come to know the First Nations players a bit. If they can't be the toughest guys on the team, they're generally treated like crap, called soft and benched [by the coach]. That's why [they] play the way they do. (Bristow, 2008, para. 11)

The expectation for all male players and Aboriginal players in particular was a gender performance that was tough, violent, and ruthless.

DISCRIMINATION

Many male Aboriginal hockey players grow up facing racism and learn to defend themselves physically against racist comments and treatment (Marks, 2008). Former NHLers Ron Delorme and Gino Odjick stated that they learned to fight in order to survive, and responded to racist comments with their fists (Marks, 2008; Spector, 1997). Willie O'Ree, the first Black to play in the NHL, said that minorities were targets for abuse and so had to fight to prove themselves, a point echoed by Terrence Tootoo, who stated that Native kids "have to be tougher in body and spirit" (Stackhouse, 2001, p. A15). In this way, Aboriginal hockey players may develop fighting skills as a direct, gendered response to racism.

SELF-SELECTION

Role models may also play a part in this stacking process, particularly with the limited numbers of Aboriginal men playing in the NHL and the fact that enforcers often receive significant media attention. For years, an Aboriginal Role Model Hockey School, featuring a number of Aboriginal enforcers as instructors, operated to introduce young Aboriginals to the game. Gino Odjick, one of the instructors and a noted NHL enforcer, cites Stan Jonathon, another enforcer, was his role model growing up. Hawkins (2002) suggests that socialization often steers youth in the direction of positions or roles where they believe they might have the best opportunity for success. Young Aboriginals may see the role of enforcer as their opportunity to make it in pro hockey as they follow in the footsteps of other Aboriginals who have made it to the NHL. This could influence the way some young Aboriginal boys play the game and perhaps limit the perceived opportunities of smaller or more skilled players.

Indeed, it is important to recognize that some form of agency is likely involved in the processes by which a hockey player (Aboriginal or otherwise) becomes an enforcer, perhaps influenced by role models, the celebration of stereotypes, and the adoption of a hypermasculine performance. Playing the role of enforcer may also therefore offer a form of cultural resistance. Robidoux (2004) argues that in Aboriginal communities, hockey is used not only as cultural expression, but also as a form of resistance to dominant Euro-Canadian sport values and culture. Playing in a specific style, such as the violent or intimidating way of the enforcer, may be a way to resist the dominant culture for some Aboriginal players.

STEREOTYPES

Finally, racist stereotypes may be a cause. The passing of the 1982 Canadian *Constitution Act* was followed by a series of land claims across Canada. Some of these resulted in highly publicized stand-offs such as those in Oka, Penticton, Ipperwash, and Gustafsen Lake. Nourbese Philip (1993) is supported by Tator, Henry, and Mattis (1998) in the assertion that racism becomes more blatant and pervasive during periods when people are more assertively claiming their rights. Roth, Nelson, and Kasennahaw (1995) argue that the media coverage surrounding the Oka crisis resulted in the blatant negative stereotyping of First Nations peoples. The *Report of the Royal Commission on Aboriginal Peoples* (1996) that followed concluded that a theme of media coverage was Aboriginal peoples as angry warriors. Henry and Tator (2002) argue that newspaper coverage depicted Aboriginals as a threat to orderly society, strengthening the dominant culture's view of Aboriginal peoples as savage. The racist media coverage may have reinforced the idea of Aboriginal peoples as savage and coincided with the peak time of the stacking of Aboriginals as enforcers.

Indeed, Hallinan (1991), and Johnson and colleagues (1999) found the determination of the position in sport most likely to be played by a racialized group was underpinned by popular and/or racist beliefs about the abilities of that population. Kanter (1977) hypothesized that when a population was underrepresented, as Aboriginal peoples are in hockey, "stereotypical assumptions and mistaken attributions made about tokens tend to force them into playing limited and caricatured roles" (p. 980). The stereotype of *warrior* continues to be associated with Aboriginal culture, even included in the titles of a documentary and book about Aboriginals in hockey (see Marks & Zubeck & Marks, 2001; Marks, 2008). Media accounts of Aboriginal hockey as a physical, aggressive, fearless style of play abound (see, for example, Peacock, 2001; Stackhouse, 2001; Swift, 2003). These stereotypes have an influence on the game.

Conclusion

While Aboriginal hockey players have consistently been underrepresented in the NHL, they have historically been overrepresented as fighters or enforcers, a position that emerged in response to expansion and the rise of the star player in the NHL. Melnick (1996) argues that when a certain role or position is specialized, one might find stacking more likely to occur. There is little evidence of the stacking of Aboriginal hockey players as fighters prior to the emergence of the enforcer era, but from the mid-1970s until the lockout of 2004–05, Aboriginal players took more penalties, were assessed more major penalties, and were much more likely to fight than non-Aboriginals. Longitudinal analysis allows us to see that differences between Aboriginal and non-Aboriginal hockey players in the NHL were more moderate before and after this time period. In light of this apparent stacking, it is perhaps not surprising that since the disappearance of the enforcer, the number of Aboriginals in the NHL has also declined.

Several theories were explored in an attempt to explain stacking of Aboriginal players as enforcers, including racism, the role of the coach, discrimination, self-selection, and stereotyping. The role of the enforcer, aligned with the Aboriginal stereotype of the savage, was used to intimidate, protect, and entertain. The stacking of Aboriginal hockey players as enforcers also coincided with the rise in Aboriginal activism and, more importantly, the negative media coverage Aboriginals were subjected to. This coverage may have contributed to the ongoing stereotyping of Aboriginal peoples as savage.

In sum, subtle forms of new racism continue to deny Aboriginal peoples opportunities for full participation in many areas of Canadian society, including hockey. The fact that hockey is seen as a natural and meritocratic part of Canadian society makes the subtle and even invisible forms of new racism an appropriate vehicle for examining racial stacking in hockey. At the least, this chapter illustrates that professional hockey may have constituted, and been constituted by, the racist stereotype of the aggressive, violent Aboriginal athlete. As a result, continued critical reflection on the role of sport in Canada in contributing to the construction of race, gender, and the institutionalization of racism is called for.

Questions for Critical Thought

1. Discuss examples of new racism that you are familiar with. How do these examples differ from more overt examples of racism? How might they be normalized and accepted?
2. How does the success of many visible minorities in North American professional sport reinforce ideas of sport as meritocratic while also undermining attempts to confront discrimination?
3. How does stacking tend to reinforce stereotypes?
4. Apply the four theories used to explain stacking to other cases of sport in North America.
5. Compare the role that agency might play in stacking to the role that structure might play.

Notes

1. When the Edmonton Oilers traded Gretzky to the Los Angeles Kings in 1988 as part of the general strategy to promote the NHL in the U.S. South, McSorley was included in the trade in order to serve as Gretzky's enforcer with his new club.
2. The 2004–05 NHL season was cancelled due to a labour dispute.
3. All fighting statistics are taken from www.hockeyfights.com
4. Six players were not considered for lack of agreement among the sources.
5. Both Maguire (1988) and Malcolm (1997) argue that qualitative data should also be gathered for stacking studies. The attempt was made to interview Aboriginal hockey players, but finding

significant numbers was difficult. In the few interviews that were completed, it became obvious that some players, particularly those who moved from the reserve to the city, were told by coaches to change roles and become enforcers.

References

Andrews, D. & Jackson, S. (2001). Introduction. In D. Andrews & S. Jackson (Eds.), *Sport stars: The cultural politics of sporting celebrity* (pp. 1–19). London: Routledge.

Barker, M. (1982). *The new racism: Conservatives and the ideology of the tribe*. London: Junction Books.

Bristow, N. (2008). Talking hockey with Scott Taylor. *NHL Digest*. Retrieved from www.nhldigest.com/2008/02/

Brown, D. (1989). The northern character theme and sport in nineteenth-century Canada. *Canadian Journal of History of Sport, 20*, 47–56.

Canadian Heritage. (2005). *Sport Canada's policy on Aboriginal Peoples' participation in sport*. Ottawa: Minister of Public Works and Government Services Canada.

Canadian Press. (2005). Nolan the target of fan abuse. *Globe and Mail* (December 19), R5.

Cardinal, W. (2008). *First Nations hockey players*. Edmonton: Eschia Books.

Castine, S. & Roberts, G.C. (1974). Modeling in the socialization process of the Black athlete. *International Review for the Sociology of Sport, 3–4*, 59–73.

Churchill, W., Hill, N. & Barlow, M. (1979). An historical overview of twentieth-century Native American athletics. *The Indian Historian, 12*(4), 22–32.

Coakley, J. (2006). *Sports in society: Issues and controversies* (9th ed.). New York: McGraw-Hill.

Cosentino, F. (1998). *Afros, Aboriginals, and amateur sport in pre-World War One Canada*. Ottawa: Canadian Historical Association.

Curtis, J.E. & Loy, J.W. (1979): Race/Ethnicity and relative centrality of playing positions in team sports. *Exercise and Sport Sciences Reviews*, 6, 285–313.

Diamond, D., Duplacey, J., Dinger, R., Fitzsimmons, E. & Zweig, E. (2003). *Total hockey* (2nd ed.). Toronto: SPORTClassic Publishing.

Earle, N. (1995). Hockey as Canadian popular culture: Team Canada 1972, television, and the Canadian identity. *Journal of Canadian Studies*, 30, 107–123.

Eitzen, D.S. & Sanford, D.C. (1975). Segregation of Blacks by playing position in football: Accident or design. *Social Science Quarterly*, 55, 948–959.

Fitz-Gerald, S. (2001). Evolution of the goon. *National Post* (December 8), B11.

Gatehouse, J. (2009). Our national blood sport. *Maclean's*, 122(19), 46–48.

Gems, G.R. (2005). Negotiating a Native American identity through sport: Assimilation, adaptation, and the role of the trickster. In C.R. King (Ed.), *Native athletes in sport and society* (pp. 1–21). Lincoln: University of Nebraska Press.

Globe and Mail. (2009). Two ways forward. *Globe and Mail* (August 17), A10.

Gordon, S. (2010). The game has changed; the roster follows as Laraque out in Montreal. *Globe and Mail* (January 22), R7.

Gruneau, R. & Whitson, D. (1993). *Hockey night in Canada: Sport, identities, and cultural politics*. Toronto: Garamond Press.

Hallinan, C. (1991). Aborigines and positional segregation in Australian rugby league. *International Review for the Sociology of Sport*, 26(2), 69–81.

Hallinan, C.J., Bruce, T. & Coram, S. (1999). Up front and beyond the centre line: Australian Aborigines in elite Australian rules football. *International Review for the Sociology of Sport*, 34(4), 369–383.

Hawkins, B.J. (2002). Is stacking dead? A case study of the stacking hypothesis at a Southeastern Conference (SEC) football program. *International Sport Journal*, 6(2), 146–159.

Henry, F. & Tator, C. (2002). *Discourses of domination: Racial bias in the Canadian English-language press*. Toronto: University of Toronto Press.

Henry, F. & Tator, C. (2005). *The colour of democracy: Racism in Canadian society* (3rd ed.). Toronto: Thomson, Nelson.

Hruby, P. (2002, May 13). Requiem for hockey's goons: The sport has evolved, and fist-first Neanderthals are a relic of a distant ice age. *Insight on the News*. Retrieved May 14, 2010 from www.highbeam.com/doc/1G1-86233304.html.

Hwang, S. (2001). Homelessness and health. *Canadian Medical Association Journal, 164*(2), 229.

Jedwab, J. (2008). Canadians have favorable opinion of Aboriginals in Canada, especially those in contact with members of Aboriginal communities. *Association for Canadian Studies*.

Johnson, D.L., Hallinan, C.J. & Westerfield, R.C. (1999). Picturing success: Photographs and stereotyping in men's collegiate basketball. *Journal of Sport Behavior, 22*(1), 45–53.

Joyce, G. (2006). *When the lights went out*. Toronto: Doubleday.

Kanter, R.M. (1977). Some aspects of proportions on group life: Skewed sex ratios and responses to token women. *American Journal of Sociology, 82*, 965–990.

Kennedy, K. (1999). Twilight of the goons. *Sports Illustrated* (March 8), 29.

Kernaghan, J. (1993). Taking our national game to the Natives. *Ottawa Citizen* (January 17), D6.

King, C. (2005). *Native athletes in sport and society*. Lincoln: University of Nebraska Press.

Klein, J. & Reif, K. (2001). *The hockey compendium*. Toronto: McClelland & Stewart.

Kohler, N. (2003). I was cut from the Olympic team because I'm Native, athlete claims. *Ottawa Citizen* (July 28), A3.

LaRocque, E. (2007). Métis and feminist: Ethical reflections on feminism, human rights, and decolonization. In J. Green (Ed.), *Making space for Indigenous feminism* (pp. 53–71). Halifax: Fernwood Publishing.

Lavoie, M. (1989). Stacking, performance differentials, and salary discrimination in professional ice hockey: A survey of the evidence. *Sociology of Sport Journal, 6*(1), 17–35.

Leonard, W.M. & Phillips, J. (1997). The cause and effect rule for percentaging tables. An overdue statistical correction for "Stacking" studies. *Sociology of Sport Journal, 14*(3), 283–289.

Maguire, J.A. (1988). Race and position assignment in English soccer: A preliminary analysis of ethnicity and sport in Britain. *Sociology of Sport Journal, 5*(3), 257–269.

Malcolm, D. (1997). Stacking in cricket: A figurational sociological reappraisal of centrality. *Sociology of Sport Journal, 14*, 263–282.

Mangan, J.A. & Ritchie, A. (Eds.). (2004). *Ethnicity, sport, identity: Struggles for status*. Abington: Frank Cass Publishers.

Marks, D. (2008). *They call me chief: Warriors on ice*. Winnipeg: Shillingford Publishing Inc.

Marks, D. & Zubeck, G. (Prod.) & Marks, D. (Dir.). (2001). *They call me chief: Warriors on ice*. Rocky Point Productions, 588 Gertrude Ave., Winnipeg, Manitoba.

Mason, G. (2006). Finding his way in San Jose. *Globe and Mail* (April 15), A4.

Mason, G. (2008). After the apology, time to move on. *Globe and Mail* (October 25), A7.

McPherson, B.D., Curtis, J.E., & Loy, J.N. (1989). *The social significance of sport. An introduction to the sociology of sport*. Champaigne, IL: Human Kinetics

Melnick, M.J. (1996). Maori women and positional segregation in New Zealand netball: Another test of the Anglocentric hypothesis. *Sociology of Sport Journal, 13*, 259–273.

Melnick, M.J. & Thomson, R.W. (1996). The Maori people and positional segregation in New Zealand rugby football: A test of the Anglocentric hypothesis. *International Review for the Sociology of Sport, 31*(2), 139–154.

Morra, N.N. & Smith, M.D. (2002). Interpersonal sources of violence in hockey: The influence of the media, parents, coaches, and game officials. In F.L. Smoll & R.E. Smith (Eds.), *Children and youth in sport: A biopsychosocial perspective* (2nd ed., pp. 235–255). Dubuque: Kendall/Hunt.

Murphy, A. (2011). Hard times in the endangered zone. *Sports Illustrated, 115*(18), 106–111.

Najak, S. (Dir.). (2007). Coach's Corner [television series episode]. In S. Najak (Exec. Prod.), *Hockey night in Canada*. Toronto: CBC.

Nixon, H.L. & Frey, J.H. (1996). *A sociology of sport*. Belmont: Wadsworth.

Nourbese Philip, M. (1993). *Showing grit: Showboating north of the 44th parallel*. Toronto: Poui.

Paraschak, V. (1989). Native sport history: Pitfalls and promise. *Canadian Journal of History of Sport, 20*(1), 57–68.

Paraschak, V. (1998). "Reasonable amusements": Connecting the strands of physical culture in Native lives. *Sport History Review, 29*, 121–131.

Paraschak, V. (2008). Native American games and sports. In *Berkshire encyclopedia of sport* (pp. 1060–1066). Great Barrington: Berkshire Publishing.

Peacock, S. (2001). Team spirit. *Elm Street* (February–March), 74–85.

Robidoux, M. (2004). Narratives of race relations in southern Alberta: An examination of conflicting sporting practices. *Sociology of Sport Journal, 21*, 287–301.

Robidoux, M. (2006). Historical interpretations of First Nations masculinity and its influence on Canada's sport heritage. *The International Journal of the History of Sport, 23*(2), 267–284.

Roth, L., Nelson, B. & Kasennahaw, M.D. (1995). Three women, a mouse, a microphone, and a telephone: Information (mis)management during the Mohawk/Canadian governments' "conflict of 1990." In A. Valdivia (Ed.), *Feminism, multiculturalism, and the media: Global perspectives* (pp. 48–81). Thousand Oaks: Sage.

Royal Commission on Aboriginal Peoples. (1996). *Report of the Royal Commission on Aboriginal Peoples*. Ottawa: Indian and Northern Affairs.

Rutherford, P. (1990). *When television was young: Primetime Canada 1952–1967*. Toronto: University of Toronto Press.

Sack, A.L., Singh, P. & Thiel, R. (2005). Occupational segregation on the playing field: The case of major league baseball. *Journal of Sport Management, 19*, 300–318.

Smylie, J. & Adomako, P. (2009). *The Indigenous children's health report*. Toronto: The Keenan Research Centre.

Spector, M. (1997). Gino was effective in curbing insults. *Edmonton Journal* (December 4), D3.

Sports Illustrated. (2009). SI players NHL poll. *Sports Illustrated, 110*(21), 19. Retrieved May 14, 2010 from http://sportsillustrated.cnn.com/vault/article/magazine/MAG1155624/index.htm

Stackhouse, J. (2001). The healing power of hockey. *Globe and Mail* (November 7), A14–A15.

Swift, E.M. (2003). On the wild side. *Sports Illustrated, 99*(6) (August 10), 52–58.

Tator, C., Henry, F. & Mattis, W. (1998). *Challenging racism in the arts: Case studies of controversy and conflict.* Toronto: University of Toronto Press.

thehockeywriters.com. (2009). The top 10 dirtiest NHL players (October 1). Retrieved from http://thehockeywriters.com/top-10-dirtiest-nhl-players

Wamsley, K. (2007). The public importance of men and the importance of public men: Sport and masculinities in nineteenth-century Canada. In P. White & K. Young (Eds.), *Sport and gender in Canada* (2nd ed., pp. 75–91). Toronto: Oxford University Press.

Wendell, S. (1996). *The rejected body: Feminist philosophical reflections on disability.* New York: Routledge.

Wiwchar, D. (2009). Native hockey stars shine in NHL. *Indian Country Today* (May 24). Retrieved from www.indiancountrytoday.com/living/sports/45843077.html

Woodward, J.R. (2004). Professional football scouts: An investigation of racial stacking. *Sociology of Sport Journal, 21,* 356–375.

PART TWO
Canadian Immigration and the Study of Race and Sport

CHAPTER 5

Gender, Immigration, and Physical Activity: The Experiences of Chinese Immigrant Women

XIN HUANG, WENDY FRISBY, AND LUCIE THIBAULT

Chapter Overview

Drawing from in-depth, multilingual interviews and a workshop with sport policy makers and 50 new Chinese immigrant women from Mainland China, Hong Kong, and Taiwan, this chapter discusses issues of gender and multiculturalism in physical activity based on Chinese immigrant women's experiences of migration and settlement. It situates the current increasing population of Chinese immigrants in the broader context of the history of Chinese immigration to Canada, and current policies and debates on multiculturalism, with specific reference to the lack of such policies in the sport arena. It highlights the important role that participation in physical activities plays in Chinese immigrant women's lives, not only in terms of physical and mental well-being, but also in terms of adjusting to life in Canada, coping with life change, and reducing social isolation. A gender analysis of the barriers Chinese immigrant women face reveals that there are age- and mother-specific issues that are compounded by race, social class, and culture.

The purpose of this chapter is to address the following questions regarding Chinese immigrant women:

1. What are the causes of the gaps in terms of gender, race, age, economic, and health status for immigrant women's participation in physical activities?
2. How do the conditions of being an immigrant woman affect one's access to physical activity services and facilities?
3. What policy and institutional changes need to be considered in order to remove the barriers for immigrant women's participation?

Gender and Chinese Immigrants in Canada

Chinese immigration from China to Canada was initially a male activity. The first group of Chinese immigrants arrived in Canada in 1858. They came as workers for the construction of the Canadian Pacific Railway and other forms of manual labour (Li, 1998). Initially women and children remained behind to sustain the family lines in the homeland, while men sent money home to ensure their survival (Chinese Canadian National Council, Women's Book Committee, 1992). However, the small number of Chinese women who also arrived in Canada were mainly wives or daughters of merchants or wives of labourers; there was a small number of prostitutes as well. The first Chinese woman, Mrs. Kwong Lee, reached the shore of Canada in 1860 (Chinese Canadian National Council, Women's Book Committee, 1992). From 1903 to 1947, various exclusion legislations, such as the *Head Tax* in 1903 and the *Chinese Immigration Act* in 1923, were enforced to limit and prohibit Chinese immigration into Canada, so the sex ratio in the Chinese community remained male biased (Li, 1998).

This situation began to change in the second half of the 20th century. The point system, introduced in 1967, selected immigrants based on their education, skills, and resources (Li, 1998). This system and the Business Immigration Program, which began in 1978 (Lee, 2005; Smart, 1994), attracted many rich and middle-class Hong Kong and Taiwanese Chinese to Canada in the 1980s and 1990s.[1] Since the 1990s, a large number of immigrants from Mainland China entered Canada, making Mainland China the largest source of immigrants to Canada since 1997. In 2009, immigrants from China accounted for 11 percent of new immigrants to Canada and 25 percent of Canada's Asian-source countries (Citizenship and Immigration Canada [CIC], 2010). Among them, those entering under the economic immigrants category numbered 19,656 or 67.7 percent of Chinese immigrants in 2009 (CIC, 2010). Immigration policies since the 1970s have favoured family reunification and targeted women as workers. As a result, women have outnumbered male immigrants since 1992 (CIC, 2011). In 2009, 27.3 percent of the 29,044 Chinese immigrants came in the family class (those who have close family already living in Canada) (CIC, 2010). Of the 797,653 Chinese immigrants who came to Canada between 1980 and 2000, 52 percent were females and 48 percent were males (CIC, 2010).

This immigration influences the makeup of Canadian society. According to the 2006 census, there are over 200 ethnic groups living in Canada, including 5 million visible minorities.[2] Statistics Canada (2010) predicted that the visible minority population of Vancouver and Toronto is expected to increase to 60 percent over the next two decades, and Chinese immigrants now represent the largest immigrant group in both Vancouver and Canada. In the 2006 census, 381,500 residents of Vancouver and Toronto—or one in every five people—identified their ethnicity as Chinese, and more than one-quarter of those residents were born abroad, mostly in Mainland China, Hong Kong, Taiwan, and Vietnam (Statistics Canada, 2008). Most of these new immigrants are either wealthy business owners or well-educated professionals, and their arrival in Canada has arguably changed the stereotypical image of Chinese immigrants as "coolies" and also restructured

Chinese-Canadian society. Their immigration has also involved changes to their family models and gender relations.

Still, Chinese immigrants to Canada often face the devaluation of their educational qualifications and labour market experience, and encounter differences in political systems, cultural traditions, and languages. Furthermore, Chinese immigrants are still perceived as racially distinct and often experience racism and other forms of social exclusion (Li, 1998). Many newcomers experience the same exclusionary, anti-Asian attitudes and practices that have long plagued Chinese settlers in Canada. Research has pointed out that the denial of jobs to immigrants and the rejection of job seekers of colour or those with an accent from high-level positions stems not from a neutral evaluation of people's skills, but from racism based on homophyly, or fear of the unfamiliar (Bauder, 2003). Statistics show that Chinese Canadians earn less than the average Canadian does. Even though over 27 percent of the Chinese people in Canada had a university degree, according to the 2001 census, the average income from all sources for Canadians of Chinese origin aged 15 and over was $25,000 in 2000, compared with an average of almost $30,000 for all Canadian adults (Statistics Canada, 2007).

The gendered and racialized immigration policies, neo-liberal social policies, professional accreditation systems, and labour market have further discriminated against immigrant women. For instance, the principal applicants of the independent class (i.e., skilled workers, entrepreneurs, investors, and the self-employed) are assessed by specific selection criteria, but their dependants are not subject to the same assessment. Man's (2004) study found that many highly educated and trained Chinese immigrant professional women entered Canada as dependants of their husbands because gender biases in definitions of education, work, and skills mean that women's abilities and personal qualities are either excluded or undervalued. As dependants, these women are not treated as potential workers in the labour market, and receive less training and support in finding employment in Canada.

On the one hand, the barriers many Chinese professional and skilled immigrant women face in continuing their careers in Canada push them toward low-status, low-paid, and part-time positions, or out of the labour force entirely. On the other hand, differences in ideal family roles, the inadequacy of child-care services, the lack of child-care subsidies, and the absence of support systems in the new country, such as extended family members, drive them to become full-time homemakers and caregivers (Salaff & Greve, 2006). Their changing social position and family roles influence their lives in Canada in general and, as we will discuss below, their participation in physical activities as well.

Gender, Culture, and Physical Activity

Even though Canada officially takes a multiculturalism approach to immigrant integration, whereby ethnic or racial groups are supposed to preserve their cultural identities rather than assimilate and adopt the dominant culture's values, norms, and customs (Ryan, 2010), Canada's roots as a White European settlers' nation have shaped its social political system and policies. As a result, Western values and beliefs are manifested in almost every aspect of life. Furthermore, criticisms of multiculturalism point out that there is often a "shallow multiculturalism" (Sandercock, 2004, p. 156) as manifested in various kinds of cultural festivals in which culture is superficially represented by food, dance, costumes, and featured as an object for display (Bissoondath, 2002). A "rich multiculturalism" (Sandercock, 2004, p. 156) involves political and policy support and encourages meaningful adjustment, intercultural exchange, and collaboration or, as DeSensi (1995, p. 36) suggests, requires an authentic internalization of multicultural frames of reference.

While Canadian multiculturalism policy encourages immigrants to preserve their cultures, in practice they often have to adjust their lifestyle to fit into the existing system. Multiculturalism thus becomes the assimilation of minority groups into the dominant culture, and this process of fitting in often evokes tensions and conflicts within families and oneself, leading to experiences of deculturation and alienation from the life one used to have and the person one used to be (Donnelly & Nakamura, 2009). Further, as immigration is a gendered process, to fit in also involves adjusting to the gendered way of being and a gendered sense of self. Through the encounter with different discourses and social policies on physical activity, gender, family, children, and women's position in Canadian society, immigrants often experience a change in family patterns, gender relations, child-raising practices, and ideas of masculinity and femininity. Newcomers have to cope with a number of issues, and undertaking physical activity often does not rank at the top of their priorities. Nonetheless, there is some research that shows participation in physical activity plays an important role in alleviating the stresses and social isolation associated with displacement and resettlement (Stodolska & Alexandris, 2004).

Our study of Chinese immigrant women in Vancouver has demonstrated that participating in physical activity not only contributed significantly to physical and mental well-being, it also helped them to socialize and share information with others, adjust to life in Canada, improve family relations, and ultimately contributed to their quality of life and happiness. However, research has also shown that new immigrants encounter significant barriers to participation in physical activity, and that immigrant women engage less in physical activity compared to non-immigrants and immigrant men (Tremblay, Bryan, Perex, Ardem & Katzmarzyk, 2006). This chapter investigates the conditions, barriers, and policies involved in Chinese immigrant women's access to physical activity.

Methods

In order to better understand the experiences of Chinese women newcomers to Canada, we interviewed 50 recent immigrant

Chinese women in their choice of Mandarin, Cantonese, or English about the role of physical activity through the public sector in their settlement. Twenty-five of these interviewees were physically inactive participants who were recruited through a social service agency in the Greater Vancouver Area called SUCCESS, which provides settlement services (e.g., employment counselling, information about health care, social housing). The other 25 participants were physically active participants who were recruited from three community centres in various neighbourhoods within the City of Vancouver. The research participants were from different socio-economic backgrounds. Interviews were transcribed verbatim, translated into English, and then analyzed.

Doing Physical Activities in a New Country

Many of the Chinese women we interviewed participated in various types of physical activities before immigration. These activities were carried out more often with friends and sometimes with family. Women participated at privately owned fitness clubs, fitness facilities provided by their workplace and their place of residence rather than community centres, which are a development of only the past decade in places like Mainland China.

Immigration brought changes in most women's lives and, consequently, a change in past habits and ideas about undertaking physical activities. Among these changes, some found that public facilities in Vancouver were better equipped, less expensive, and more accessible, especially in terms of policies that encouraged the participation of economically disadvantaged groups. Some felt that in Canada, ordinary citizens could enjoy many facilities and services that would be available only to people in the upper echelons in China. Coming to Canada also provided them with opportunities to learn about popular Canadian sport and physical activities. A number of women thought that the physical culture in Canada had a positive influence that led to their increased participation. Several explained that they were more conscious about participating in sport after coming to Canada. Some interviewees were encouraged to do more physical activity by their family doctors; others became more involved because of their children, or were motivated by aging and health concerns.

Not all changes were positive, however. There were observable differences in the ways recreational facilities and services are organized and delivered between China and Canada. For example, barriers to participation were caused by social and economic downward mobility, changes in family structure, language, and differences in policies, practices, and patterns of physical activities between their former and new homeland. Many women changed their habits because of their new living conditions following immigration due to considerations of cost, time, transportation, child care, social support, and companions.

We also found that many participants lacked information about services available, knowledge of the Canadian recreation and physical activity service system, and the skills needed for participating in the programs offered. Many were also unaware of the opportunities and subsidy policies of which they could take advantage, such as the City of Vancouver's Leisure Access Policy and the federal government's Children's Fitness Tax Credit. Some also reported they were unfamiliar with the ways in which services were provided. For example, community centres often assume that its users know their rights, entitlements, and ways to access these services and subsidy policies, and have the skills to utilize the facilities and programs offered. However, our research participants were unfamiliar with the neo-liberal approach to Canadian recreation and physical activity program delivery in which individuals are responsible for their own participation and well-being. Several women also reported that some programs offered at the community centres were too "Canadian," meaning that they had little knowledge about, or skills required to take part in, the activity. This was considered a barrier, particularly when programs and instructions were conducted in English, a language most of the women were still struggling to master, and few programs were tailored to their needs in terms of types of physical activity, scheduling, child care, and cost. From our perspective, these barriers reflect a deeper level of disjuncture between Chinese immigrant women's understandings and the dominant Canadian ways of conceptualizing and engaging in physical activity. There is also an apparent disjuncture between meanings of citizenship and responsibility, rights, and entitlements, and the role and relationship between the individual and the state. Below is a sample quotation from one of the women that illustrates this point:

> Usually the weekend is better because as you can see after the working hours, I have to take care of the meals. So it is already late so we can go out only on the weekend. I think Sunday is better as our family also played badminton in the community centre, I think one or two years ago, the community centre closed on Sunday. I don't know why they close on Sunday and then we can no longer go for the badminton activity. It is bad. (S5, age 48, from Hong Kong, immigrated eight years ago; family income: $50,000–$100,000, own income: $30,000)

Cultural differences regarding the appropriate time to engage in physical activity and, consequently, when community centres could be expected to provide services were salient.

Physical Activity and Changing Family, Socio-economic, and Gender Models

Some research participants referred to the challenges associated with immigration to Canada. The deskilling of immigrants in the job market due to the devaluation of their educational qualifications, negative labour market experiences, and cultural and language barriers were cited. Consequently, many immigrant families who were affluent in China experienced both a social and economic downturn following immigration.

CHANGING GENDERED CAREER PATTERNS

For many women, these changes were compounded by the pressure to remodel their lives to fit into a different employment market, gender norms, and a social welfare system. Most of the women we interviewed worked outside of the home and contributed to the family income. Among the 50 women we interviewed, 62 percent of them had education at the college level or above. After immigration, some of them changed from being career women to stay-at-home mothers.

Contrary to the negative stereotypes that immigrants' countries of origin are "backward," "traditional," and "oppressive to women" compared to a "modern" Canada, immigrant women from many socialist countries such as Mainland China grew up in a socialist women's liberation tradition, which encouraged their participation in the formal labour force and promoted equal pay for equal work. As research has demonstrated, immigration to Canada often leads to the reinforcement of gender inequality (Li & Findlay, 1999; Man, 1995, 1997; Silvey & Lawson, 1999; Waters, 2002). In our study, we asked immigrant women not only about the annual income of their families, but also about their own income in Canada. While most of the 50 women worked before immigration—60 percent indicated they had some level of income—only one-fifth of them now earned more than $20,000 a year, an amount significantly lower than the Canadian female average wage of $29,200. Even though 64 percent had a college level or higher education, 40 percent did not have their own income, 16 percent earned less than $10,000 a year, and over half did not have formal full-time employment, making them financially dependent on their husbands.

Therefore, when these women immigrated to Canada, in addition to the employment disadvantage from the discrimination against immigrants and the downward movement of their social capital, they also often experienced a gendered downward movement of their economic position in the family, which in turn affected the power relations and resource distribution within the family. In some cases, as illustrated in the quotation below, working women who were liberated from housework in their country of origin by hiring cheap domestic service provided by other women and other social support now had to assume the traditional gender role to absorb the family's economic downturn.

> But one thing is different from Hong Kong is that I didn't have to care much about the housework. We had some helpers, part-time helpers. But here, we don't hire any part-time workers. And every day I have to spend some more time on the cooking, cleaning up the kitchen, and then the children are young, they need more attention. So I think the spare time is less here. (S5, age 48, immigrated eight years ago; family income: $50,000–$100,000, own income: $30,000)

CHANGING MOTHERING AND CHILD-CARE PATTERNS

Among the 50 women we interviewed, 77 percent were between 31 and 50 years of age and 91 percent had children, with 30 percent having more than one child. Interestingly, over half of the women from Mainland China, a country where the one-child population policy was strictly implemented, had more than one child. On the one hand, social policy in Canada enabled them to enjoy more reproductive freedom, but on the other hand, it also prolonged their child-bearing and child-rearing period; the lack of affordable child care, compounded by unpromising job prospects for immigrant women, kept them at home.

For some professional women, being a stay-at-home mother is an alternative lifestyle choice that was not previously available where the dual working parents model was dominant, and social and parental expectations of their career development were high. Many women, either voluntarily or reluctantly, adopted the mainstream femininity in North America that puts women's family roles before their careers. The neo-liberal turn within the Canadian state since the 1980s has brought about privatization, decentralization, individualization, government downsizing and deregulation, and consequently led to the withdrawal of state-led social support and the erosion of welfare programs (Brodie, 2002). These changes have disproportionately affected women who, as default primary caregivers, often have to subsidize the loss of social provisions with their unpaid reproductive labour. The hollowing out of the welfare state and the cutting back of social services have been especially devastating for immigrant women, who have fewer economic and social resources in a new country to cope with these challenges.

While a few women we interviewed participated more in physical activity since immigrating because they had older children, less stressful jobs, part-time jobs, or no job at all and thus more spare time, this was not the case for the majority. Having children and staying at home did not necessarily stop mothers from undertaking physical activity since many of them were also active in China. From our research, we learned that women with children were much more likely to hear about community centre programs through schools or from their children's programs provided by the community centres. However, while their children brought them to the community centre, they were there, for the most part, passively watching their children play rather than participating themselves.

As many Chinese immigrants had a two-income family model in China and had affordable child-care service or extended family to provide free substitute child care, women in general had more free time and could attend physical activity sessions by themselves or with their friends even after they had children. However, since immigrating, they had to adjust their previous child-rearing practices and often became stay-at-home mothers to fit into the male breadwinner nuclear family model that Canada's neo-liberal social policies were designed to support.

I came, started to work, and then had children. And then I take care of kids, buy food, cooking. I am a yellow-faced old woman (*huanglianpo*). [Laughs] Now I don't have that chance, and no time because the kids are young. That is the way most people live through. You can't do much. (C21, age 31, immigrated six years ago; family income: Less than $20,000, no own income)

Though she tried to laugh it off, this woman's comments reveal her reluctance to be a stay-at-home mother and her disapproval of this gendered position. The term *huanglianpo* is used to describe housewives who are older, often from the countryside, illiterate, backward, unattractive, and who know and care only about domestic affairs, as opposed to the desired image of the young, urban, chic, and attractive career-oriented, cosmopolitan Chinese woman. Women as socialist labourers during the Maoist period represented the image of liberated Chinese women, while housewives were stigmatized. They were regarded as the leftovers from the old China who failed to keep up with the times and transform themselves into the new women of China, and thus were victims of the old gender order and embodiments of tradition. They were referred to as "women of the family" (*jiatingfunü*) as opposed to "women of the nation" (*funü*). This negative perception is evident in the comments made by another interviewee from Mainland China:

Staying at home it would be too dull and outdated! Without more contact with the community, women barely learn anything new at home. (C26, from Mainland China, age 37, immigrated four years ago; family income: $20,000–$50,000, own income: $4,000)

In this way, life is harder in Canada for immigrant women because they face different child-care practices and institutional settings. For example, in Mainland China, because of the high percentage of women's participation in the labour force, there are convenient and affordable child-care services provided by the state or workplace, and many of the women interviewed could get child-care help from close family or friends. However, in Canada, many Chinese immigrants could not afford to pay for child care in order to go out and engage in physical activity, which is clearly a Canadian middle-upper-class practice. The policy that children under age 13 have to be supervised by adults is also a Canadian practice that differs from Chinese conventions. For many immigrant women from Mainland China who grew up in double-income families in the Mao era, children were often on their own after school. In the cities, there was a generation of children who were the so-called "key on the neck children" (Chen & Wang, 2002). Chinese immigrant women who have this historical cultural background, and who experienced a childhood in which adults were frequently absent, find it even harder to spend money on babysitting in order to go out.

> At that time I was at home all day taking care of my kid. She has to arrange her time well at the first place, and then she can have time to do sports. Also, when you stay at home, at least your husband needs to be willing to help you taking care of the kids, or someone at home can take care of the kids for you, then you can go out. (S25, age 45, immigrated nine years ago; family income: $20,000–$50,000, no own income)

CHANGES TO SOCIO-ECONOMIC STATUS AND PHYSICAL ACTIVITY

Generally speaking, most families who immigrate to Canada come with some savings, but the interviewees in this study felt uneasy spending money on physical activity because of their unstable income and uncertain future. The cost of undertaking physical activity was a concern for women who were stay-at-home mothers because they were financially dependent. However, they were also the group who arguably needed to be involved in physical activity the most as their new environment and changing role as homemakers often led to social isolation and depression.

> I aspire to do exercises together with others, but currently I cannot make it. It seems that every day I am just living in the small world of myself. I cannot integrate into the society ... still the same problems. One is that I have to take care of my kids. The other is financial consideration. (C5, age 41, immigrated two years ago; family income: $20,000–$50,000, own income: $12,000; she used to bowl and play tennis for free)

As mentioned earlier, the cost of child care is a significant concern for immigrant women as physical activities outside the house often require not only spending money on program fees (usually between $5 and $15 per hour), but also on child care, which is at least another $5 an hour, and public transportation, which costs another couple of dollars. As stay-at-home mothers who do not bring money into a financially struggling family, interviewees were often much more conscious about cost and did not feel entitled to spend this money on themselves.

> Although the community centre in my neighbourhood offers daycare service, it is $3 per hour. If we also take some classes or use the facilities, we have to pay double costs for our kids and ourselves. You know because we don't work, it feels like we have more financial pressures than those moms who work. I feel I need to save up money since I am not making any money. I don't feel ok to spend money on myself. So it is very rarely that we will spend money on ourselves to do exercise and sports. (S18, age 29, immigrated three years ago; family income: $20,000–$50,000, no own income; she used a fitness centre with an annual pass that cost about RMB 300–400 or CAD $50–$60 a month)

By comparison, when asked how much they spent on their physical activities in China, some women had free or very affordable access to facilities through their school, workplace, or residence, while others used public or private facilities. Some wealthier women from Taiwan and Hong Kong spent $40–$80 a month on fitness, but considered it to be a small expense in light of their previous salaries. In the case of women from Mainland China, it was common for them to spend RMB 200–500 (CAD $30–$70) annually on physical activities, accounting for up to 5 percent of their own monthly income. For instance, a woman who had a well-paying job (CAD $2,000/month) in Taiwan and spent CAD $40–$80/month on physical activities claimed the cost "was really nothing." In general, when the immigrant women in this study discussed the cost of undertaking physical activity in China, they did not express concern about the spending, even though most of them raised the issue of cost when they noted being physically active in Canada, and many of them mentioned the cost issue more than once during their interviews. The women felt comfortable spending money on physical activity in China partly because they had their own incomes, yet in Canada they became more conscientious about spending money on themselves because many of them were now financially dependent and did not feel entitled to having such luxury.

For women who are unemployed, economic dependence often leads to an unequal distribution of household labour, with women returning to traditional gender roles, and a deterioration of power both inside and outside the home (Man, 1995). When facing unemployment or underemployment and the high cost of child care, many Chinese immigrant women in this study became stay-at-home mothers, taking care of their children, often without a sufficient support network. This posed time and economic constraints for many immigrant women to participate in physical activity.

Chinese Women's Diverse Physical Activities

Notably, the Canadian way of life changed not only immigrants' family and gender models, but also dominant ideas about the body and perceptions of desirable femininities and masculinities. These ideas impacted immigrant women's bodily experiences in terms of what activities to do, how to do them, when, and where. Many women we interviewed had been involved in various kinds of physical activities before immigration and recalled doing more exercise, especially when they were in school, where participation in physical activity was largely free. Some popular activities included badminton, table tennis, swimming, and dancing. Some of them also cycled to commute.

There is a common stereotype among some Canadian service providers and policy-makers that Chinese women prefer less intense and aggressive sports, and like playing table tennis and badminton (Frisby, 2011). The underlying assumption is that to serve Chinese needs, all that is required is to add programs such as table tennis and badminton, and then multiculturalism in sport and recreation services has been achieved. We argue that these stereotypes are a result of cultural essentialism involving the Othering and homogenizing of certain groups of people in Canada.

The Chinese immigrant women with whom we worked were not a homogeneous group as they differed significantly in terms of culture, language, geographic location, economic status, age, marital and parental status, education, and English proficiency levels (Creese, Huang, Frisby & Ngene Kambere, 2011). They also had diverse habits and needs in terms of undertaking physical activity that cannot be subsumed under one singular category of Chinese women. These observed Chinese-specific preferences in physical activity have more to do with cultural and environmental factors than with inherent bodily differences or an essence of culture. Rather than taking certain phenomena for granted, we need to situate them in the social and political contexts in which they occur. For example, table tennis and badminton are not originally Chinese sports, as table tennis originated in Britain during the 1800s, and British military officers stationed in India in the mid-18th century invented badminton. Various forms of Western modern sport were introduced into China and integrated into the imported modern education system in the early 20th century, along with the heated nationalist discourse of strengthening Chinese people's bodies in order to build a strong and modern Chinese nation (Brownell, 1995). Physical activities that require relatively simple and cheaper equipment, facilities, and training were promoted to the general public. While playing table tennis is one of the popular physical activities among women from Mainland China, few immigrant women from Hong Kong listed it as their favourite during our interviews. The popularity of table tennis and badminton in Mainland China thus has more to do with its accessibility and China's historically marginal economic status rather than with some distinct element of Chinese culture.

In fact, during our interviews, many women recalled learning various types of physical activities at school, laying the foundation for their knowledge, skills, and preferences for their future physical activity habits. It is thus reasonable to argue that when the women interviewed immigrated to Canada, they often kept doing the activities they grew up with, not out of a desire to retain their cultural heritage, but because they already knew how to play them and because these activities typically cost less.

If we take a social constructionist rather than essentialist approach to culture and understand it as not fixed in time but evolving, and not closed but open, we could argue that after a century of promotion and practice, table tennis and basketball have become part of contemporary Chinese sport culture. In turn, this approach to culture also opens up space for cultural exchange and the development of new content in culture. It is this understanding of culture that makes multiculturalism possible, and this open attitude was observed in the women we interviewed. For instance, rather than bearing the burden of culture, many Chinese immigrant women wanted to learn and participate in new physical activities, including those that are popular in Canada, such as skiing, skating, jogging (e.g., joining the Vancouver Sun Run), yoga, swimming, hiking, golf, and even hip-hop dance. They also perceived getting involved in Canadian activities as a way of learning about their new environment. As our research findings demonstrated, their lack of participation in these activities was largely attributed to constraints in cost and accessibility (such as transportation, lack of knowledge and skills, lack of child care, and language barriers). An essentialized understanding of Chineseness thus would inhibit policy-makers from seeking ways to assist Chinese immigrant women to learn and explore new activities to encourage their participation and cross-cultural learning.

Furthermore, if the women in our study have some preferences for certain activities, in addition to the factors such as knowledge and accessibility, these preferences may also relate to gender or other factors such as age and socio-economic status, rather than simply to an essentialized culture. This is because physical activities are often highly gendered and ideas of what are suitable and desirable activities for women are tied to a notion of femininity, which, again, is a social construction rather than a culturally essentialized fact. Contrary to the usual stereotype that Chinese women prefer soft, gentle, feminine activities, some Chinese women in our study expressed interest in more gender-neutral, or even traditionally masculine, physical activities such as skiing, jogging, basketball, golf, and hiking. Other women we interviewed also expressed interests in activities such as yoga and dancing, which could improve their flexibility and give their body a more feminine appearance. Considering the seemingly gender-neutral but actually more masculinized physical education training many women received at school in China, especially in the Maoist era when women were encouraged to emulate men physically, these preferences may be understood as a rejection of the suppression of their femininity in the world of sport and physical activities, and a pursuit of activities that comprise feminine ways of connecting with one's body (Vertinsky, McManus, Sit & Lui, 2005).

I think the exercise class that I took in China in which we learned ballet was quite good for body extension and enhancement of women's temperament. My parents couldn't afford to let me learn ballet when I was young. So I could make it up by learning from an instructor in the ballet class. (C17)

In badminton, we can trim our, what is it, *Lin-Huo*? What is it in English? ... Yes, flexibility ... I think it [the change of habits in doing physical activities] is not mainly because I changed place from Hong Kong to Canada, but it is because of my age. [Laughs] When I was younger, I just wanted to lose more weight. And then I go for exercise to look more fit. But now because I am getting older and then the focus of health is how high is your blood pressure and those things. Yup, so when I was young, I just focused on looking better. (S5)

Some Chinese women's preferences for less competitive and intensive physical activities, rather than attributions to an essentialized Chinese culture, can be interpreted as a preference for more female-centred activities, in connection to certain ideals of femininity, which are not necessarily or only Chinese.

Conclusion: Beyond Culture, beyond Physical Activities

In this chapter, we demonstrated that in order to better understand the barriers for immigrant women's participation in physical activity, we need to go beyond physical activity per se and examine differences in the social, political, and cultural systems and the ideologies between Canada and immigrants' countries of origin, which often are the roots of these barriers. One important aspect we have explored in this chapter is that differences in social institutions such as the labour market, family structures, gender roles, and ideas of femininity and masculinity between Canada and China have a gendered impact on immigrant women's participation in physical activities. We demonstrated how Canada's welfare state history and the current neo-liberal social policies, in conjunction with the gender inequality in education and employment in both countries, pushed some immigrant women to adopt the gender roles of the traditional nuclear family model, which led to their social isolation and contributed to barriers that limited their participation in physical activities.

This chapter also revealed that in order to remove the barriers for participation, service providers need to consider solutions beyond physical activity by engaging more with immigrants to better understand their histories, situations, and interests. Still, while we could suggest that community centres provide free or affordable child care for young mothers or have child–parent programs, community centres should not be the only ones to bear the cost and be blamed for policy failures such as the lack of affordable child care in Canada. Rather, we need to tackle the roots of these problems, such as the neo-liberal policy of the Canadian state and its philosophical foundations that inform such policy. In addition, some authors suggest that we should move beyond multiculturalism to interculturalism in order to learn cultural practices from one another instead of living in ethnic enclaves (Sandercock, 2004). While immediate solutions such as child–parent programs are necessary, to truly improve immigrant women's participation in physical activities, we need to address issues of racism and sexism in employment, social welfare policies, and social conventions of gendered divisions of labour at home. We also need to think about the connections between recreational policy and other social policies, and how the change of one entails the change of another.

In sum, we have demonstrated that contrary to some Canadians' assumptions that immigrants' countries of origin are backward and traditional, that Canada is modern, and that by immigrating, women are saved from the burden of their patriarchal and backward culture or nation, many Chinese immigrant women benefited from the women's liberation of socialist China, where they received equal opportunity for education and employment, had high-status jobs, enjoyed a social institution that supported their life path as professional women, and had more leisure time and financial resources for physical activities. Conversely, the gendered immigration process, racist and sexist labour market, and neo-liberal social policy in Canada reinforced gender inequality, and pushed immigrant women back to more traditional gender roles of being financially dependent, stay-at-home mothers. In addition to the downward movement of their social capital, many Chinese immigrant women also experienced a gendered downward movement at home, with changing power relations and resource distribution within the family. The changes of their gendered positions in society and at home often increased the barriers to their participation in physical activities in Canada.

An essentialized notion of Chinese culture will limit rather than expand the opportunities for Chinese immigrant women's physical culture in Canada, whereas a social constructionist approach can open up opportunities for immigrant women to explore other activities and extend their horizons, as well as foster cross-cultural learning, and ultimately move toward interculturalism, which is understood as a process of mutual learning. In light of the discussion on multiculturalism, we suggest that rather than pushing immigrants to integrate into the European-Canadian system and way of life (which is currently the case in spite of the multiculturalism rhetoric), building an intercultural Canada relies on understanding and challenging the ways in which the Canadian state incorporates different political and cultural values and practices into its policy. We must re-examine and transform the White, Eurocentric values and practices that are the foundation of social policies in Canada.

Questions for Critical Thought

1. How are gender inequalities compounded with immigration? How does immigration impact the lives and experiences of women newly arrived in Canada?
2. How can sport, physical activity, and recreation contribute to the successful settlement of newcomers?
3. What roles can leaders and policy-makers within governments and non-profit sport and recreation organizations play to ensure an environment where newcomers have affordable and easily accessible sport and physical activity services and programs that meet their needs?

Notes

1. See: http://cicnet.ci.gc.ca/English/immigr/guide-be.html for details on Citizenship and Immigration Canada's immigration requirements.
2. The *Canadian Employment Equity Act* defines the "visible minority" as "persons, other than aboriginal peoples, who are non-Caucasian in race and nonwhite in colour." As Graham and Phillips (2007) point out, the visible minority label privileges the Whiteness of early English/French settlers and is no longer meaningful in many cases as minorities are increasingly becoming majorities in Canadian neighbourhoods. For instance, one of the participants in our research program on Chinese immigrant women challenged this label and said, "In Vancouver, we Chinese are the majority."

References

Bauder, H. (2003). "Brain abuse," or the devaluation of immigrant labour in Canada. *Antipode, 35*(4), 699–717.

Bissoondath, N. (2002). *Selling illusions: The cult of multiculturalism in Canada*. Toronto: Penguin Books.

Brodie, J.M. (2002). The great undoing: State formation, gender politics, and social policy in Canada. In C. Kingfisher (Ed.), *Western welfare in decline: Globalization and women's poverty* (pp. 90–110). Philadelphia: University of Pennsylvania Press.

Brownell, S. (1995). *Training the body for China: Sports in the moral order of the People's Republic*. Chicago: University of Chicago Press.

Chen, H. & Wang, Y. (2002). *Born in the 1960s (Shenyu Liushi Niandai)*. Chengdu: Sichuan People's Publishing House.

Chinese Canadian National Council, Women's Book Committee. (1992). *Jin Guo: Voices of Chinese Canadian women*. Toronto: Women's Press.

Citizenship and Immigration Canada (CIC). (2010). *Annual report to Parliament on immigration*. Retrieved from http://www.cic.gc.ca/english/resources/publications/annual-report2010/section2.asp

Citizenship and Immigration Canada (CIC). (2011). *Facts and figures 2008 — Immigration overview: Permanent and temporary residents, 2009*. Retrieved from http://www.cic.gc.ca/english/resources/statistics/facts2008/permanent/01.asp

Creese, G., Huang, X., Frisby, W. & Ngene Kambere, E. (2011). Working across race, language, and culture with African and Chinese immigrant communities. In G. Creese & W. Frisby (Eds.), *Feminist community research: Negotiating contested relationships* (pp. 116–144). Vancouver: UBC Press.

DeSensi, J.T. (1995). Understanding multiculturalism and valuing diversity: A theoretical perspective. *Quest, 47*(1), 34–43.

Donnelly, P. & Nakamura, Y. (2009). Multiculturalism and sport participation: The dynamics of social inclusion. Paper presented at the North American Society for Sociology of Sport Conference, Ottawa.

Frisby, W. (2011). Learning from the local: Promising physical activity inclusion practices for Chinese immigrant women in Vancouver, Canada. *Quest, 63*, 135–147.

Graham, K. & Phillips, S.D. (2007). Another fine balance: Managing diversity in Canadian cities. In K. Banting, T.J. Courchene & L. Seidle (Eds.), *The art of the state: Belonging, diversity, recognition, and shared citizenship in Canada* (pp. 155–194). Montreal: Institute for Research on Public Policy.

Lee, S.M. (2005). Physical activity among minority populations: What health promotion practitioners should know—a commentary. *Health Promotion Practice, 6*(4), 447–452.

Li, L. & Findlay, A. (1999). To follow the chicken or not? The role of women in the migration of Hong Kong professional couples. In P. Boyle & K. Halfacree (Eds.), *Migration and gender in the developed world* (pp. 172–185). London: Routledge.

Li, P.S. (1998). *The Chinese in Canada* (2nd ed.). Toronto: Oxford University Press.

Man, G. (1995). The experience of women in Chinese immigrant families: An inquiry into institutional and organizational processes. *Asian and Pacific Migration Journal, 4*(2/3), 303–327.

Man, G. (1997). Women's work is never done: Social organization of work and the experience of women in middle-class Hong Kong Chinese immigrant families in Canada. *Advances in Gender Research, 2,* 183–226.

Man, G. (2004). Gender, work, and migration: Deskilling Chinese immigrant women in Canada. *Women's Studies International Forum, 27*(2), 135–148.

Ryan, P. (2010). *Multicultiphobia.* Toronto: University of Toronto Press.

Salaff, J.W. & Greve, A. (2006). Chinese immigrant women: From professional to family careers. *Social Transformations in Chinese Societies, 2*(1), 75–106.

Sandercock, L. (2004). Sustaining Canada's multicultural cities. In C. Andrew (Ed.), *Our diverse cities* (pp. 153–157). Ottawa: Metropolis.

Silvey, R. & Lawson, V. (1999). Placing the migrant. *Annals of the Association of American Geographers, 89*(1), 121–132.

Smart, J. (1994). Business immigration to Canada: Deception and exploitation. In R. Skeldon (Ed.), *Reluctant exiles? Migration from Hong Kong and the new overseas Chinese* (pp. 98–119). Armonk: M.E. Sharpe.

Statistics Canada. (2007). The Chinese community in Canada. Retrieved from http://www.statcan.gc.ca/pub/89-621-x/89-621-x2006001-eng.htm

Statistics Canada. (2008). *Canada's ethnocultural mosaic: 2006 census.* Ottawa: Minister of Industry.

Statistics Canada. (2010). *Projections of the diversity of the Canadian population*. Ottawa: Canadian Ministry of Industry.

Stodolska, M. & Alexandris, K. (2004). The role of recreational sport in the adaptation of first-generation immigrants in the U.S. *Journal of Leisure Research, 36*, 379–413.

Tremblay, M.S., Bryan, S.N., Perex, C.E., Ardem, C.I. & Katzmarzyk, P.T. (2006). Physical activity and immigrant status: Evidence from the Canadian community health survey. *Canadian Journal of Public Health, 97*(4), 277–282.

Vertinsky, P., McManus, A., Sit, C.H.P. & Liu, Y.K. (2005). The gendering of physical education in Hong Kong: East, west, or global? *The International Journal of the History of Sport, 22*(5), 816–839.

Waters, J.L. (2002). Flexible families? "Astronaut" households and the experiences of lone mothers in Vancouver, British Columbia. *Social and Cultural Geography, 3*(2), 117–134.

CHAPTER 6

Understanding Structural Barriers in Amateur Sport and the Participation of Immigrants in Atlantic Canada

LORI A. LIVINGSTON AND SUSAN TIRONE

Introduction

Nova Scotia's Department of Health Promotion and Protection, and its recent integration (i.e., in 2006) of the sport and recreation bureaucracy with that of population and public health, has theoretically laid the foundation for enhanced provincial linkages between sport and recreation policy, physical activity, and health-related issues (Pitter, 2009). The timing, if not deliberate, is nonetheless important as declining sport participation has become a global concern, with waning participation and greater levels of physical inactivity being linked to growing health-related issues (e.g., obesity, diabetes, heart disease), social issues (i.e., increasing rates of crime, drug use), and the decreased financial viability of existing sport organizations (Vail, 2007). In Canada, where health care costs are borne by the state, the importance of developing the capacity to deal better with health risks and their associated costs is a must. Creating and enacting policy with the goal of getting more Canadians involved in sport, either as active participants (i.e., athletes) or in key support roles (i.e., coaching, officiating, administration) to enhance the capacity of the sport delivery system, seems both logical and warranted.

Canada's sport delivery system relies heavily on volunteer support, especially at the recreational and grassroots levels, with the demand for volunteers to help plan and run amateur sport expected to grow in years to come (Costa, Chalip, Green & Simes, 2006). In 2005, over 2 million Canadians volunteered their time to sport as administrators, 1.8 million as coaches, and approximately 800,000 as umpires, referees, or officials (Ifedi, 2008). Put another way, this means that approximately 18 percent of Canadians—or about one in every five Canadians—contributed in some way to the recreation and sport delivery system. Coincidentally, in 2006, one in every five Canadians (i.e., 19.8 percent) was an immigrant to Canada (Martel & Caron Malenfont, 2007), yet immigrants were much less likely than those born in Canada to participate in sport or sport-related activities (Ifedi, 2008; Tirone & Shaw, 1997). The reasons for these lowered participation rates are many and well documented (Karp & Yoels, 1990; Paraschak & Tirone, 2008; Stodolska, 1998, 2000; Stodolska & Alexandris, 2004; Tirone, 2000; Tirone & Pedlar, 2000; Tirone & Shaw, 1997). The key point, however, is that if the global trend in declining participation in sport is to be reversed, and if Canada's existing recreation and sport delivery system is to be sustained, current and future recruitment of immigrants into the sport volunteer ranks is a must.

To this end, in 2006, the Coaching Association of Canada (CAC) issued a call for research proposals to assist them in finding ways to effectively engage new Canadians in coaching and, more specifically, in the National Coaching Certification Program (NCCP). Two separate investigations were funded, one involving youth sport coaches from Ontario and Quebec (Erickson, Wilson, Horton, Young & Côté, 2007; Wilson, Erickson, Horton, Young & Côté, 2007) and the other incorporating sport key informants (i.e., employees or volunteers with local, provincial, and national sport governing bodies responsible for administering or delivering coaching programs) and newcomer key informants (i.e., volunteers with local newcomer organizations, as well as newcomers involved in coaching) from Atlantic Canada (Livingston, Tirone, Smith & Miller, 2008). Although a full recounting of these two studies is beyond the scope of this chapter, both investigations yielded strong evidence of what Livingston and others (2008) identified as "systemic or organizational obstacles" within Canadian sport that act as barriers to immigrant involvement (p. 414). However, neither investigation thoroughly discussed or critiqued these conclusions.

In this chapter, our purpose is to begin a dialogue on what others (e.g., Danisman, Hinings & Slack, 2006; Macintosh & Whitson, 1990; Pitter, 1996) have identified as the formal structures that exist within our federal and provincial sport delivery systems and how they interact with the circumstances often experienced by newcomers in ways that either enhance or detract from their sport participation. To do this effectively, we begin by establishing the context for further discussion through the inclusion of a brief history of Canadian sport policy and the structural systems and cultures that have emerged from it. We then suggest that the issue of getting more new Canadians involved in sport-related roles falls neatly into what has been conceptualized as a "wicked" problem; that is, one that is difficult or impossible to solve because of incomplete, contradictory, and changing requirements (Rittel & Webber, 1973, p. 160). Such problems are often difficult to recognize, and efforts to solve one aspect of a wicked problem may reveal or create other problems (Brown, Harris & Russell, 2010). Thereafter, we revisit the findings of our earlier investigation in an attempt to better understand the receptivity (or lack thereof) for immigrant involvement within our existing amateur sport systems and make suggestions on how to move forward in addressing the issues at hand.

Historical Context

In their book *The Game Planners* (1990), Macintosh and Whitson provide a brief yet detailed account of the history of government involvement in the creation and oversight of Canada's amateur sport system. They note that for much of Canada's history, state involvement in sport was extremely limited, yet this began to change following World War Two, when the Soviet Union "began to conceive of sport as a means of demonstrating the achievements of its socialist society" (p. 3). Unexpected athletic losses (e.g., Canada's losses in international hockey championships) were but one of many factors that fuelled international rivalries and provided the impetus for the Canadian government to embrace sport as a priority. Direct federal involvement began in 1961 with the passage of the *Fitness and Amateur Sport Act* (Bill C-131), an Act that led to the establishment of federal–provincial cost-sharing agreements to promote fitness and sport programs and the provision of grants to national sport organizations (NSOs).

According to Macintosh and Whitson (1990, p. 4), "as sport assumed an increasingly important role in Canadian popular culture, the government's attitude changed." In 1968, newly elected Prime Minister Pierre Trudeau fulfilled an election promise and established a Task Force on Sport. The task force's report, in turn, generated a number of recommendations, which formed the basis upon which the government would later openly support and establish a bureaucratic sport system to promote high-performance sport. The report criticized the NSOs on multiple levels, including their reliance on a "kitchen table" style of operation (p. 4); that is, an overwhelming reliance on part-time volunteer coaches, officials, and administrators, recruitment of national executives from only one or two regions of the country, and what was deemed to be a high degree of inefficiency. The federal government responded to these issues by establishing the Ottawa-based National Sport and Recreation Centre (NSRC) and by creating two new divisions within the Fitness and Amateur Sport Branch: that is, Sport

Canada and Recreation Canada. The NSRC literally and figuratively provided a new structure for the administration of sport in Canada by providing office space, support services, and funds to hire full-time executive personnel, directors, and national coaches for the NSOs. But the NSOs also experienced a reduction of their autonomy between 1970 and 1984 as increases in funding support led to an eightfold increase in the number of administrative, clerical, and technical staff housed at the NSRC (Macintosh, Bedecki & Franks, 1987) and new levels of organizational complexity within the NSOs. By 1990, the general framework by which the federal government interacted with the NSOs in making and enacting policy for high-performance sport in Canada had evolved to include the following five levels of formal structure:

- the "federal government," including the Cabinet and those appointed to official roles (e.g., Minister of State for Fitness and Amateur Sport)
- the "federal sport bureaucracy," including the director-general of Sport Canada and the sport consultants who work with the NSOs
- the "sport bureaucracy" at the NSRC, including the executive, technical, and program directors of the NSOs
- the "NSOs and umbrella associations," such as the Canadian Olympic Association and the Coaching Association of Canada
- the "key actors" outside the aforementioned who influence policy-making, such as influential members of provincial sport organizations (PSOs), current and former sport participants, and other influential national figures (Macintosh & Whitson, 1990, pp. 5–6)

Over the past 40 years, Canada has gradually built an integrated high-performance sport system that has increasingly adopted a "professional bureaucratic form of organizational design" (Danisman et al., 2006, p. 304), one in which priority was given to formal planning and the centrality of professionals in decision-making processes (Kikulis, Slack & Hinings, 1992). Interestingly, formal planning, including the identification of explicit goals and desired outcomes, had emerged in the early 1960s and quickly became the desired *modus operandi* in both business and government circles. This approach was popular because it was seen as efficient and it afforded the notion that the professional's job was to solve problems that were always "definable, understandable, and consensual" (Rittel & Webber, 1973, p. 156), but it was also flawed as it focused exclusively on what the systems should do (e.g., goals, outcomes) rather than on their complexity (e.g., multiple constituents) or context (e.g., what it is versus what it ought to be). As a result, we now have a well-entrenched high-performance sport system in which the NSOs value and conform to:

- high performance in international events rather than domestic development (i.e., recreational, provincial, or national-based sporting opportunities)
- professional staff involvement rather than volunteer control
- organizational rationalization and efficiency
- planning in all aspects of strategy and operations
- corporate sponsorship and other forms of financing
- commitment to government oversight and involvement as strategic leaders (Danisman et al., 2006; Kikulus et al., 1992)

While there has been some shifting of priorities with respect to high-performance sport over the past two decades, the aforementioned five-tiered bureaucratic system essentially remains in place, albeit with some individual roles at each level renamed, redefined, or eliminated. There has also been some mirroring of these five levels within each of the provincial and territorial sport bureaucracies, although regional diversity in economics and geography, and provincial government autonomy in decision-making, have created variations at this level (Pitter, 1996). It is perhaps most important to recognize that the bureaucratization of sport has not diminished the roles of volunteers in our amateur sport system, nor has it "solved the 'problem' of traditional 'kitchen table' administration but rather raise[d] other emerging dilemmas" (Sam, 2009, p. 501).

Sport Policy Problems as Wicked Problems

Formal planning is a process that aligns well with the classical paradigm of the natural sciences (i.e., the scientific method) and private sector manufacturing (Osborne, 2010), where problems are definable, solutions are findable, and it is clear when a solution is found. However, there are other instances, according to Rittel and Webber (1973), where planning is bound to fail and especially so when an attempt is made to use formal planning to solve a problem in an open societal system where the "plurality of objectives held by pluralities of politics makes it impossible to pursue unitary aims" (p. 160). In particular, these authors suggest that social policy problems do not lend themselves to being resolved using planning methods because they are characteristically difficult to define and solve, because they are underpinned by multiple and often conflicting causal relationships, and because they are relentless (i.e., their solutions or remedies inevitably create new issues or unanticipated, unintended consequences). In essence, then, societal problems are by their very nature "wicked" (Rittel & Webber, 1973, p. 160) (i.e., circular, tricky, and aggressive as they generate further problems to be addressed) and need to be recognized as such in order to be adequately addressed.

An extensive search of the literature revealed only one examination of the public management of sport that aimed to demonstrate that sport policy problems do indeed display the characteristics of wicked problems. Importantly, Sam (2009), in focusing on the Canadian federal government's identification of the problem of "kitchen table" administration and its creation of Sport Canada and Recreation Canada as the solution, illustrates that the solution to the problem (i.e., the creation of a professional sport bureaucracy) led to a "relentless" wave of previously unanticipated consequences, including a focus on elite, high-performance-oriented and corporately funded athletes versus grassroots participation, a valuing of professional versus volunteer control of sport, and an efficiency of operation versus democracy (i.e., addressing inequalities concerning race, gender, language, or disability) trade-off.

These consequences align with what we previously reported as the values espoused, and conformed to, by Canada's NSOs (Danisman et al., 2006; Kikulis et al., 1992). In turn, we suggest that they have contributed to and created what we now conceptualize as a next wave or emerging wicked problem; that is, the underrepresentation of new Canadians in the volunteer coaching, officiating, and administrative ranks of the amateur sport system. We also argue that if this next wave problem is to be effectively understood and managed, then it must be seen as what it is—the product of a wicked problem.

The 2008 Study

The research in this chapter draws upon the findings of a study conducted in 2007 and subsequently published in 2008 in which our aim was to examine the lived experiences and thereby the issues related to participation in coaching of those who identified with the newcomer and minority ethnic communities in a city in Atlantic Canada (Livingston et al., 2008). Our efforts were funded by a grant from the Coaching Association of Canada (CAC). The study used a qualitative research approach and, through individual and focus-group interviews, we sought to understand the coaching-related and sport-related experiences of immigrant newcomers who had settled in Atlantic Canada within the last five to 10 years. We also interviewed a number of individuals who were currently employed or volunteered as sport leaders, coaches, and administrators in badminton, soccer, and basketball (i.e., those sports identified as the most popular among immigrant newcomers in the region), as well as others who worked with local recreation departments or immigrant-support organizations. These latter groups were included as we sought to understand their experiences in facilitating newcomer integration into the existing sport system. Seventeen individuals, including four females and 13 males, participated in the study via a series of semi-structured, one-on-one interviews. Three participants were new Canadians, whereas five identified as having previously immigrated to Canada. In terms of ethnicity, the majority were Caucasian (n = 8), with several others of African-Canadian (n = 3), Middle Eastern (n = 3), Chilean (n = 1), Trinidadian (n = 1), and Greek (n = 1) descent. Responses gathered from a follow-up focus-group interview of five participants were used to confirm our initial interpretation of the data and to establish trustworthiness in our findings.[1]

In our initial analysis, three major themes emerged from the data. These included the discrepancies in expected versus actual levels of involvement; the barriers to, responsibility for, and importance of inclusion; and disconnects in, as well as suggestions for improving, communication and information flow between sport organizations and potential newcomer groups. Although we (Livingston et al., 2008, p. 414) identified that "systemic or organizational obstacles" existed within Canadian sport itself, we did not elaborate on, discuss, or thoroughly critique their impact on newcomer involvement in sport. The purpose of the remainder of this chapter is to explicitly evaluate our findings in this regard, and to do so by conceptualizing the problem at hand as a wicked problem and thereafter suggest how best to move forward in an attempt to increase the participation of new Canadians in all aspects of Canada's sport delivery system.

Newcomer Involvement as Influenced by the Existing Sport Delivery System

Canada's existing sport delivery system, spawned from Bill C-131 and repeatedly influenced by the imposition of formal planning processes, has evolved over the past four decades to become what has been characterized as a high-performance-oriented entity that values elite rather than grassroots participation and professional staff involvement over volunteer control in a milieu in which government oversight and involvement as strategic leaders has become the norm (Danisman et al., 2006; Kikulis et al., 1992; Sam, 2009). Evidence of the aforementioned was readily apparent within the responses received from our study participants. With reference to the elite bias of the system, we repeatedly heard that newcomers arriving with impressive athletic abilities or coaching credentials were markedly advantaged over their lesser skilled peers when they sought to enter the Canadian sport system. One of our participants referred to this bias as "systematic racism" and went on to add that "it's sad to say, but right now it's what's happening." While this phenomenon is perhaps better labelled as systematic elitism and may be viewed as a phenomenon that affects newcomers and native-born Canadians alike, one individual spoke about having been "blessed or fortunate enough to have been one of the better athletes in [his] sport, both provincially and nationally" and went on to reveal that "if you're fortunate enough to have [the skill and] experience ... your colour becomes less of an issue when you're skilled as long as you do excel." Similarly, in instances where personal circumstances (e.g., poverty) might otherwise preclude participation, we were told "if someone is really, really good ... you usually find a way to work around it." In these cases, elite privilege intersected with race and class to nullify discrimination. Non-elite racialized and poor athletes, however, suffered from significant exclusions.

The elitism bias also emerged as a topic of discussion during the focus-group interview, when another participant espoused "if you're good, then the grapevine is like that [snaps fingers]. He's from so and so [country] and he's really good ... the next thing you know, he's in a club and he's in a provincial program." This comment and others provide evidence that an individual's country of origin, intelligible as a construct connected to race, contributed to the privileging of some over others in entering the sport system. For example, with reference to the sport of soccer and one's home country, one respondent indicated that "It was perceived that I had more knowledge than I actually had" and "If they're from Europe, they've been involved in the professional academy, they're probably going to be [more highly qualified] ... but it really depends on the country." Importantly, some of our participants acknowledged that less talented newcomers—individuals to some extent disadvantaged by their country of origin—had more difficulty in gaining entry into the playing and coaching ranks. For example, "it really depends on the country. A lot of kids come from Africa who have very good technique, but just played street soccer" and "[they] think that they're better based on the way they played back home. Then they come here and then they realize that they're not as good as they thought they were and I think that really discourages them to keep pursuing [the game]." When asked what they could do to assist these individuals, some suggested that they themselves or their sport organization lacked the knowledge and skill needed to reach out in a proactive way to newcomers. Many of our participants suggested that responsibility for including newcomers was more likely that of the PSOs, NSOs, or the CAC as the organization responsible for designing, offering, and delivering the NCCP's coaching education programs.

This response provides a rather salient example of the extent to which Canadians have learned to defer responsibility to our sport governing bodies and their professional staff for strategic direction and oversight. Some were adamant about this with comments like "I think too that [the PSO] has to ... step up to the plate now and start advocating for all," and "it needs to be done at a national level ... then it becomes a set program." Others were more moderate in saying "I think we have to partner with [the PSO] and work with them because they have the knowledge of the NCCP program. We have new Canadians that come to us. So if we linked as partners, we could channel those people who are interested into that existing program that they have."

In a related vein, another individual discounted responsibility at the local and provincial level altogether and suggested that "I think it's [best] to pass these people on to Sport Canada and the provincial sport associations to get them involved, otherwise it might get too confusing." While some participants suggested that they must personally bear some of the responsibility to ensure inclusion for newcomers within sport, this often came with an important caveat; that is, success was seen as closely associated with availability of resources, be they human or financial in nature. For example, success was associated with the presence of professional staff (i.e., "There are a lot of sports that can't afford full-time persons in the office and I really believe that there is money available for at least one person in each sport to make a living out of promoting the sport in the community or elite level"). Success also depended on the provision of financial resources (i.e., "I'll start with resources. We as an association receive $5,000 a year for our provincial block funding. Everything else we are on our own to fundraise for, which kind of means that clubs ... leave it up to the clubs themselves to fundraise to pay for facility costs if you don't have it for free"). Ironically, with respect to the particular focus of the study, one individual indicated that "Other resources we don't have are the amount of volunteers we need."

Changes in the national economy and political agenda over time have demanded organizational rationalization and efficiency in all government departments, including those with responsibility for sport (Thibault & Harvey, 1997). To this end, the sport delivery system has, like others, been forced to opt for operating approaches based on business models that emphasize efficiency of operation, designing and offering programs on a common single model, and an often inflexible platform (e.g., weekend clinics for coaches) without an eye to addressing the growing diversity (e.g., language, socio-economic status) of the Canadian population. It has also been forced to continue to rely heavily on volunteers to support its operations. But despite this, the cost of sport participation continues to rise and is known to be a barrier to participation for immigrants (Paraschak & Tirone, 2008) and especially so in the early years of settlement in their new country.

In our study, we frequently heard that the cost of sport participation was a barrier for newcomers. While there was recognition that financial subsidies were available for those who needed support (including native-born Canadians), we also heard that such funding was limited and difficult to learn about and apply for. We heard frustration expressed about the funding priorities dictated by various players within the national sport delivery system, with little, if any, room for local and provincial organizations to redefine their priorities. As one participant identified relative to the Canada Games, "Look at the waste of money ... from a soccer perspective, a complete waste of our resources, and ... we could take that money when it comes and take those kids on ... and then stretch it between all of our programs, not just our lead program." Hence, we have a sport delivery system that is often too expensive for newcomers to access while at the same time being somewhat inflexible in redefining its priorities.

Discussion

The purpose of this chapter was to begin a dialogue on what have been identified (e.g., Danisman et al., 2006; Macintosh & Whitson, 1990; Pitter, 1996) as the formal structures within our federal and provincial sport delivery systems and how they interact with the circumstances often experienced by newcomers that either enhance or detract from their sport participation. To accomplish this task, we revisited the findings of an earlier investigation (Livingston et al., 2008) in which we explored the lived experiences and thereby the issues related to participation in sport by those who identified with the newcomer and minority ethnic communities in a city in Atlantic Canada. In particular, we were interested in identifying how the sport delivery system's valuing of and conformity to certain practices (e.g., high-performance orientation, government oversight and professional control, efficiency and rationalization of operations) shaped newcomer involvement in sport.

While newcomers were able to access the sport system, we found evidence to support Pitter's (1996) observation and Sam's (2009) respective propositions that the bureaucratization of the NSOs and the mirroring of the same within the PSOs is effectively wicked because it has introduced unexpected challenges, dilemmas, and trade-offs for participants. For example, the sport delivery system provides some access for new Canadians by preferentially welcoming those who fit the bill as elite athletes and coaches, but provides little support for access to the majority who are less skilled or qualified. While it is recognized that the elitism bias is also applicable to native-born Canadians, this dichotomy of practice is problematic when one considers the importance for newcomers in being able to find a sense of community during the early stages of settlement. Young immigrants from the African continent, for example, may place great value on soccer as both a pastime and as a profession (Poli, 2010), yet we were told of specific examples whereby this generally skilled group is likely to be turned away or disadvantaged in their initial efforts to enter and explore opportunities for success within the sport. Given the extent to which soccer is valued by many within this cultural group, failure to gain entry into the system can be devastating (Poli, 2010).

In seeking ideas from our study participants on how to rectify this problem of exclusion, another dilemma emerged in the form of a lack of consensus on whose responsibility it is to ensure newcomer participation in sport. We heard multiple suggestions, ranging from a few individuals indicating a preference to take it on themselves or to initiate it at the community level to many suggesting that responsibility fell within the purview of the PSOs, the NSOs, the CAC, or the provincial and federal governments in general. The provision of funding from the province and or the federal level was also a commonly heard theme. Placing the onus on a provincial or national organization is a traditional top-down sport development strategy that aims to increase participation uniformly across regions (Vail, 2007) and one that Canadians have become used to with the emergence of our professional sport bureaucracy. Sadly our study sheds light on the notion that it is an oft-used fallback position, perhaps one that is best characterized as a state of learned helplessness (Peterson, Maier & Seligman, 1995), and one that effectively shifts the onus (and possibly the blame) to a different level of the sport delivery system when resources are hard to come by at the regional or local level or when the complexity of the problem is too great for comprehension.

In a similar vein, some of our study participants saw the solution to the problem as hiring professionals, implicitly valuing the efforts of paid staff, while also explicitly suggesting that volunteers often did not have the required skill set to effectively address the needs of new Canadians. And, ironically, some also identified that with the current shortage of volunteers within their organizations, it would be virtually impossible to shift any resources to address the issue of how to get greater numbers of new Canadians involved in sport.

With all of that said, it is clear that in attempting to overcome the inefficiencies of our sport delivery system's "kitchen table" administration (i.e., the problem) through the creation of a professional sport bureaucracy (i.e., the solution), our sport delivery system has come to value and conform to a series of standards (i.e., emphasis on high-performance sport, professional staff, government oversight, etc.) and unanticipated consequences that continue to impact all aspects of program delivery some 40 years later. Nowhere is this more apparent than in the current system's relative inability to welcome new Canadians into important roles within the overall operation, thus creating a next generation problem (i.e., How do we get new Canadians more involved in sport?). To this question we see that there are two potential answers, the first of which would be to work within the existing sport delivery system to effect change.

Our participants and others (Erickson et al., 2007; Wilson et al., 2007) view working with the NSOs and the PSOs as a viable option, but we worry that the effectiveness of such an approach may not match expectations. The reasons for this are twofold. First, the limitations of the current system, as outlined in our findings, will not be easy to overcome. Moreover, lessons learned in Great Britain provide valuable insight into the challenges that Canadian sport would encounter in moving forward. National sport agencies and organizations in the United Kingdom came together in the early part of this decade to create and introduce a Racial Equality Standard to address issues of diversity and equality in sport (Long, Robinson & Welch, 2003). In evaluating the impact of the Standard on organizational change, Spracklen and co-authors (2006) recently concluded that the impact of the Standard was disappointing, having been largely ineffective in supporting racial equality within the system. The Standard's objectives, while well espoused and readily embedded within top-down policies and plans, were in their estimation not translated into practice. Moreover, these same authors observed that little effort had been invested in monitoring and managing diversity efforts beyond producing sport-specific equity policies. Clearly, addressing these shortcomings of the existing sport delivery system through mandated policy, action, practice, and concerted management and evaluation would be a must if this was the chosen path to make the existing Canadian system more receptive to all newcomers.

Alternatively, a second possible solution to ensure inclusion would be the use of a participatory community development approach to increase and sustain sport participation. As Vail (2007, p. 593) has suggested, "It is time to rethink sport delivery" if we want to effectively support Canada's dual interest in securing gold medals while simultaneously addressing socially inclusive participation. The value of such an approach is that it addresses the complexity of issues at hand and the multiple needs of a community's constituents by having diverse people from within the community invested in self-determined, bottom-up change processes. For grassroots development to work effectively, sport development opportunities must be provided for newcomers and people from other underrepresented groups to participate as stakeholders at the kitchen table meetings. As well the value of volunteer participants in the process of sport development needs to be reassessed and prioritized as an essential component of the sport delivery system. Wicked problems need to be addressed by multiple stakeholders from multiple disciplines and diverse backgrounds so as not to perpetuate limited or linear answers to problems that require more complex solutions (Brown et al., 2010).

Our study and the conclusions that we draw from it are necessarily limited in their generalizability as a result of drawing the participant sample from only one Atlantic province. We believe, however, that it provides enough evidence to suggest that extensive change is required within the existing national and provincial sport delivery systems if participation by, and the multiple needs of, newcomers to Canada are to be adequately addressed. Although administrators of local sport are interested in facilitating the involvement of new Canadians, they often do not know how to ensure access for those who identify with minority ethnic cultures, and/or those who lack racial and class privileges. This is a complex and perhaps wicked problem as there is no readily available or simple solution. The existing sport delivery system is inadequate in its current form to address the needs of all Canadians.

Questions for Critical Thought

1. Who are all of the stakeholders in the sport delivery system you know? (*Hint:* One approach to this question would be to identify a local sport organization, its funders, and to whom it is accountable at provincial, national, and international levels.)
2. What is the responsibility of each stakeholder for including

new immigrants and people of diverse cultural or religious traditions?
3. Define what is meant by the elitism bias. Do you think it affects native-born Canadians and new Canadians equally? Can you identify examples from your own experiences?
4. What strategies could the sport system use to create a welcoming environment for new immigrants?

Note

1. For a more detailed description of the sample and methods followed, please see the original published study (i.e., Livingston et al., 2008).

References

Brown, V.A., Harris, J.A. & Russell, J.Y. (2010). *Tackling wicked problems: Through the transdisciplinary imagination.* London: Earthscan.

Costa, C.A., Chalip, L., Green, B.C. & Simes, C. (2006). Reconsidering the role of training in event volunteers' satisfaction. *Sport Management Review, 9,* 165–182.

Danisman, A., Hinings, C.R. & Slack, T. (2006). Integration and differentiation in institutional values: An empirical investigation in the field of Canadian national sport organizations. *Canadian Journal of Administrative Sciences, 23,* 301–317.

Erickson, K., Wilson, B., Horton, S., Young, B. & Côté, J. (2007). Involving immigrants in youth sport coaching: Part 1. A literature review and quantitative profile. *International Journal of Sports Science & Coaching, 2,* 435–448.

Ifedi, F. (2008). *Sport participation in Canada, 2005.* Ottawa: Statistics Canada.

Karp, D.A. & Yoels, W.C. (1990). Sport and urban life. *Journal of Sport and Social Issues, 14,* 77–102.

Kikulis, L.M., Slack, T. & Hinings, C.R. (1992). Institutionally specific design archetypes: A framework for understanding change in national sport organizations. *International Review for the Sociology of Sport, 27,* 343–369.

Livingston, L.A., Tirone, S.C., Smith, E.L. & Miller, A.J. (2008). "They just don't know where to go, what to do": Connecting newcomers to sports and coaching opportunities in Atlantic Canada. *Our Diverse Cities* (Spring), 121–125.

Livingston, L.A., Tirone, S.C., Smith, E.L. & Miller, A.J. (2008a). Participation in coaching by Canadian immigrants: Individual accommodations and sport system receptivity. *International Journal of Sports Science & Coaching, 3,* 403–415.

Long, J., Robinson, P. & Welch, M. (2003). *Raising the standard: An evaluation of progress.* Leeds: Leeds Metropolitan University.

Macintosh, D., Bedecki, T. & Franks, C.E.S. (1987). *Sport and politics in Canada.* Kingston & Montreal: McGill-Queen's University Press.

Macintosh, D. & Whitson, D. (1990). *The game planners: Transforming Canada's sport system.* Kingston & Montreal: McGill-Queen's University Press.

Martel, L. & Caron Malenfont, E. (2007). *Portrait of the Canadian population in 2006, 2006 census.* Ottawa: Statistics Canada.

Osborne, S.P. (2010). Delivering public services: Time for a new theory? *Public Management Review, 12,* 1–10.

Paraschak, V. & Tirone, S.C. (2008). Race and ethnicity in Canadian sport. In J. Crossman (Ed.), *Canadian sport sociology* (2nd ed., pp. 79–98). Toronto: Nelson.

Peterson, C., Maier, S.F. & Seligman, M.E.P. (1995). *Learned helplessness: A theory for the age of personal control.* New York: Oxford University Press.

Pitter, R. (1996). The state and sport development in Alberta: A struggle for public status. *Sociology of Sport Journal, 13,* 31–50.

Pitter, R. (2009). Finding the Kieran way: Recreational sport, health, and environmental policy in Nova Scotia. *Journal of Sport and Social Issues, 33,* 331–351.

Poli, R. (2010). African migrants in Asian and European football: Hopes and realities. *Sport in Society, 13,* 1001–1011.

Rittel, H.W.J. & Webber, M.M. (1973). Dilemmas in a general theory of planning. *Policy Sciences, 4*, 155–169.

Sam, M.P. (2009). The public management of sport: Wicked problems, challenges, and dilemmas. *Public Management Review, 11*(4), 499–513.

Spracklen, K., Hylton, K. & Long, J. (2006). Managing and monitoring equality and diversity in U.K. sport: An evaluation of the sporting equals racial minority standard and its impact on organizational change. *Journal of Sport and Social Issues, 30*, 289–305.

Stodolska, M. (1998). Assimilation and leisure constraints: Dynamics of constraints on leisure in immigrant populations. *Journal of Leisure Research, 30*, 521–551.

Stodolska, M. (2000). Changes in leisure participation patterns after immigration. *Leisure Sciences, 22*, 39–63.

Stodolska, M. & Alexandris, K. (2004). The role of recreational sport in the adaptation of first-generation immigrants in the United States. *Journal of Leisure Research, 36*, 379–413.

Thibault, L. & Harvey, J. (1997). Fostering interorganizational linkages in the Canadian sport delivery system. *Journal of Sport Management, 11*, 45–68.

Tirone, S.C. (2000). Racism, indifference, and the leisure experiences of South Asian teens. *Leisure, 24*, 89–114.

Tirone, S.C. & Pedlar, A. (2000). Understanding the leisure experiences of a minority ethnic group: South Asian teens and young adults in Canada. *Society and Leisure, 23*, 145–169.

Tirone, S.C. & Shaw, S.M. (1997). At the center of their lives: Indo-Canadian women, their families, and leisure. *Journal of Leisure Research, 29*, 225–244.

Vail, S.E. (2007). Community development and sport participation. *Journal of Sport Management, 21*, 571–596.

Wilson, B., Erickson, K., Horton, S., Young, B. & Côté, J. (2007). Involving immigrants in youth sport coaching: Part 2. A qualitative analysis of the barriers, facilitators, and motivators for involvement. *International Journal of Sports Science & Coaching, 2*, 449–465.

PART THREE
The Study of Race and Sport beyond Canada's Borders

CHAPTER 7

Managing Whiteness in Sport for Development and Peace Internships

SIMON C. DARNELL

I. Introduction

Sport is now understood to be of use in meeting the goals of international development.[1] A host of organizations and programs—state-supported, non-governmental, and/or corporate—mobilize sport and physical activity in support of development, a sector often referred to as Sport for Development and Peace (SDP) (see Kidd, 2008).

Canadians and Canadian-based organizations are increasingly involved in SDP. For example, Right to Play, a sport-focused refugee-assistance program, is headquartered in Toronto. Athletes for Africa, also based in Toronto, supports youth education and includes Canadian NBA star Steve Nash as a board member. This increasing profile of SDP attracts volunteers from the North to serve overseas as "global citizens" (see Tiessen, 2011). As a result, the experiences of Canadians within the SDP sector have implications for understanding sport and physical activity and its connections to Canadian identity, particularly within the transnational relations of power that permeate development initiatives.

This chapter examines the ways in which young Canadian sportspeople recognized and responded to the racialized subject position of Whiteness into which they were hailed while serving abroad as volunteer interns within Commonwealth Games Canada's (CGC) International Development through Sport (IDS) internship program. Understanding Whiteness as a subject position recognizes the social construction of White identity and the experience of being positioned as White in relation to Others. It also draws attention to Whiteness as a form of privilege, both material and discursive, that is (only) constructed through intersections of race with other forms of dominance like social class and gender. Given that one can be included or excluded in Whiteness in a host of geopolitical contexts (Arat-Koc, 2010), service in SDP offers young Canadians a chance to discover and/or decode their racial privilege. Drawing on their reflections, I consider the implications of the ways interns "managed" Whiteness within the material and discursive hierarchies of race they encountered.

II. Theoretical Framework

Three overlapping theoretical approaches make up the framework of analysis for this chapter: (1) the social construction of Whiteness; (2) the study of race within international development; and (3) the importance of space and spatial analyses for understanding the experiences of development volunteers. Each is briefly described in this section.

THEORIZING WHITENESS

Constructed largely to counter the notion that "race" references and speaks of people of colour exclusively, theories of Whiteness have been used to understand and deconstruct how race (and its intersections with class, gender, sexuality, etc.) constitutes the subject positions of White people (Frankenberg, 1993). Studies of Whiteness remind us that White people are *raced*, though never in the same ways, or with the same effects, as people of colour. Unlike outward White supremacy or malicious racial hatred, Whiteness often proceeds from benevolence and/or a disavowal of dominance in the name of universality, a discursive construction that, in turn, secures the stewardship, privilege, and normativity of White identity. Munificence, respectability, claims to worldly, humanist values, and the socio-political interventions that follow serve the construction and maintenance of Whiteness and White privilege (see Mahrouse, 2010), even in countries like Canada with large immigrant and visible minority populations.

At the same time, Whiteness is not reserved for White bodies. Rather, by interlocking with other forms of privilege, like material wealth, as well as social codes of respectability, Whiteness becomes a position of dominance into which all are invited through hegemonic relations. In a culture where race and, indeed, racism are fundamental and intelligible, social actors—or *subjects* in reference to how people understand themselves—are regularly and routinely hailed into Whiteness to secure a socially dominant position. As a result, Whiteness is not simply constructed through knowing the Other, but produced within an aspirational framework of striving for a position of superiority and normativity. Achieving Whiteness depends on the construction of the self as not-Other, and therefore standard and dominant (Schick, 2002).

For this chapter, understanding Whiteness is important for two reasons. First, despite enduring myths of idyllic multiculturalism, racial hierarchies and the privileging of Whiteness continue to structure Canadian society (Thobani, 2007). The normative intelligibility of White bodies interlocks with dominance based on wealth and class, patriarchy and heteronormativity, to produce White culture as quintessentially Canadian, and vice versa. Second, and as I have argued elsewhere, overlapping discourses that position sport and development as universal, accessible, politically palatable, and largely benevolent contribute to the construction of Whiteness as a racially dominant subject position within SDP (Darnell, 2007, 2010b). That is, the relatively conservative response to inequality often proffered by the SDP movement, one that tends to seek the empowerment of individuals rather than structural changes (Darnell, 2010a), obscures, yet solidifies, claims to innocence among dominant people. These claims to innocence rely on the rarely acknowledged ways in which many Canadians disproportionately benefit from processes of deregulated trade and capital, southern resource extraction, and/or military interventions that sustain poverty and displacement in the global South. International experiences, like SDP volunteering, which proceed from a position of non-implication in global inequality, can reify the racialization of poverty and sustain race-based hierarchies.

RACE AND "WHITENESS" IN INTERNATIONAL DEVELOPMENT

In recent years, increased critical attention has been paid to the social construction of race and racial hierarchies within international development initiatives and discourses (see Kothari, 2005; McEwan, 2009; White, 2002). This literature challenges the "taboo" of race and racism within development and argues for critical understandings of the ongoing implications of colonial-informed development hierarchies, the ways in which race and racism are swallowed up through technical explanations of inequality, and Whiteness as a symbolic form of authority and expertise (Kothari, 2005).

Building on this focus, critical development research has looked specifically at racialized identity construction among northern development workers serving overseas (e.g., Baaz, 2005; Goudge, 2003; Heron, 2007; N. Razack, 2005; Tiessen, 2011). Baaz (2005, p. 85) has likened development work for northern volunteers to a process of racial discovery in two specific ways: recognizing Whiteness as a marker of difference, and the (re)discovery of relative privilege despite an ostensible politics of unity within development efforts. There is an opportunity, if not a tendency, for Whiteness to be normalized through the transnational encounters of development service.

Whiteness also speaks to the reasons that northerners are drawn to development. Heron (2007) has argued that a history of colonialism and the material inequalities of global capitalism that benefit the global North construct and sustain a White, middle-class Canadian urgency to respond as a "good person." Heron's research is particularly relevant to this chapter because of its focus on the experiences of *Canadians* within development work. Her analysis of innocence suggests that within social hierarchies—including racialized ones—development provides a means of "anti-conquest" or the act of being interested in, or concerned for, the welfare of those understood to be exotic or relatively powerless. Hers is also one of the few studies that consider how race interlocks with class, gender, and sexuality in development service. Heron (2007, p. 94) argues that for White Canadian women in development (a research sample that included herself), "it was almost impossible for us to extricate gender from whiteness in the development context" because notions of preferred femininity were constructed in and through identities of race and racialized Others.

At the same time, this literature reminds that the construction of Whiteness among development workers is not automatic, nor is it necessarily linear or intuitive (Baaz, 2005). "Dominant" does not constitute the complete subject position of development workers; rather, identity construction in the development context is often marked by irony and contradiction (Heron, 2007). Still, a commitment to global social justice and equality that characterizes the progressive nature of international development and SDP is complicated by a "professional hegemony" based on racialized *and* spatialized notions of superiority (N. Razack, 2005, p. 101).

RACE AND TRANSNATIONAL SPACES

The SDP interns interviewed in this research travelled from Canada to the Caribbean or Africa as part of their internship; it is salient, therefore, to consider the ways in which the act of transnational border crossing contributed to interns' construction and management of racialized identity. The social configurations of space have historically served in the institutionalization and normalization of racism(s) (Goldberg, 1993; S. Razack, 2002; Teelucksingh, 2006). Historians of empire have shown how Europeans came to know the colonial world and its inhabitants largely in spatial terms, through an imperial presence, as well as by researching strange lands (see Pratt, 1992; Said, 1978; Smith, 1999; Stoler, 1995, among others).

Space is also implicated in contemporary racialized subjectivities. A cosmopolitan subject is brought into focus through experiences of border crossing or claims to border transcendence made increasingly possible through a globalized economy (Grewal, 2005). I suggest that sport's globally commercialized organization and appeal, in which both high-performance elite sport (Smart, 2007) and participatory lifestyle sport (Wheaton, 2005) are globally intelligible and transnationally fluid, offer an entry point for the cosmopolitan subject. Global sport facilitates the transnational reach of SDP and the development subject, who understands himself or herself as "a subject privileged enough to choose to be in unfamiliar landscapes" (S. Razack, 2002, p. 12). It is here that space becomes race, as Whiteness is identified as mobile and unattached in opposition to static bodies of colour (S. Razack, 2002).

Nestel (2002) offers a particularly lucid example of this process through her analysis of the experiences of White midwives in Ontario who travelled to clinics along the U.S.–Mexico border in order to attend births and meet the requirements for Canadian midwifery certification. She found that despite claims to a global feminist solidarity, Ontario midwives used their relative privilege to secure their own personal and professional benefits with Mexican women's bodies as the physical and discursive source. Such "midwifery tourism" renders the Third World woman and southern space as a material supply for northern entitlement and benefit. Nestel's analysis illustrates how such activities are possible only through, and thus serve to secure, a myopic reading of unequal relations of power and a discursive commitment to midwifery tourism as a benevolent and moral project, rather than evidence of "collusion with the violent effects of globalization" (2002, p. 250). Her analysis draws attention to the *process* by which race becomes intelligible and subjects hailed into Whiteness in and through transnational spaces and experiences.

III. Methodology

Studying Whiteness and White privilege is difficult methodological terrain. On the one hand, failing to analyze and confront Whiteness maintains its invisibility and supports its social and political normativity. On the other hand, to reference Whiteness as visible, experiential, tangible, or "real" runs the risk of essentializing race and solidifying the very hierarchies that critical studies set out to challenge (Gallagher, 2000). In addition, the subject conducting the research is also implicated in such politics. Heron (2007, p. 19) cautions that there is an opportunity for the critical researcher of Whiteness to assume the moral high ground, particularly in analyses of subjectivity, that problematically overlooks the complexities of racial identity and power, or offers little explanation of the subject's social antecedents.

In response, I position this chapter as a way to understand how CGC interns made sense of the racial positions in which they found themselves while serving abroad and to consider the sociopolitical implications of these processes. The goal is not to expose racism or demonize privileged people, but to contribute to a critically informed analysis of race, privilege, and SDP. Indeed, my own position as a White researcher likely afforded me the access, authority, and trust of participants to discuss their experiences, but also the responsibility to deconstruct and challenge relations of racial dominance.

Semi-structured interviews were conducted with 27 former interns of the CGC's IDS program. Interview methodology aligns with the post-positive commitment to understanding human experiences not simply as evidence of social reality but rather constitutive of political relations and the workings of power (Scott, 1991). All the interviewees had served for at least eight months with a CGC partner organization in a Commonwealth country in the Caribbean or Africa between 2002 and 2007. The partnership orientation of the CGC program—in which interns work for a local sport/health/education organization facilitated by a relationship between the organization and CGC—meant that each intern worked in a different area of sport, physical education, and/or health, depending on the organizational and strategic focus and needs of their placement. Some interns held administrative positions, such as event planning or fundraising, while others were more directly involved in sport through coaching youth, training community leaders and volunteers, or organizing sport to facilitate critical health or education initiatives.

Most interns were under 30 years of age, university-educated (often in sport- or health-related disciplines such as physical education or kinesiology), and had extensive sport and physical education backgrounds. Twelve served in countries in the Caribbean and 15 in Africa. Twenty-one of the interviewees were women, and of the total sample of 27 interns, two self-identified with an ethnic identity that was not White.[2] Pseudonyms are used in the results section to protect the anonymity of the interviewees.

IV. Results

All CGC interns interviewed for this study agreed that social understandings of race and Whiteness permeated their efforts to support local capacities and mobilize sport in the service of international development goals. These experiences suggest that interns were hailed into Whiteness in and through their service time abroad. Yet, they also tended to respond to this through the management of Whiteness more than its deconstruction. The section is separated into four thematic parts: (1) the importance of sport and/in space; (2) recognizing and experiencing Whiteness; (3) managing Whiteness; and (4) reflexive considerations.

PART 1: THE IMPORTANCE OF SPORT AND/IN SPACE

Understandings of, affinities for, and experiences with sport were central to CGC interns' decisions to serve abroad in an SDP program. Interns' positive sporting experiences drew them into development work where they could mobilize their knowledge of sport and of a (sporting) self into tangible and practical action. As Stella described, a love of sport and fascination with the physically active body, combined with a desire to travel, attracted her to the use of sport for development:

> I think [my decision to volunteer] came out of a desire to travel and just a real interest in the social side of the sport world. [I saw] this sign "Do you like to travel? Do you like sports? Apply for the Commonwealth Games internship." So I read it through and I was like, ohmygosh, this is exactly what I want to do even though I didn't know it. (Stella)

For many CGC interns, sport was a catalyst for development. In turn, the opportunity to do an SDP placement solidified interns' understanding of themselves as conduits of positive sporting experiences between and across the transnational divide of development. Heron (2007) has argued that White women benefit from development work by publicly assuming a respectable and proper femininity; here sport and physical educators took up subject positions as reputable, respectable, and service-oriented. In this sense, "sport as a vehicle" referred not only to the benefits of sport for SDP participants and partners, but also to the utility of sport in establishing the subject position of the intern:

> What interested me about the program was actually doing the development work and this particular program geared towards sport, development through sport ... kind of

seemed to be, when I came across it, the best way for me to gain the experience and to use the skills that I had learned so far and to apply it in a positive way. (James)

James's description shows that sport was central to what made development and SDP attractive to CGC interns. Development *through sport* was a preferred type of development because interns were able to connect their development interests to their sporting competencies.

In addition to sport, the element that interns cited regularly as a "reason to go" was the chance to travel and experience other cultures. Travel in this regard was specifically related to the opportunity to see exotic locales and have adventurous experiences. Such imagined spaces of underdevelopment are not only rendered tangible and real, but can be dominated through discursive practices of knowledge and authority (Said, 1978). Sport offered a means of facilitating, supporting, and justifying interns' interest in travelling to such spaces, and their interests in experiencing the development context constructed a northern subject position of worldliness and mobility (see Baaz, 2005; Heron, 2007; N. Razack, 2005):

I'll be totally blunt with you, my real interest was kind of going and working in development and working in Africa. I'd just grown up with this dream to just go to some part of Africa; it's quite strange because it was quite vague as to exactly what I wanted to do, but I just sort of had this desire to go there and just sort of experience it. So luckily for me, I had a huge sort of sporting background and it was sort of ... a good excuse. Not that I ever lied, but I definitely sort of used my sporting background to get me to Africa. (Randall)

Sport afforded opportunities for CGC interns to fulfill their desires to travel, and they drew on notions of sport as a universal language and a catalyst of individual and social change as a means to support their spatial mobility. Heron (2007, p. 46) suggests that for northern subjects interested in development, "altruism becomes our passport to the south." Sport similarly secured this passport of development benevolence for SDP interns. Not only were their motivations and desires connected to the spaces of the development context and the act of travelling, but space was central to the process by which interns fortified and implemented the helping imperative of their SDP placement.

The desire to do SDP service was also tied to the understanding that it would be a trip across a social and spatial dichotomy—from privilege to underprivilege, from rich to poor, from fortunate to unfortunate—and that the experience of exploration in underprivileged, poor, unfortunate spaces could confirm one's sense of self. Such knowledge required a prior imagination of Africa as the socio-political space of scarcity, and the North as affluent and dominant, socially and politically:

> I just feel so fortunate to have just grown up in [suburb of major Canadian city], to have been given a free education and a good quality education.... But I also had a sense of some guilt because of it, and I thought, OK, I want to do something good, and there's obviously this North American perspective to go to Africa. Go to Africa. (Amanda)

There was an intimate relationship, then, between the SDP volunteer placement and interns' recognition, acknowledgement (and enjoyment) of their own privilege. Amanda described a paradox between the quest for a morally superior subjectivity (superior not only in relation to the global South, but also to those northern subjects who do not choose to "do something good") and the fact that these activities *require* celebrating and acting upon one's position of social and spatial privilege. The next section illustrates that this spatial dimension of the internship, facilitated by sport, did not preclude awareness of racial identity and privilege; interns recognized and experienced Whiteness in the spaces of their internships.

PART 2: RECOGNIZING AND EXPERIENCING WHITENESS

The development experience for northern subjects is a relational one; knowledge of self is intelligible and dependent on racial and spatial relations with Others (Heron, 2007). For many CGC interns, the SDP placement constituted one of, if not the, first time(s) that they experienced being White. This took place largely because they were recognized in the development context as privileged, and often by people of colour. Some interns, though, were unprepared for the knowledge and power associated with their skin colour and its history in the development context, and often found the experience of being White more difficult than anticipated:

> And there's a lot of assumptions about White people there, about our wealth, like a Mzungu—that's the name—like immediately you're branded and you're unknowable, like you're just way above them or just way too different than them and so trying to implement a program when you're trying to make it like it's not "coming down" on them is really, really difficult. (Stella)

Stella's racialized identity, in which Whiteness was associated with affluence and power, clashed with her desire to implement programs that did not assume or reproduce such a hierarchy. Her challenge was to take up the racialized benevolence—the Whiteness—that supported the development worker subject position without invoking the same hierarchy in the name of achieving development goals. While no satisfactory way out of this position was readily apparent for Stella, for other interns the recognition of Whiteness illustrated its *utility* in implementing programs to meet development goals. For example, Carol reacted with "bad feelings" to her position of Whiteness and the privilege it afforded her, but was willing and able to reconcile these feelings against the access it provided.

SD: Some of the other interns were the only White person in a very non-White place....

Carol: I definitely experienced that. And that was part of me being able to have access to things, which is totally weird.

SD: What was that like?

Carol: Well, you feel bad, to be honest. I felt bad. I wanted to use it because it's for the good of the program. I mean it's not like I could change what I looked like, um, but it's strange. I remember thinking about having something going for me and something going against me. I'm a White foreigner so I can, like I said, have access to certain people and perhaps some people think I know something about something.

This process that Carol described offered an opportunity for critical reflection on racial hierarchies, but the chore of attaining international development goals, and the utility of Whiteness therein, took precedence. The dominance of Whiteness is reified in such a process, and even justified as a means to development and SDP. Schick (2002, p. 108) argues that identifying with ideologies of "rationality and objectivity" serves in the process of securing White entitlement. In this case, the central development ethic of the will to improve (Li, 2007) and a helping imperative (Heron, 2007) trumped anti-racism.

Other interns had similar experiences to Carol in terms of the benefits of Whiteness. Marie, for example, described how the novelty of Whiteness in her placement community afforded her a profile that allowed her to build partnerships and relationships and accomplish development goals more efficiently:

I think [being a White woman] might have been an advantage in most circumstances. I think I was mysterious to them. So, for example, when we were trying to meet with the village elders ... [usually] women are at the end of the list, but ... I do feel that like this exoticness of [being] this young White girl might have enabled me to make things happen a little bit faster without having to ever ask. (Marie)

Interns understood that the people they encountered in SDP made presumptions about their privilege. As Heron (2007, p. 85) suggests, from the perspective of the overseas development worker, "it must be assumed that [locals in development] negotiate our presence unceasingly, in ways that are either not perceptible to participants or not mentioned in our narratives." Particularly through a lens of Gramscian hegemony, in which it is understood that subordinates negotiate the relations of their domination, it makes sense that people of colour in the development context participated in SDP by negotiating with White development workers to their own benefit. There were seemingly few fissures in the racial hierarchy of development and SDP to challenge these structures of material and discursive dominance.

Still, some interns recognized Whiteness not as an opportunity for facilitating development, but more for the way it underpinned their status while abroad, status imbued with notions of relative prosperity, real and/or imagined. For example, Joanne's placement community offered tangible examples of the intersections of race and class that hailed her into a dominant subject position. In this sense, perceptions of Whiteness drew on examples of Whiteness. Joanne's reflections suggest that the multicultural ethic of racial equality brought forth to the development context was challenged by the racially informed disparities and inequalities into which she was hailed. She described a shadow of Whiteness attached to SDP interns.

So I think there's this perception that White people have money, which you kind of understand it to be true because in relation, people are coming with huge [amounts of] money. So it always feeds this idea that White people have money. And in general, it is true. Like around the world it is true. [And] I'm not any different so I think it's always with me. That kind of is a shadow kind of following me, of people's conceptions. (Joanne)

Such shadows cohere around privilege, wealth, and the ethic of "doing good" (Slocum, 2007), but not necessarily around White bodies because Whiteness is not essentially tied to White skin or even White identity (Schick, 2002, p. 104). The biological slipperiness of Whiteness suggested by such a theoretical perspective was evident in this study to the extent that *all* interviewees acknowledged that they were hailed into racialized privilege, even the two interns who did not identify as White. The social politics of the SDP experience were complicated and highlighted by discourses that equate foreign wealth and privilege with Whiteness. Florence's experiences were illustrative of this:

When they met me, they saw me as a foreigner—right?—this kind of White person and whatever goes along with a White person, even though I'm not White. But anybody who's not Black or Indian is White. And me as a female—obviously there's a lot of stereotypes that come with it, and when they first saw me, they just literally looked down on me. [But] as soon as we got on that court and we just played, everything dropped. All the stereotypes [were gone] and it was just everybody was equal in a sense that I can play, you can play, let's all have fun. (Florence)

In Florence's recounting, race was subsumed not through the deconstruction of dominance and subordination, but through a renewal of the dream of reciprocity—the belief that presuming, recognizing, or "practising" sameness among different people, no matter their relative privilege, leads to the achievement of equity. Such discourses are constitutive of Whiteness within the liberal logic of racial equality and aided by social activities like sport, which ostensibly level the metaphorical racial playing field.

The opportunities for recreation, play, and physicality that sport afforded within SDP went a significant way toward establishing a sense of reciprocity with those in less privileged positions.

In this case, sport did not solidify White supremacy outright (see King, Leonard & Kusz, 2007), but it did prove useful for coming to terms with—and in some cases absolving—racial privilege. As a result, the reification of Whiteness in SDP was rarely challenged, and the power and privilege (material and discursive) ascribed to Whiteness, if not directly to White bodies, remained relatively intact. Interns' management of Whiteness, explored in more detail in the next section, further supported this process.

PART 3: MANAGING WHITENESS

Interns' various responses to racial privilege were largely constitutive of the management of Whiteness and not of anti-racism. Two techniques of the management of Whiteness emerged. One was to draw on "equality" or "belonging" in transnational development encounters in which the White intern travelling to the South is presumed to have a minority experience in a manner akin to being a person of colour in Canada. The other was turning to the act of caring and an ethic of compassion for the Other. Patricia reflected on the "equality" thesis:

> Dealing with stereotypes and other things that people held, especially about international development workers, I found hard to overcome and difficult to deal with. Learning to deal with racism—that's something that someone in my position doesn't deal with a lot back home. It was difficult to develop strong friendships. (Patricia)

Patricia's response to Whiteness was to position her racial minority status as a difficulty, if not a liability. "Standing out" due to White skin colour was a new, challenging, and destabilizing experience, particularly given the dominant understanding of Canada as a nation of belonging for people of European descent, even amidst multiculturalism (see Thobani, 2007, p. 87). Her recognition that she is rarely racially visible in Canada brought the racial politics of the development context to the fore and potentially destabilized the normativity of Whiteness in meaningful ways. Still, the discourse of reverse racism proved the most attractive and palatable rejoinder, even though the minority status of White bodies does little to challenge the dominance of Whiteness (see N. Razack, 2005).

James negotiated Whiteness by invoking notions of race relations in which his friendly engagement with the local people of colour absolved him of the privileged position he inhabited. While Baaz (2005) argues for a focus on the reification of Whiteness in development, here Whiteness was rendered invisible because interns were deemed not responsible for the ways in which being White, and acting White, underpins the social and political apparatus of international development.

> I would say race relations, particularly in the area that I was in, were negligible in the sense that there was me who was White and everyone else was ethnic [nationality]. I was very close to the border with [country], it's all the same kind of tribes, so in terms of race relations and language, that wasn't an issue at all. Overall, everyone was very friendly and very welcoming, which was nice. So [problems with] race? No. (James)

From an anti-racist perspective, the presence of Others is not proof of emancipation, but rather calls into question the ways in which dominance is sustained in spite of Others' presence (Schick, 2002, p. 110). Similarly, the presence of White people as minorities in communities or nations does not equate with racial equality or justice. Rather, dominance is sustained in James's reflections by the use of acceptance in the community as evidence of a lack of racial hierarchy, even though such a hierarchy served in the process by which James came to be in the village in the first place.

James suggested that given that his presence in his placement community was generally accepted and relatively unchallenged, he became another tribe in that part of the world. James's claims to sameness—as a member of another, yet equal, racial group—served as the basis from which to assume the development benevolence of the SDP movement and the CGC internship.

The second approach to managing Whiteness was through the act of caring and an ethic of compassion for the Other. This was a form of the anti-conquest (Pratt, 1992). In Esther's description, the SDP experience was a process distinct from saviourship and the problematic of stewardship. Instead, compassion was invoked to signify that Whiteness does not seek to dominate, only to understand and care. Such an approach is particularly connected to a Canadian national identity of global concern and benevolence (Heron, 2007, p. 117) and demonstrated interns' efforts to establish themselves as exemplars of the Canadian ethic of responsibility and empathy.

> In some cases [SDP] may have been a racialized [process] because to think of the White person who actually cares about kids from wherever [was significant]. [I'm] coming from Canada, and I actually care and want to teach them and coach them and develop these programs ... the look on their faces when they realized that I'd come [was amazing], and they're just so excited that someone else is actually trying to break down those barriers. (Esther)

According to Slocum (2007, p. 520), "Whiteness coheres precisely ... in the act of doing good." To this end, Whiteness was clearly on display and, to an extent, reified in the SDP context. Interns set out to construct and know themselves as "good people," similar to what Heron (2007) has argued. Yet, interns also recognized the difference through privilege that embodying Whiteness established for them in the development context, and they turned to different strategies to maintain their status and subject positions as helpers despite their privilege. This is the untenable position of Whiteness in the SDP context; Whiteness is constitutive of the need to do development work—and it facilitates its accomplishment—but it simultaneously compromises the objectivity and sanctity of the experience.

PART 4: REFLEXIVE CONSIDERATIONS

Despite the management of Whiteness, several interns did offer critical reflections around its discursive and material implications, and some struggled to find a way to support development without trading on privilege. For Steven, this tension was evident in both the preferential ways he was treated because he came from the North, and the notion of development workers as saviours. He was left to question the extent to which his presence as expert was beneficial in meeting development goals or whether it was a hindrance to the social organization of his placement community.

> Starting with race, ... I felt that as coming from a Western country into that kind of situation, I was perhaps given more respect than was warranted and perhaps even justified, as if my views were worth taking into account just because [I'm White], rather than for any value of what I had to offer. And I think that is a matter of a lot of development workers going there and speaking about how great everything is at home because our way is somehow superior and our education and ability is somehow superior. So sometimes I was wondering if I was a benefit or a hindrance in terms of [local] empowerment in that way. (Steven)

Steven's reflections illustrate the historical ambivalence of the development worker subject. Li (2007, p. 14) has argued that the tension of colonial rule stemmed from the colonialists' inability to reconcile their view of the Other. If the colonized were fundamentally different, then there was no moral basis for development; it was merely dominance and subordination. If, on the other hand, the colonized were essentially the same, "developing" them would eliminate the lack that constituted the right to rule. In Li's analysis, governmentality, or a focus on the conduct of the Other, was a means out of this colonial quagmire. Yet in Steven's recount, Whiteness prevented governmentality as a recourse to privilege; he questioned whether his privilege undermined the effective implementation of governmentality. He was not the only one who struggled in this way.

> Sometimes I wonder, wouldn't it be better for everyone just to leave, like what happens if we just all left? Like there are so many aid organizations in [country] ... what good are we doing here? The people really just want to live and they just want to do their thing.... Why do we have to be there? Is sport getting into something that's just going to end up being the same [as traditional development]? Should we get out of there? (Stella)

The ethic that attempted to position interns and development partners on equal footing in the process of using sport to facilitate equality was confronted by the fact that the markings and barriers that sustain inequality were so clear. For interns like Stella, it was very difficult to reconcile SDP as an act of solidarity and benign knowledge transfer amidst such stark hierarchies.

Finally, interns like Jessica challenged the spatially informed notion that development and SDP affords First World subjects an opportunity to experience the subject position of racial minorities and underclasses. For her, the experience of Whiteness in SDP was the experience of recognizing relative privilege. Her description of positive racism speaks to the experience of being racialized, of having a racial identity beyond the invisibility of Whiteness in Canada, but one that is never the same as that of a person of colour at home or abroad.

> Before I went to [country], it was like I was going to

understand what it means to be a minority because I'm going to be the only White person in this country. And very quickly I realized I will never understand what it means to be a marginalized minority. Because being the only White person, I received a lot of positive racism. I received a lot of attention, but it's not like it's bad, it's often like "Oh, can I take your picture?" (Jessica)

Jessica's perspective speaks to, I would argue, an imagination or ethic of development that is closest to an anti-racist paradigm. She illustrated that it may be possible to use the cross-cultural experience that development and SDP affords to illuminate the racialized power relations that sustain inequality in the development context and on a global scale. Questions remain as to the political approach taken toward addressing these inequalities, but it does suggest that SDP may offer an initial opportunity to challenge racial hierarchies rather than use or manage them.

V. Conclusion: The Implications of Whiteness in SDP

This chapter has focused on experiences of, and responses to, Whiteness within Sport for Development and Peace (SDP) internships. Commonwealth Games Canada interns who served abroad were understood, recognized, and situated in their placement communities as "White," a historicized and racialized position of benevolence, affluence, power, privilege, and prestige. Whiteness was connected to space as travelling to the development context served in the processes by which interns came to know where and why their work was needed.

For CGC interns, this produced a tension given that their privileged social position (of race, space, and class), and the benefits it afforded them in the development context, often clashed with their desire to implement sport-based programs without presuming or reproducing racial hierarchies. Interns struggled to take up the social and material benefits of Whiteness in post-colonial spaces without invoking the same hierarchy in order to meet development goals. Sport was particularly useful in this regard because it was understood to have a utility in meeting development goals given its cross-cultural appeal and presumed universality and fairness. In this way, sport, as an everyday, fun, and attractive activity and social institution offered interns a means by which to secure a subject position of redemption amidst privilege. It also, though, forced interns to confront and negotiate their own racialized privilege, an often destabilizing effect of international development service (see N. Razack, 2005).

The critical issue, then, is that CGC interns were privileged within the social relations and spaces of development and SDP, but were rarely able or encouraged, either socially or institutionally, to reflect and/or act upon their experiences in such terms. With a few notable exceptions, they relied on disavowals of racial hierarchies or deference to the dominant tradition of Canadian liberal multiculturalism. This is understandable but problematic if inequality and racial hierarchies are overlooked in the rush to attend to the material effects of racism and social injustice. As Mahrouse (2010, p. 169) argues, the ability of social justice interventions to enact sustainable change is compromised by "white hegemony and the liberal paradigm," which actively work to prevent shifts in relations of power. SDP appears particularly susceptible to such logic. This does not mean that sustainable change is impossible, but it does draw attention to the deconstruction of power and privilege as an alternative to attempting to secure the preferred conduct and prosperity of the world's marginalized peoples.

In sum, if identifying with ideologies of "rationality and objectivity" serves in the process of securing Whiteness (Schick, 2002, p. 108), then a commitment to international development and SDP needs to be accompanied by a political and ethical commitment to anti-racism and resisting social hierarchies. The issue is not the appropriateness per se of meeting the goals of SDP, but rather the extent to which meeting such goals trades on Whiteness, solidifies it as a regime of truth, constructs White innocence, and absolves privileged people of an ethical responsibility to the benefits of their position. The results of this chapter illustrate the extent to which notions of sport as fun, apolitical, and useful in development serve in the process by which transnational Whiteness is secured as moral and helpful. This is particularly the case for young, middle-class, sport-minded Canadians who have been raised in an environment of liberal multiculturalism. As such, it is worthy of ongoing discussion and scrutiny within SDP and sport culture in Canada.

Questions for Critical Thought

1. Why is Whiteness more recognizable or intelligible in spaces of international development and Sport for Development and Peace volunteering as compared to Canadian and other sport settings? What does this suggest for Canadian culture and policies of multiculturalism?
2. In what ways can race and racism interlock with other forms of privilege in the fields of sport, international development, and Sport for Development and Peace? Consider gender, class, sexuality, and ability.
3. What strategies for responding to the privilege of Whiteness can be identified that go beyond the management or strategic use of such a position? How might these be implemented within Sport for Development and Peace?

Notes

1. For example, in 2003, the United Nations adopted resolution 58/5, which formally recognized the contributions that sport can make to meeting international development goals, and followed this with the International Year of Sport and Physical Education in 2005.

2. I use "White" to refer to a fluid, socially produced identity of ethnicity connected to pale skin colour and implicated in dominance, but distinct from a fixed biological state.

References

Arat-Koc, S. (2010). New whiteness(es) beyond the colour line? Assessing the contradictions and complexities of "whiteness" in the (geo)political economy of capitalist globalism. In S. Razack, M. Smith & S. Thobani (Eds.), *States of race: Critical race feminism for the 21st century* (pp. 147–168). Toronto: Between the Lines.

Baaz, M.E. (2005). *The paternalism of partnership: A postcolonial reading of identity in development aid*. London & New York: Zed Books.

Darnell, S.C. (2007). Playing with race: Right to play and the production of Whiteness in development through sport. *Sport in Society, 10*(4), 560–579.

Darnell, S.C. (2010a). Power, politics, and sport for development and peace: Investigating the utility of sport for international development. *Sociology of Sport Journal, 27*(1), 54–75.

Darnell, S.C. (2010b). Race, sport, and bio-politics: Encounters with difference in "Sport for Development and Peace" internships. *Journal of Sport and Social Issues, 34*(4), 396–417.

Frankenberg, R. (1993). *White women, race matters: The social construction of Whiteness*. Minneapolis: University of Minnesota Press.

Gallagher, C.A. (2000). White like me? Methods, meaning, and manipulation in the field of White studies. In F.W. Twine & J.W. Warren (Eds.), *Racing research, researching race: Methodological dilemmas in critical race studies* (pp. 67–92). New York: New York University Press.

Goldberg, D.T. (1993). *Racist culture: Philosophy and the politics of meaning*. Cambridge: Blackwell.

Goudge, P. (2003). *The power of whiteness: Racism in Third World development and aid*. London: Lawrence & Wishart.

Grewal, I. (2005). *Transnational America: Feminisms, diasporas, neoliberalisms*. Durham: Duke University Press.

Heron, B. (2007). *Desire for development: Whiteness, gender, and the helping imperative*. Waterloo: Wilfrid Laurier University Press.

Kidd, B. (2008). A new social movement: Sport for development and peace. *Sport in Society, 11*(4), 370–380.

King, C.R., Leonard, D.J. & Kusz, K.W. (2007). White power and sport: An introduction. *Journal of Sport and Social Issues, 31*(1), 3–10.

Kothari, U. (2005). Authority and expertise: The professionalisation of international development and the ordering of dissent. *Antipode, 37*(3), 425–446.

Li, T. (2007). *The will to improve: Governmentality, development, and the practice of politics*. Durham: Duke University Press.

Mahrouse, G. (2010). Questioning efforts that seek to "do good": Insights from transnational solidarity activism and socially responsible tourism. In S. Razack, M. Smith & S. Thobani (Eds.), *States of race: Critical race feminism for the 21st century* (pp. 169–190). Toronto: Between the Lines.

McEwan, C. (2009). *Postcolonialism and development*. London: Routledge.

Nestel, S. (2002). Delivering subjects: Race, space, and the emergence of legalized midwifery in Ontario. In S. Razack (Ed.), *Race, space, and the law* (pp. 233–255). Toronto: Between the Lines.

Pratt, M.L. (1992). *Imperial eyes: Travel writing and transculturation*. London & New York: Routledge.

Razack, N. (2005). "Bodies on the move": Spatialized locations, identities, and nationality in international work. *Social Justice, 32*(4), 87–104.

Razack, S. (2002). Introduction: When place becomes race. In S. Razack (Ed.), *Race, space, and the law* (pp. 1–20). Toronto: Between the Lines.

Said, E.W. (1978). *Orientalism* (1st ed.). New York: Pantheon Books.

Schick, C. (2002). Keeping the ivory tower White: Discourses of racial domination. In S. Razack (Ed.), *Race, space, and the law* (pp. 100–119). Toronto: Between the Lines.

Scott, J. (1991). The evidence of experience. *Critical Inquiry, 17*(4), 773–797.

Slocum, R. (2007). Whiteness, space, and alternative food practice. *Geoforum, 38*, 520–533.

Smart, B. (2007). Not playing around: Global capitalism, modern sport, and consumer culture. In R. Giulianotti & R. Robertson (Eds.), *Globalization and sport*, Malden: Blackwell.

Smith, L.T. (1999). *Decolonizing methodologies: Research and indigenous peoples*. London & New York: Zed Books & Dunedin: University of Otago Press.

Stoler, A.L. (1995). *Race and the education of desire: Foucault's* History of Sexuality *and the colonial order of things*. Durham: Duke University Press.

Teelucksingh, C. (2006). Toward claiming space: Theorizing racialized spaces in Canadian cities. In C. Teelucksingh (Ed.), *Claiming space: Racialization in Canadian cities* (pp. 1–17). Waterloo: Wilfrid Laurier University Press.

Thobani, S. (2007). *Exalted subjects: Studies in the making of race and nation in Canada*. Toronto: University of Toronto Press.

Tiessen, R. (2011). Global subjects or objects of globalization? The promotion of global citizenship in NGOs offering sport for peace and/or development programmes. *Third World Quarterly, 32*(3), 571–587.

Wheaton, B. (2005). Selling out? The commercialisation and globalisation of lifestyle sport. In L. Allison (Ed.), *The global politics of sport: The role of global institutions in sport* (pp. 140–161). New York: Routledge.

White, S. (2002). Thinking race, thinking development. *Third World Quarterly, 23*(3), 407–419.

CHAPTER 8

Playing in Chinatown: A Critical Discussion of the Nation/Sport/Citizen Triad

YUKA NAKAMURA

Introduction

The North American Chinese Invitational Volleyball Tournament (NACIVT) is an annual event that has occurred on Labour Day weekend since the 1930s. The event has been held regularly in Toronto, Washington, New York, Montreal, San Francisco, and Boston. Though attempts have been made to establish teams in Vancouver, neither the game nor the tournament has taken root despite the city's large Chinese population. Nevertheless, the growing popularity of the tournament is undeniable; the event attracts over 1,000 players from 90 men's and women's volleyball teams, as well as their family, friends, and fans from cities across Canada and the U.S.

The tournaments generally begin with a parade of teams, led by a lion dance and words of welcome from local dignitaries. The tournament space is divided into several courts, marked out with lines of masking tape. The posts holding the nets are secured by ropes and cinder blocks or water tanks. A chair or ladder is placed by the net for the referee. Upon the referee's signal, players line up at the back of the court, bow to each other, and then proceed to jog along the outside boundary, greet opposing players at the net, and then return to their side of the court to do a team cheer. The starting lineup prepares, and with the blow of the whistle, the first serve is delivered and the game begins. Players must play close attention as there are several matches in both the men's and women's division taking place at the same time. Due to the close quarters, balls from other matches or players warming up enter the court frequently, temporarily stopping play. Limited space means that fans have to pay close attention in order to deflect, retrieve, and return balls, as well as to avoid players who come running out of bounds in an attempt to save an errant ball, inevitably crashing into a distracted observer.

There are a number of unique elements of the NACIVT. For example, the NACIVT is known for nine-man volleyball, which is played in the men's division, unlike the women, who play regular sixes volleyball. As the name suggests, there are nine rather than six players on the court, the nets are lower, and the court is also larger than dimensions outlined by the Fédération Internationale de Volleyball regulations. In addition, the tournament has historically been held in the streets or a parking lot in an urban Chinatown, and it is this connection between the NACIVT, Chinatown, and citizenship that is the focus of this chapter.

My multi-sited ethnography of the NACIVT "takes unexpected trajectories in tracing a cultural formation across and within multiple sites of activity" (Marcus, 1995, p. 96). By asking what trajectories map out the NACIVT, I identified various data collection sites, including the tournaments, the awards ceremony, the fundraising events, the social activities, and tournament websites and booklets. Based on this framework, I conducted participant observations of three tournaments (Toronto, September 2005; New York Mini, July 2006; and Washington, September 2006); held 31 semi-structured, in-depth interviews with current and retired participants; and carried out textual analysis of tournament-related texts, such as the program booklets and tournament websites.

Data were analyzed to interpret meaning and to demonstrate the complexity of the NACIVT through open coding. I considered the content of statements, how they are delivered; the message they try to communicate; the narrative, characters, storyline, impact, links to broader themes, the relationships between individuals and each other, groups and contexts, and patterns of conflict and negotiation (Hsiung & Raddon, 2005). I also examined what or who are the actors, actions, activities, places, ways of participating, interactions, associations, and meanings (LeCompte & Schensul, 1999). Connections, themes, and patterns were identified in the data, and similar pieces of information were grouped and categorized. These categories were then analyzed for a logical sequence (Glesne, 1999) by asking what the recurrent patterns mean; under what conditions the patterns occur; how the patterns complicate commonsense understandings; and what variations, interconnections, and exceptions to the rule mean (Hsiung & Raddon, 2005).

The data and subsequent analysis illustrate that Chinatown itself has multiple meanings and is used in different ways for varying purposes. For example, it is the presumed site of so-called authentic Chineseness, a symbol of anti-Chinese sentiment, a safe haven, a springboard into middle-class suburbia, a nostalgic home-sweet-home, a knot of kinship ties, a depoliticized tourist destination, a symbol of multiculturalism, a place to develop citizenship skills, and a diasporic node within a transnational field, among others. For the participants of the NACIVT, Chinatown is home to an authentic Chineseness, not a replacement for an unknown homeland, and a place to play a sport they love. In this chapter, I demonstrate the significance of this claim to Chinatown. That a sporting event provides an opportunity to make this assertion is particularly important because Asian bodies are frequently constructed as inept at sport. Thus, by playing sport in public, in Chinatown, NACIVT participants destabilize racialized understandings of the nation/sport/citizen triad and the question of who may claim citizenship in Canada.

Social Construction of Chinatown and White Settler Society

Spadina and Dundas, Canal Street, H and 7th ... for those familiar with Toronto, Manhattan, or Washington, these streets and intersections are discursively linked to Chinatown. Although I take the position that Chinatown is socially constructed, it is important to recognize that it also refers to an actual place (even while its location and boundaries may change), with Chinese signage, services that cater to Chinese people, and architectural features that reference Chinese culture and art, a place that has been and is home to many Chinese people. It is also a place associated with dynamic, diverse, and contradictory images, stereotypes, meanings, and associations. Despite its shifting social construction, that Chinatown is also a real place is likely what allows contradictory assumptions about Chinatown to take root so easily.

Common explanations for how Chinatowns were formed include the view that they formed in response to discrimination that Chinese people faced in Canada and the U.S., the result of social organization of migrants, a launching pad for assimilation, a traditional Chinese practice, and a product of racial segregation, among others. Anderson (1987) identifies a critical weakness in a number of these explanations, namely, the reliance on discrete Chineseness as the explanatory principle for the formation of Chinatown or, in other words, the assumption that there is a real Chineseness, which is the driving force for the formation of Chinatowns. Instead, Anderson (1987) argues that "Chinatown is a social construction with a cultural history and a tradition of imagery and institutional practice that has given it a cognitive and material reality in and for the West" (p. 581). Chinatown is not a reflection of some inherent and essential Chineseness or Chinese culture but the result of an active process of racial classification. Using the case of Chinatown in Vancouver during the late 19th to 20th century, Anderson (1987) illustrates how the space where Chinese people settled was "apprehended and targeted by European society through that society's cognitive categories [resulting in] a boundary between 'their' territory and 'our' territory" (1987, p. 583). Through this process of connecting and embedding a racial ideology to a material space, a socially constructed place like Chinatown was "given a local referent, became a social fact, and aided its own reproduction" (p. 584). The state too was directly involved in "sanctioning the arbitrary boundaries of insider and outsider and the idea of mainstream society as 'white'" (Anderson, 1987, p. 584) by racializing Chinese people as unsanitary and immoral, legitimizing the creation of Chinatown, and assigning these outsiders to this space and vice versa.

For example, Vancouver's Chinatown was viewed as diseased and there was a subsequent move to prevent it from spreading. Thus, in 1887, when 10 of 13 laundries owned by merchants from Chinatown were found to be outside the border of Chinatown, City Council moved to contain this infiltration of Chineseness into the city. Since civic authorities could not deny business licences to certain nationalities, other indirect strategies were used to restrict Chinese laundries and prevent them from crossing the boundary of Chinatown. A bylaw was passed preventing laundries from being built outside certain boundaries. During an outbreak of cholera, houses along the main street of Chinatown were targeted based on the view that residents along this street would naturally not abide by sanitary practices. As a result, shacks and houses were destroyed. The poor living conditions in Vancouver's Chinatown that could result in a cholera outbreak were not linked to the constraints on the lives of Chinese people, including job and pay discrimination, and the deteriorating physical condition of the area; rather, they were explained by the assumption that Chinese people were dirty. "Whether or not the image of Chinatown as unsanitary was accurate, the perceptions of image makers intent on characterizing the area as *alien* were the ones that continued to have consequences" (Anderson, 1987, pp. 587–588; emphasis added).

A second key perception was of Chinatown and Chineseness as immoral. Chinese people were viewed as chronic gamblers who were lawless, inscrutable, evil, and addicted to opium. Immorality was seen as naturally a Chinese characteristic and a feature of Chinatown. Thus, when prostitutes moved in, "an especially evil construction was cast upon the practice only in 'Chinatown'" (Anderson, 1987, p. 592), even though there were other niches where prostitution was tolerated. Likewise, the anti-opium league of Chinatown also called for federal assistance to prohibit the importation, manufacture, and use of opium, "[b]ut try as some merchants did to counter the idea of Chinatown, the drug that Britain had introduced to China in the 1840s was now a powerful metaphor for neighborhood definition" (Anderson, 1987, p. 592). Even when White people abused opium, this confirmed "the belief that Chinatown was a menace to civilized life" (p. 592). Thus, because Chinese people were racialized as unsanitary and immoral, Vancouver's Chinatown came to signify "all those features that seemed to set the Chinese irrevocably apart....[Chinatown] embodied the white Europeans' sense of difference between immigrants from China and themselves" (Anderson, 1987, p. 594).

Similarly, with respect to San Francisco's Chinatown, Craddock (1999) documents how Chinese people and Chinatown were pathologized by medical discourse that located smallpox and syphilis within the Chinese community and thus constructed Chinese bodies as "intrinsically diseased" (p. 352) because of their "un-American practices, physical characteristics and language" (p. 357). Even the ways that the Chinese body occupied space (i.e., overcrowding and poor living conditions in Chinatown) "confirmed its subhumanness" (p. 359; see also Ealham, 2005) in the eyes of medical experts at the time. Chinatown in San Francisco subsequently occupied a "marginalized position within San Francisco's political cartography" (Craddock, 1999, p. 353). This is a key contribution of Craddock's work (1999) and one that is especially relevant for this chapter, for not only was Chinatown marginal, but it was also undesirable and therefore needed to be excised because it "endanger[ed] the otherwise healthy city" (p. 349). Likewise, Ealham (2005) shows how Chinatown in Barcelona was portrayed as an alien space that "defied the mores and civic spirit that prevailed in the rest of the city" (p. 376). Constructing Chinatown as a cancerous tumour that needed to be removed and/or as a space that was in complete opposition to the civilized city and even the nation "[recast] urban America as racially homogeneous (i.e., white)" (Craddock, 1999, p. 353). Coupled with Anderson's (1987) demonstration of how Vancouver's Chinatown was viewed as a menace to society, these examples illustrate how this space was perceived as outside of the nation and its residents as foreigners and not citizens.

Recently, there has been a shift or, more accurately, an additional dimension in how Chinatown is being constructed. Anderson (1990) discusses the case of Chinatowns in Melbourne and Sydney. These spaces are now being held up as "ethnic expressions par excellence" (p. 137), and that within a context of celebrating multiculturalism, Chinatown has become "a symbol of difference to be protected rather than censured" (p. 138). Indeed, the same could be said for Chinatowns in Canada, such as in Toronto or Vancouver. Anderson (1990) illustrates, however, that despite this relatively positive view of Chinatown, White Australia continues to approach Chinatown and Chinese people based on the assumption of a singular Chinese race, and Chinese people remain an Other against which White Australians are defined. While Chinatown is being embraced as proof of a multicultural, non-racist Australia, the Chinese body remains necessarily outside of the nation through racialization and multiculturalism rhetoric, which reproduces the view of mainstream society as White and Others as merely contributors but rarely as primary authors or decision-makers. Furthermore, in the case of the revitalization of two Chinatowns in Australia, how this redevelopment was imagined, the acceptable symbols of ethnic diversity, and the process through which Chinatown was reinterpreted continued to be based on "the belief in a Chinese race—and the sense of separation upon which that belief relied" (Anderson, 1990, p. 8). Chinatown was viewed as a "product and symbol of some essential 'Chineseness,' some inherent difference against which mainstream Australia was set" (Anderson, 1990, p. 11). Thus, even within a context of celebrating diversity and official multiculturalism, Chinese people and Chinatown continue to be constructed as outside of the nation.

Though Anderson's (1990) argument is specific to Australia, it is reasonable to suggest that the simultaneous production of White, normative citizens, of the foreign and alien Chinese, and of Chinatown as outside of the nation are applicable to other contexts as well. Furthermore, the emergence of Severe Acute Respiratory Syndrome (SARS) in 2003 demonstrated how the historic construction of Chinatown as diseased continues to resonate. Eichelberger (2007), for example, shows how SARS and Chinatown came to be conflated in New York because of the ongoing depiction of Chinese communities as diseased and dangerous. Similar findings were reported in a study of the social impact of the SARS crisis on the Chinese and other Asian communities in Toronto. Specifically, respondents reported being victims of alienation, discrimination, and harassment due to stereotypes of Chinese people being dirty and the source of disease (Leung & Guan, 2004).

It is important to recognize that while Chinatown is constructed as homogeneous both within and between different Chinatowns, there is considerable variability among them. In particular, Chinatowns that have emerged in the suburbs are quite different from the downtown Chinatowns, in terms of the language spoken, periods of migration, and socio-economic status, to name a few. Furthermore, these downtown Chinatowns have also changed considerably over time. In Toronto, for example, the urban Chinatown has shifted a number of times before its establishment at the Spadina and Dundas intersection. In addition, Toronto's downtown Chinatown is now dominated by Chinese-speaking Vietnamese, with only a few Toisanese patriarchs remaining (Pon, 2000). Despite the heterogeneity of urban and suburban Chinatowns, the construction and representation of Chinatown remain surprisingly uniform across time and space. Chinese people and Chinatowns, be they urban or suburban, are still constructed as foreign and outside of the nation, and looked upon with suspicion. For example, with the development of Pacific Mall in a suburb of Toronto, Pon (2000) describes the local mayor's speech on behalf of White residents who felt besieged by the influx of Chinese residents, businesses, and visitors. In other words, there were too many Chinese. This feeling resulted in an exodus or White flight out of the neighbourhood.

Still, the ongoing social construction of Chinatown does not exclusively exemplify how race has and continues to structure the lives of Chinese people in Canada. Rather, the long history of Chinatown's social construction and the tenacity of these representations signal the continuous production of Canada as a White settler society. A White settler society is one that begins with "the dispossession and near extermination of Indigenous populations by the conquering Europeans ... [and] continues to be structured by a racial hierarchy" (Razack, 2002, p. 1). In such a society, White people are automatically conferred the benefits of citizenship, while people of colour must earn their citizenship through appropriate behaviour, only to have it revoked at any time because they represent a potential threat to the calm, orderly space of the original citizens. That Chinatown is consistently defined and represented as external to the nation—a place to contain alien residents and their strange culture, and where foreigners should stay (as opposed to citizens, who can move freely throughout the nation)—illustrates how the social construction of Chinatown helps to reinforce the image of Canada as a White settler society.

Nevertheless, Chinatown can also serve as a site to destabilize this image and narrative of a White settler society. Though Chinatown is socially constructed, it is actively used, lived in, and claimed by its residents or those who are thought to or feel that they belong there. For example, despite the White flight resulting from the development of Pacific Mall, Pon (2000) presents the mall as a site of resistance and of Chinese consumption, as a refusal to be erased or to defer to White flight, and as Chinese entrepreneurs' claim to Canada. Specifically, Pon (2000) focuses on Chinese youth he observes at Pacific Mall who seem to demonstrate comfort and pride in their Chineseness, particularly through their consumption of Cantopop. Based on these observations and an analysis of a popular Cantopop song, Pon (2000) concludes that the Chinese listeners of Cantopop "seem to remark 'Too bad! We're here and we won't be erased! We love who we are, our community, our Chineseness, our language, and our Cantonese pop singers! So get over it!'" (pp. 228–229). Such resistance is important because, as Pon (2000) notes, it counters the model minority stereotype that is consistently applied to Chinese people specifically and to Asian people in general as a way to simultaneously commend a minority group while marginalizing them and reproducing the notion that Canada is a White settler society into which minority groups must constantly seek acceptance. I suggest that this resistance and claim to the nation and citizenship is reflected in the relationship between the NACIVT participants and Chinatown.

CHINATOWN AS HOME

Just as the Chinese youth in Pon's (2000) study project an image of resistance and bold assertion of confidence, pride, and presence within a Canadian context, the NACIVT participants, in their relationship to Chinatown, also make a claim of belonging to the nation. For many participants, Chinatown is the home to which they return. They describe Chinatown and their relationship to this place in a way that articulates a homing desire (Brah, 1996), and in doing so they root themselves within the nation. The feeling of nostalgia for Chinatown-as-home has grown in recent years as the traditional tournament sites are less able to accommodate the rising popularity of the event. Frequently, the tournament is held in a convention centre or a parking lot that is close to Chinatown. However, playing in Chinatown creates an atmosphere that cannot be reproduced in other spaces. Lisa (all names are pseudonyms), for example, explained how playing in the streets of Chinatown felt "more authentic" since shopkeepers would watch the games, and the backdrop of her opponents would be "a Chinese restaurant with, you know, barbequed duck in the window [laughs]." Because of this unique atmosphere, one that cannot be recreated, tournament organizers and long-time players expressed regret over not being able to hold or attend the tournament in the heart of Chinatown, and nostalgically recalled previous tournaments that were held on the streets of Chinatown and supported by Chinatown residents.

For others, the significance of Chinatown as the site of the tournament went beyond ambience as described by Lisa. In Michael's words, the tournament "brings back the Chinese Americans that have no contact with the Chinese, that move out into the suburbs.... This is the first time that they have a chance to go back to their roots." Implicit in his comment is the view that the tournaments are for those Chinese who have moved away from the urban core, and by participating in the NACIVT, are returning to their roots in Chinatown. Situating the downtown Chinatown as the home of Chinese suburbanites was reinforced by participants who viewed the suburbs as devoid of Chineseness. James explained that he grew up in an outlying area of Toronto and consequently had never heard of the NACIVT. He was introduced to the sport as a university student. However, he was certain that had he grown up in downtown Chinatown, he would have automatically learned of and played the sport. Adam reiterated this point, claiming that those Chinese volleyball players who grew up in the suburbs would have no knowledge of the NACIVT. Thus, the suburbs were interpreted by a number of participants, and portrayed within the stories repeated in the tournament booklet, as a location that lacked authentic Chineseness, while the urban Chinatown was the site of Chinese people and their roots.

The significance of rooting Chinese people in Canada and the U.S. in downtown Chinatowns and this homing desire for urban space becomes apparent in relation to literature that focuses on migration and immigrants, specifically those that take a transnational approach. There is a tendency to privilege the relationship between home and away, or the "home one migrates *from* and the home one migrates *to*" (Trotz, 2006, p. 40; emphasis in original). The result is a concentrated exploration of the duality of immigrant life, and of how immigrants are caught in, negotiate, or flexibly traverse the dyad of home and away, origin and settlement, sending and receiving country, and so on (Trotz, 2006). This home-and-away binary is complicated by the positioning of Chinatown in the imaginations of the informants. Several participants indicated that they or other Chinese youth in the tournament lived in suburban areas that were far from the historic downtown Chinatown. The tournament, therefore, offered them an opportunity to be in Chinatown again. It was a place seen as authentically Chinese—not a stand-in for the China they had never known.

Destabilizing the home-and-away binary is also critical for undermining the forever immigrant trope that is prevalent within the narrative of a White settler society. People of colour are frequently presumed to be immigrants. Providing answers like "Winnipeg" or "Boston" to the question "Where are you from?" are often brushed aside with a follow-up query of "Where are you *really* from?" By claiming urban Chinatown as home, the presumed sites of *home* and *away* shift away from, and therefore call into question, racist assumptions about who is a citizen. The NACIVT participants are thus rejecting the forever immigrant/never a citizen category because the place to which they are rooted is not away but rather firmly entrenched within Canada and the U.S.

PLAYING VOLLEYBALL AS A CLAIM TO CITIZENSHIP

Just as racism formed the foundation of the social construction of Chinatown and, in turn, located and bound Chinese people within its confines, racism also plays a role in constructing physical activity spaces as White and Asian bodies as incongruous with these spaces. This relationship is enacted by stereotyping Asians as effeminate, cowardly, weak, physically inept, and therefore unsuited for physical education or sport. Furthermore, this generalization is made to seem innocuous and natural through the model minority myth, which constructs Asian people as high achievers with a strong interest in education. While complimentary, this stereotype subsequently naturalizes the presumption that Asians are disinterested in physical activity and sport. As a result, Asian bodies can be prevented from using or even evicted from physical activity spaces through outright hostility, as recounted by Millington (2006, as cited by Millington et al., 2008; Pon, 2000). In fact, social exclusion is precisely the reason why the NACIVT began on the streets of Chinatown.

The earliest NACIVT players were Chinese male laundry workers, whose leisure time and disposable income were limited because of their socio-economic circumstances. Volleyball was an ideal sport because it allowed a large number of people to participate and did not require specialized equipment. Players used a rope or string in lieu of a net, marked out the boundaries of the court by using stones or drawing lines, and fashioned a ball out of cloth. As the years passed, players attempted to access mainstream physical activity spaces, but were excluded or were denied permits to host the tournament in mainstream facilities (see also Yep, 2010), leaving them no choice but to continue playing in the streets. Though such experiences of blatant exclusion were not personally recounted by current players, they nonetheless continued to encounter and even internalize stereotypes about their Asianness and physical and sport capabilities.

For example, John belonged to mainstream teams outside of the NACIVT and was often the only Asian player on the team, club, or even league—as is the case of many NACIVT players. He recalled feeling "singled out, 'Oh yeah, the Chinese guy, [John]' or whatever and just the stigma attached to it. Like with any other team too they'll say, 'Okay, Asian guy's on the court, don't serve [to him], you know he's a good passer.'" He explained that Asian players are often perceived to be good only at defence because they are small and therefore quick, but have limited offensive skills. In John's case, even though his Asian physicality was constructed in narrow and limited ways, he was still able to access and excel in the mainstream volleyball system. Other players, however, may not be able to overcome these stereotypes. This struggle is reflected in Christie's attempt to join a Regional Volleyball Association (RVA) when she was 18:

> I think that the RVA is racist too. If you're not 5'10", blonde hair and blue eyes, you will not make an RVA team. Okay, I'm generalizing and making assumptions, but honestly, when I tried out, they know that I had skill, but I wasn't tall enough.

Christie proceeds to explain that now, several years later, she is approached by RVA players who admire her skill and talent and is asked what RVA team she plays for, assuming that she must have developed her abilities in the mainstream volleyball system. She recalled with pride how surprised these players were to learn that she has never played on an RVA team, and that it is her NACIVT coach who saw her potential and took the time to mould her into the athlete she is today.

This story helps to illuminate the perceived importance of the NACIVT for Asian players whose physiques may not fit the ideal image of talented volleyball players. Through high-level coaching and intense practices, the NACIVT provides opportunities for "athletes who don't fit the cookie cutter mold of 6 feet tall, 5'11" volleyball players" (Christie) who dominate mainstream White volleyball leagues and circuits. For example, Christie remarked that an increasing number of NACIVT players who are below or just 6 feet tall are playing key roles on men's interuniversity volleyball teams. She believes that through the NACIVT, "they've had the opportunity to learn technique and training so they can get their vertical that tall or get their blocks down so they can compete against guys who are 6'5". So that's a big difference." On mainstream volleyball teams, Asian players may not even get selected, let alone learn and develop their abilities, because of stereotypes of limited or lack of skill. This exclusion could lead to internalization of these stereotypes, even among those players who resist such generalizations. For example, having successfully competed among White players for most of his volleyball career, Kyle joked that when he first learned about the NACIVT, he assumed that he was "probably better than any other Asians out there." Similarly, John expected the calibre of play in the NACIVT to be low precisely because it was an all-Asian setting.

Being stereotyped as disinterested in physical activity or sport or, worse, incapable, while still evidence of racism, may seem relatively minor compared to, for example, racial violence or being denied housing or employment. The significance of being stereotyped as inept at physical activity and sport participation becomes apparent when considered through the prism of the nation/sport/citizen triad. Nation-building, sport, and citizenship-building are connected to one another in a number of ways. For example, sport has been used as a vehicle for civilizing natives and building the nation in imperial projects. In the case of volleyball, this activity is rooted in a history of imperialism through its relationship to the Young Men's Christian Association (YMCA). The game was invented in 1895 at a YMCA in the U.S. and quickly spread across the world through the various YMCA schools and societies in Canada, the Philippines, China, Japan, Burma (Myanmar), India, and several Latin American countries (McGehee, 1997; The volleyball story, www.fivb.org/EN/volleyball/story.htm). Volleyball was perceived as critical in building the character of foreign and immigrant men and spreading muscular Christianity, or the "Christian commitment to health and manliness" (Putney, 2001, p. 11). When the U.S. colonized the Philippines, the YMCA worked closely with the colonial government to ensure that the sport curriculum civilized the natives, uplifted those who were deemed inferior, and imparted American values. Volleyball, in particular, was seen as an ideal vehicle for teaching values such as democracy, teamwork, sacrifice for the good of the whole, obedience to a coach, and a strong work ethic (Gems, 1999). Sport thus serves as a medium for teaching and performing citizenship (and civilized) skills.

NACIVT participants take advantage of this relationship, using sport to simultaneously debunk stereotypes about Asians, demonstrate citizenship, and gain social status. The significance of being skilled at sport as a marker of social status (Bourdieu, 1978; White & McTeer, 1990) is reflected in Michael's story of his son and his experiences in sport:

> My son is very smart and very capable. You know when he was in high school, he was a good student. He gets As. But he doesn't participate in sport. He says "The only way I could outdo the Caucasians is through sport because that's the only thing they look at. They know the Chinese is smart." So he played baseball and football and he became a good player. So now he gains the confidence. "I can beat you in anything." You know so [the NACIVT] is one way for us to take pride in ourselves and say, "Hey, we're good at something," have that knowledge.

Later, Michael explained that his family was the first Chinese family to move into the neighbourhood where his children grew up. When his son began attending school, Michael asked him if there were other Chinese children in his class. His son responded, "What do they look like?" Michael laughingly said that at the time, his son did not know he was Chinese. Clearly, he later came to understand himself and who Chinese people were in relation to Caucasian students based on stereotypes that were imposed and voluntarily taken up. Thus, the NACIVT provides an opportunity for his son and for other Asian players to debunk these stereotypes and to demonstrate that they are more than academically oriented—they are also skilled and confident athletes.

The demonstration of Asian athleticism is a critical way to illustrate citizenship because sport is a way through which the strength of citizens can be conditioned, performed, and assessed. Not surprisingly, physical education has historically been considered a key element of nation-building because the vitality of citizens is believed to measure and reflect the strength of the nation (Harvey, 2001; McNeill, Sproule & Horton, 2003; Okay, 2003). Through sport and physical activity participation, individuals demonstrate strength, health, vigour, and athleticism, and these qualities are perceived to project an image of a nation that is strong and that can defend itself and win against others. Thus, success at international sporting events, especially the Olympics, is inextricably tied to nation-building as athletes demonstrate the physical primacy of their nation in a legitimate and universally sanctioned forum.

In addition to physical prowess, good citizenship has come to be linked to certain moral qualities and skills, such as responsibility and productivity (Harvey, 2001), characteristics that can be learned through sport. For example, Eley and Kirk (2002), in their study of the psychosocial characteristics of participants in a sport-based volunteer program, conclude that "sport provides an avenue to learn social responsibility, leadership skills and confidence for life" (p. 165). In the case of the NACIVT, players from hosting cities, for example, are expected to take up leadership positions such as coaches, tournament chairs, or organizing committee members; to volunteer their time for fundraising, set-up, marketing, and other tasks; and to train and manage volunteers. In doing so, they exhibit the qualities associated with good citizenship. When Asian people are denied the chance to participate in sport, they are also prevented from developing and demonstrating citizenship skills. While they are excluded from mainstream sport opportunities, particularly institutionalized sport, players' participation in the NACIVT gives them an opportunity to learn organizational leadership and management skills, which facilitate development of citizenship.

Yep's (2010) study of Chinese playground women basketball

players provides additional evidence of the value of sport for Asian people in accessing citizenship. Through their participation, these women "[carved] out an empowering space against the context of poverty, racism, and the multiple forms of patriarchies in their lives" (Yep, 2010, p. 123). Furthermore, their experiences illustrate important ways through which sport provided a chance to demonstrate citizenship skills, an invaluable opportunity in light of the exclusion the women faced in sport and beyond. Specifically, these working-class women were "unwelcome on their school teams" (Yep, 2010, p. 123), and racially segregated in Chinatown. They were paid low wages, lived in poor housing conditions, and faced negative representations of Chinese-American women in the media, racial prejudice, and limited gendered expectations. Participation in basketball helped the women create a sense of community, self-esteem, assertiveness, and self-confidence, as well as develop decision-making abilities. The women also crafted through their sport participation what Yep (2010) calls different kinds of femininities, such as forming unions, joining labour movements, organizing strikes, joining clubs, fundraising, and public leadership, activities that I suggest also demonstrate citizenship skills.

While I have argued that the NACIVT provides a medium for teaching and exhibiting citizenship, it is necessary to recognize that sport and citizenship do not always promote social inclusion (Harvey, 2001). That the nation/sport/citizen triad provides the rationale for using sport as a vehicle for projects to colonize foreign bodies has already been noted. Harvey (2001) adds that sport can also "divert citizens away from their civic duties, distract the underprivileged classes, or provide fertile terrain for the spread of chauvinism" (p. 25) and other forms of oppression. Importantly, the presumed positive aspects of the relationship between sport and citizenship are usually unquestioned, thus contributing to the oppression that can result from the nation/sport/citizen triad. For example, through participation in the NACIVT, it is a masculinist citizen that is being claimed. Women's matches continue to be less valued, and women often take up supportive roles, such as fan, team manager, or "mother hen" as one former player-turned-supporter described herself, so that men may continue to play or participate in respected leadership roles. Admittedly, the vitality, strength, athleticism, power, and speed that were most celebrated in the NACIVT were those of the male players and of the men's nine-man game. Nevertheless, there are an equal number of women's and men's teams; many established clubs have both men's and women's teams; efforts are made to ensure that men's and women's final championship matches are not scheduled simultaneously; and there were observed instances of fans admiring the skills, power, and abilities of women players at the Toronto tournament.

Conclusion

The inability to access recreational spaces, which ultimately led to the formation of the NACIVT, and the marginalization of Asian players within mainstream White volleyball structures need to be contextualized within a history of exclusion. Lowe (1996) argues that the American institution of citizenship necessitated the legal exclusion and disenfranchisement of Asian immigrants, making their citizenship within national culture an impossibility. This is especially true in the case of Chinese people in Canada and the U.S., since they were excluded from entering these nations because of race. They have, therefore, been constructed outside of the nation, historically barred from its soil and its citizenry (see also Leung & Guan, 2004; Li, 2003). In light of the historical links between physical education and nation-building (Okay, 2003; McNeill, Sproule & Horton, 2003), the perception that Chinese men did not belong in recreational spaces during the early beginnings of the NACIVT, and the continued perception that Asians do not belong in physical education spaces (Millington et al., 2008), are manifestations of the eviction of Asian bodies out of the nation in both the U.S. and Canada (Park, 2007).

With this nation/sport/citizen triad in mind, I suggest that the model minority myth, which positions Asians as not sporty, unfit, passive, and timid, reinforces the view of Asians as outside the nation and justifies equating Asianness with foreignness by the implication that they are unfit to be citizens. Together with the exclusion of Chinese men from physical activity spaces that marked the beginning of the NACIVT, the model minority myth plays a role in the continuity of Asian exclusion from the nation. By looking through the lens of the nation/sport/citizen triad, it is clear that the NACIVT and Chinatown are alternative cultural spheres (Lowe, 1996) that illuminate how exclusion from mainstream sport and racialization both within and outside of sporting realms occurs. The NACIVT is a site where claims to citizenship and national belonging can be demonstrated. First, participants can learn, practise, and hone a number of aspects of hegemonic citizenship, such as volunteerism, community-building, and co-operation, and exhibit strength, vitality, health, and victory. Second, participation in the NACIVT is also a sign of citizenship in the nation because its history provides evidence of the rootedness of Chinese and Asian people in Canada and the U.S. and their role in nation-building. It also magnifies the participants' homing desire for Chinatown. The significance of this marker of roots is undeniable when considered in relation to the persistent question "Where are you *really* from?" This query presumes that one has no history in Canada and the U.S. The NACIVT, along with its history and connection to Chinatown, root Asian people in the nation and acts as a claim of belonging. It is an alternative cultural space that calls into question narrow and racialized understandings of who counts as a citizen.

Questions for Critical Thought

1. This chapter suggests that playing sport in public spaces is a way to make a claim to the nation and demonstrate citizenship, and that this is particularly relevant for racialized people

who are constructed as outside the nation and therefore not citizens. Does this argument hold true for other racialized groups, such as young Black men who play basketball on an outdoor public court?
2. The nation/sport/citizen triad can reproduce masculinist citizens through the celebration of the strong, aggressive, powerful athlete. Women athletes who display these characteristics may feel pressure to prove their femininity. Consider how race, gender, and sexuality intersect through the nation/sport/citizen triad to produce a White, masculinist, and heternormative citizen.
3. Consider racialized athletes like Ben Johnson, Carol Huynh, and Daniel Igali. How does the nation/sport/citizen triad operate differently in these instances?

References

Anderson, K.J. (1987). The idea of Chinatown: The power of place and institutional practice in the making of a racial category. *Annals of the Association of American Geographers, 77*(4), 580–598.

Anderson, K. (1990). "Chinatown re-oriented": A critical analysis of recent redevelopment schemes in a Melbourne and Sydney enclave. *Australian Geographical Studies* [Now *Geographical Research*], *18*(2), 137–154. Retrieved from http://onlinelibrary.wiley.com/doi/10.1111/j.1467-8470.1990.tb00609.x/pdf

Bourdieu, P. (1978). Sport and social class. *Social Science Information, 17*(6), 819–840.

Brah, A. (1996). *Cartographies of diaspora: Contesting identities*. London: Routledge.

Craddock, S. (1999). Embodying place: Pathologizing Chinese and Chinatown nineteenth-century San Francisco. *Antipode, 31*(4), 351–371.

Ealham, C. (2005). An imagined geography: Ideology, urban space, and protest in the creation of Barcelona's "Chinatown," c. 1835–1936. *International Review Social History, 50*, 373–397.

Eichelberger, L. (2007). SARS and New York's Chinatown: The politics of risk and blame during an epidemic of fear. *Social Science & Medicine*, 65(6), 1284–1295.

Eley, D. & Kirk, D. (2002). Developing citizenship through sport: The impact of a sport-based volunteer programme on young sport leaders. *Sport, Education, and Society*, 7(2), 151–166.

Gems, G.R. (1999). Sports, war, and ideological imperialism. *Peace Review*, 11(4), 573–578.

Glesne, C. (1999). *Becoming qualitative researchers: An introduction* (2nd ed.). New York: Addison Wesley Longman.

Harvey, J. (2001). The role of sport and recreation policy in fostering citizenship: The Canadian experience. In Canadian Policy Research Networks (Ed.), *Building citizenship: Governance and service provision in Canada* (pp. 23–46). Canadian Policy Research Networks Inc. Retrieved from www.cprn.org/documents/29305_en.pdf

Hsiung, P. & Raddon, M. (2005). Lives and legacies: A guide to qualitative interviewing. Unpublished manuscript. Retrieved January 8, 2005 from http://courseware.utoronto.ca

LeCompte, M.D. & Schensul, J.J. (1999). Analyzing and interpreting ethnographic data. Book 5 of Ethnographer's Toolkit. Walnut Creek: AltaMira Press.

Leung, C. & Guan, J. (2004). Yellow peril revisited: Impact of SARS on the Chinese and Southeast Asian Canadian communities. Chinese Canadian National Council. Retrieved from www.ccnc.ca/secionentry.php?entryid=6&type=campaign

Li, P.S. (2003). The place of immigrants: The politics of difference in territorial and social space. *Canadian Ethnic Studies*, 35(2), 1–13.

Lowe, L. (1996). *Immigrant acts: On Asian American cultural politics*. Durham: Duke University Press.

Marcus, G.E. (1995). Ethnography in/of the world system: The emergence of multi-sited ethnography. *Annual Review of Anthropology*, 24, 95–117.

McGehee, R.V. (1997). Volleyball: The Latin American connection. *International Council for Health, Physical Education, Recreation, Sport, and Dance*, 33(4), 31–35.

McNeill, M., Sproule, J. & Horton, P. (2003). The changing face of sport and physical education in post-colonial Singapore. *Sport, Education, and Society, 8*(1), 35–56.

Millington, B., Vertinsky, P., Boyle, E. & Wilson, B. (2008). Making Chinese-Canadian masculinities in Vancouver's physical education curriculum. *Sport, Education, and Society, 13*(2), 195–214.

Okay, C. (2003). Sport and nation building: Gymnastics and sport in the Ottoman state and the Committee of Union and Progress, 1908–18. *International Journal of the History of Sport, 20*(1), 152–156.

Park, H. (2007). Constituting "Asian women": Canadian gendered Orientalism and multicultural nationalism in an age of "Asia rising." Unpublished doctoral thesis, Ontario Institute for Studies in Education of the University of Toronto, Toronto.

Pon, G. (2000). Beamers, cells, malls, and Cantopop: Thinking through the geographies of Chineseness. In C. James (Ed.), *Experiencing difference* (pp. 222–234). Halifax: Fernwood Publishing.

Putney, C. (2001). *Muscular Christianity: Manhood and sports in Protestant America, 1880–1920.* Cambridge: Harvard University Press.

Razack, S. (2002). When place becomes race. In S. Razack (Ed.), *Race, space, law, and the unmapping of a White settler society* (pp. 1–20). Toronto: Between the Lines.

The volleyball story. (n.d). Retrieved from www.fivb.org/EN/volleyball/story.htm

Trotz, D.A. (2006). Rethinking Caribbean transnational connections: Conceptual itineraries. *Global Networks, 6*(1), 41–59.

White, P. & McTeer, W. (1990). Sport as a component of cultural capital: Survey findings on the impact of participation in different types of sport on educational attainment in Ontario schools. *Physical Education Review, 13*(1), 66–71.

Yep, K.S. (2010). Playing rough and tough: Chinese American women basketball players in the 1930s and 1940s. *Frontiers: A Journal of Women Studies, 31*(1), 123–141.

CHAPTER 9

An Intersectional Analysis of Black Sporting Masculinities

JANELLE JOSEPH

Black masculinities form a prominent aspect of Canadian sporting culture. Mainstream sport icons, sport apparel advertising, and televised sport are conservative institutions that largely reproduce a narrow view of Black athletic masculinity, including hypermasculine, apolitical characters. Highlighting activities on the periphery—that is, non-dominant sport, sideline behaviours, or the narratives of retirees—allows us to recover alternative models of Black masculinity (Carrington, 2010; McKay, Messner & Sabo, 2000) because it brings attention to the many other social categories that influence the performance of racialized, gendered cultural scripts. The purpose of this chapter is to show that a study of Black sporting masculinities in Canada requires an intersectional analysis that recognizes (1) the interdependence of race and gender performances; (2) the importance of thinking beyond nations, since the borders of the nation-state do not contain Black communities; and (3) the significance of generational differences (i.e., age and immigration status) among members of a diaspora. I examine Black masculinity by drawing on two ethnographic research projects with Black Caribbean-Canadian male athletes in non-dominant sport—cricket and *capoeira* (Brazilian martial arts).

This chapter highlights similarities and differences within what is conceptualized as a unified and uniform "Black Atlantic." I draw from the theories of Paul Gilroy (1993), who conceptualizes the Black Atlantic as a region encompassing the Caribbean, the United States, and the United Kingdom, and argues that streams of migrants, experiences of economic exploitation and political racism, feelings of displacement, and flows of transnational Black vernacular culture within this region account for a shared sense of community and identity. For example, he describes music as the "'raw materials' supplied by the Caribbean and black America" (p. 81) that created a distinct mode of lived Blackness among Britain's Black settlers. This musical heritage was the primary expression of "cultural distinctiveness, which this population seized upon and adapted to its new circumstances" (p. 82). I similarly use sport supplied by the Caribbean and Brazil to examine the (c)overt racial, political, and gendered messages shared among men who perform a Black identity in Canada. Sport, like music, was "instrumental in producing a constellation of subject positions that was openly indebted for its conditions of possibility to the Caribbean, the United States, [Brazil] and even Africa" (Gilroy, 1993, p. 82). Here, I move beyond Gilroy's work to explore not merely the unifying elements of Black diasporas, but also their internal differences and the ways they are indelibly marked by local Canadian conditions.

I begin with a review of literatures concerning intersectional analyses and sporting Black diasporas. I then summarize the research methods used before showing alternative sport as settings for Black men's identity performances, which are informed by the national and diasporic affiliations, class positions, age, and generation (of immigration).

Intersectional Analyses of Racialized Masculinities

Masculinity and femininity are not based on innate biological categories; rather, they are performances contingent on shared cultural scripts (Butler, 1990; Alexander, 2006); for instance, staged gender drag performances highlight ways of doing gender (Connell, 2005). As Butler states, in *"imitating gender, drag implicitly reveals the imitative structure of gender itself.…* [W]e see sex and gender denaturalized by means of a performance which avows their distinctness and dramatizes the cultural mechanism of their fabricated unity" (1990, p. 175; emphasis in original). In other words, staged gender drag exaggerates quotidian gender performances and decouples them from biological sex, drawing our attention to the performative nature of gender.

Similar to gender drag, the social construction of race is revealed in the spectacle of Black(face) performances, which depend upon cross-racial interactions and Black performative cultural capital (Alexander, 2006). Majors (1990) and Ross (1998) have suggested that Black male performances as tough, strong, cool, and aloof operate as defensive responses to White racism. However, Alexander (2006) argues that Black masculinities should not be understood merely as reactions to racism and feelings of powerlessness. Despite structural oppression, Black men have agency and perform their identities in relation to a constellation of cultural resources, historical scripts, and gender privileges.

Sport provides a central stage to both reiterate and challenge gender and racial scripts. Those sports associated with the British Empire were established as a means of inculcating not only masculinity, but also Whiteness. For example, cricket in the 19th and early 20th centuries is commonly described as a key male homosocial institution, a space for the middle classes to learn the manly virtues of war without weapons, fair play, mental vigour, obedience, and determination. Cricket participation also enabled men to understand a legitimate claim to dominance over women—particularly in the face of first-wave feminism—and importantly, dominance over Blacks within the British Empire (Hall, 2002; Seecharan, 2006). In contrast, the Brazilian sport of *capoeira*, in this same time period, has been shown to be a venue for Black and lower-class men's indoctrination into the important values of *malandragem* (trickiness), *cultura da rua* (street culture), *vadiação* (idleness), and *liberdade* (freedom) (Assunção, 2005; Talmon Chvaicer, 2008). In this context, Black performances cannot be understood outside of societal racism, which limited opportunities for employment and power, and cultural scripts that restricted women's and gays' participation in street activities.

In 1982, Hazel Carby noted that much of the literature on masculinity fails to explore the relationship between gender and race, racism, ethnocentrism, and sexual politics. The intersections were first articulated as a theory by Crenshaw in 1989. Since then, many scholars, particularly within diaspora studies (Abdel-Shehid, 2005; Anthias, 1998; Hall, 2006), have echoed the importance of intersectional understanding—that is, a simultaneous examination of the influence of multiple social categories on power, culture, and politics.

To date, issues of age or generation receive short thrift within intersectional analyses. Yet, the transnationalism literature (e.g., Portes & Rumbaut, 2001; Park, 1999; Levitt & Waters, 2002) has repeatedly demonstrated that older and younger immigrant men may eat different foods, listen to dissimilar music, have a wide or narrow range of ethnic diversity among their friends, and carry more or less influence from the homeland. As this chapter will show, age and generation of immigration are central to leisure practices, the particular ways in which sport is engaged, and the discourses that accompany sport performances.

In addition, nation and diaspora are critical dimensions of Black Caribbean identity given the legacy of the trade in enslaved Africans, subsequent migratory flows, and transnational cultural currents that create Black subjects within and across many nation-states. In 1998, Floyas Anthias directed the study of race and ethnicity to a diasporic framework. Rather than focus on processes of assimilation and integration on one hand, or ethnic conflict and structural disadvantage on the other, Anthias (1998) examines racial and ethnic groups in terms of their internal diversity because "different groups within the overall category will have different political projects; this may include the crosscuttings of gender, class, political affiliation and generation" (p. 564) and different external connections that result in "a new identity becom[ing] constructed on a world scale which crosses national borders and boundaries" (p. 560). Similarly, Edwards (2001, p. 64) excavates the intellectual history of the term "Black diaspora" and reminds us that it was "introduced in large part to account for difference among African-derived populations." A diasporic framework draws attention to migratory and cultural currents and the ways differently positioned members of the group variously take up certain cultural resources. Therefore, any study of diaspora necessitates an intersectional analysis. In the following section, I show how the notion of diaspora has been applied in the study of Black nationalisms and the sociology of sport.

Sporting Black Diasporas

The concept of the Black diaspora has recently been used by scholars who foreground issues of multiple- and supranational attachments in discussions of the ways race is linked to the production of nationalisms. To draw from Paul Gilroy's (1993) text, *The Black Atlantic*, is now customary in studies of Black cultures. Gilroy's work highlights the creation of a racial subjectivity that "cannot be confined within the borders of the nation state" (1993, p. 85). Carrington (2010, p. 58) notes that "most of the iconic moments in African American sporting history occurred *outside* of the United States." He adds that the politics of race and sporting successes of Americans Jack Johnson in Australia or Muhammad Ali in Zaire (now Democratic Republic of the Congo), for example, must be read "diasporically in order to understand how nominally 'national' star athletes come to have a global significance that both alters their relationship to their countries of origin and enables transnational forms of identification to be established" among members of the Black diaspora. Carrington (2010) explains that beginning in the late 19th century, racist logic defined Black men as inferior to Whites in every way, including physically. But sport afforded otherwise marginalized men a powerful cultural platform from which to publicly display their masculine traits, including strength, stamina, and sacrifice, within an otherwise limited structure of opportunity (Majors, 1990). It was through undeniable physical prowess, particularly pugilism, that Black men rallied marginalized ethnic communities and struck fear among Whites globally, secured a sense of manhood, and challenged racist stereotypes of Black inferiority (Carrington, 2010). In turn, sporting success, explosive physical expression, and rounds of verbal sparring came to be characteristic of performances of Black masculinity.

Research on the Canadian setting addresses a major gap in Gilroy's formulation. For example, Abdel-Shehid (2005) has incorporated a Black diaspora framework into Canadian sport studies to demonstrate the complex relationship between colonial histories, nation-states, racism, diasporic connections, and racialized athletic performances. Abdel-Shehid shows that a "both/and" (not an "either/or") position—with respect to roots (attempts to establish permanence) and routes (experiences of travel)—is essential to understanding Black athletic masculinities in Canada. He argues that "in addition to rarely referencing the world outside the United States, much of the work on black male athletes largely neglects black masculine performativity and complicity within other systems of domination" (Abdel-Shehid, 2005, p. 20). Using a Black diaspora framework combined with queer and feminist theory, Abdel-Shehid demonstrates that Black masculinity is defined in mainstream discourses as occupying the realm of the natural, as opposed to the cultural. McKittrick (2006, p. 99) also argues that Black Canadians are outernational, that is, always named as "Caribbean or U.S. [which] unhinges black people from Canada . . . it also reifies ideologies around nation-purities by insisting that black communities are non-Canadian, always other, always elsewhere, recent, unfamiliar and impossible" (McKittrick, 2006, p. 99).

The success and failure of sprinter Ben Johnson highlights the outernational discourse that accompanies media representations of Black masculinities in Canada. At the time of the 1988 Olympics in Seoul, Korea, Johnson was not only a young Canadian man, he was also a Jamaican-born Black immigrant. Many Caribbean Canadians, especially Jamaicans, other Canadians, and Blacks around the world worshipped Johnson as a hero. After testing positive for steroid use and being stripped of his gold medal, Johnson's disgrace cast a shadow on all Caribbean-born Black sprinters (Jackson, 2004) and, arguably, all Black Canadians. Jackson demonstrates how "the Ben Johnson crisis [was] constituted by, and constitutive of, the broader crisis of identity" in Canada (1998, p. 22). A diasporic analysis of the Johnson case would take into consideration multiple simultaneous national attachments and supranational, racial identities. Such an analysis was conducted of Black Canadian-British boxer, Lennox Lewis. McNeil (2009) uses Gilroy's themes of nationalism, double (or poly)consciousness, and Americocentricity to chart the polyvalent Black identity Lewis performs in and through sport.

The Black diaspora concept was also helpful for James (2005) to denote the attachment to more than one national space in a case study of a 21-year-old Caribbean-Canadian athlete in Toronto, Canada. He demonstrates the complicated nature of ethnicity and national belonging, de-territorialized home(s) and identities, youth and the importance of sporting success as cultural capital. James does not consider the development of a masculine sporting identity as a gendered response in racist Canadian society, however. The importance of the intersections between gender and race, along with age and diaspora, are explored in two sport ethnographic case studies below.

Research Methods: Mavericks Cricket and Ginga *Capoeira* Case Studies

The first case study involves older men aged 44–74 (mean age 61 years), who are members of a group I call the Mavericks Cricket and Social Club (MCSC; all group and individual names are pseudonyms used to protect participant anonymity). These men migrated to the Greater Toronto Area (GTA) in Ontario, Canada, from various Caribbean territories (mainly Antigua, Barbados, Guyana, Jamaica, and Trinidad). They grew up obsessed with playing and watching cricket, a sport described by Yelvington (1995) as a signifier of regional pride and masculine aptitude in the Caribbean. Because of the international success of the West Indies team and "the prominence and prowess of West Indians who were otherwise racially and economically marginalized," cricket also became "a crucial cultural form—or forum—for West Indian racial issues" (Hartmann, 2003, p. 459). MCSC members brought their passion for cricket with them when they migrated and continue to play friendly (non-league) games, primarily with other men from their homelands. For 21 months in 2008–2009 I carried out 29 formal (digitally recorded) interviews, made systematic observations, engaged in casual conversations at MCSC weekend games, participated in social activities such as dances and picnics, and made two-week tours to Caribbean (and diasporic) locations (e.g., Christchurch, Barbados and London, England) along with MCSC members.

The second case study presents an assembly of younger Black Caribbean-Canadian men who play, teach, and perform the Brazilian martial art, *capoeira*, in the GTA with a multicultural group I call *Ginga Capoeira* (GC). These men were of the 1.5 (i.e., child migrants) and second generations (i.e., born in Canada to migrant parents), and were of Barbadian, Jamaican, and Vincentian heritage. All were between 28 and 42 years of age. They encountered *capoeira* in their twenties and have been playing and, in some cases, teaching for over a decade. I have participated in this *capoeira* group since 2001, and the data presented below are based on ongoing ethnographic research since 2004. I conducted nine interviews in 2005 and 13 in 2010 with GC members of many ethnicities, and made observations when I attended classes two or three times each week; went to special workshops with *mestres* (masters of the art) visiting from Brazil and the United States; observed and performed in presentations at festivals, weddings, on the street, and in parks; and participated in social events such as group members' birthday parties and barbecues.

In both cases, interviews were transcribed verbatim and my observations, conversations, and reflexive thoughts were recorded daily in field notes. Transcripts and field notes were subsequently analyzed for emergent themes. These two case studies were selected more for their similarities than their differences. The participants engage in two completely different sports—cricket is a bat-and-ball game of colonial English origins, while *capoeira* is a dance and martial art of African descent—and are of two different age groups and immigration statuses (when MCSC members were migrating to Canada in the 1970s, GC members were just being born). However, all use their sporting practices to perform what they believe to be authentic Blackness; to navigate dominant and subordinate forms of masculinity; and to negotiate their Canadian and supranational identities. In the following sections I show ritualized, imaginative rediscoveries of Black masculinities that must be read as celebrations of culture, resistance to dominant racisms, performative reactions to gendered social expectations, age-specific social worlds, and manifestations of national and diasporic affinities.

Adopting Dominant Gender and National Discourses

Hegemonic masculinity is a constellation of practices that articulate White male dominance over women and subordinate (working-class, Black, homosexual) men. Sport is a homosocial environment within which masculine superiority—defined by characteristics such as physical strength, mental acuity, successful competition, heroic leadership, and personal self-sacrifice—is supported and reproduced (Connell, 2005). Black men use success in sport settings to access and express their masculine traits. Distinctive of Caribbean men's sports is how the audience receives (attempts at) athletic feats. Burton's (1995) analysis of the social history of Caribbean cricket demonstrates that the carnival or *fête* (party) style of playing and watching cricket is part of masculine Caribbean identity and heritage; cricket crowds exaggerate street culture, spending their afternoons in loud and unruly jesting and joking. Games in the Caribbean diaspora are sites for similar gender performances.

During the Mavericks' cricket games, I observed spectators celebrating achievements, often yelling out in surprise, "Hey, he still got it!" when players hit balls for fours and sixes (over the boundary marker that surrounds the field), ran or threw the batsman out, or dove to make a catch. The spectators also found great joy in deriding players who made on-field mistakes. "I tink him hit a home run off you!" one player yelled out to another who was bowling. His reference to the baseball term "home run" suggested that the ball had been bowled so poorly it was "pitched." The bowler yelled back, "What would you know about home runs?" alluding to the innuendo between "hitting a home run" and having sexual intercourse. Everyone within earshot chuckled, but not as loudly as after they heard the spectator's retort: "You mus' ask you wife." The intersecting performances of the men's cultural heritage, age, gender, and sexual identities are revealed here. To say he is a baseball player rather than a cricket player casts doubt on an older Black Caribbean man's athletic, gender, and racial authenticity. As far as they are concerned, cricket is the only sport a real Black man of their generation plays. Second, claiming sexual possession of another man's wife is a means of asserting heterosexual status and constructing women as sexual objects, thereby reinforcing their patriarchal privilege.

These men define their cricket spaces in relationship to who is *not* playing—that is, women. Women's exclusion from and subordination within male sporting cultures is another means of reproducing masculinity among the Mavericks. One spectator exclaimed, "A woman dat! [That is a woman!]" when a fielder dropped an easy catch. In C.L.R. James's (1963) description of Caribbean culture, he recounts his aunt Judith's creation of regular feasts after local cricket matches. The fact that she died sitting at the festive table after working from the early morning to prepare the meal goes without a gendered analysis; however, socially constructed masculinity and femininity are key to the ways MCSC cricket is enjoyed. After most games, the club provides all players and spectators with a free traditional Caribbean meal that a few of the players' wives have spent the day preparing. In their cricket spaces, masculinity is defined as those who eat but do not cook curry goat and rice. There are some exceptions to this. For example, Ciskel, an older Guyanese man, is well known for his jerk pork specialty, which he prepares for some of his close friends. And if there is a barbecue, male club members are typically the ones standing in front of the fire. Nevertheless, female club members, excluded from playing, contribute to the creation of a Caribbean home space at the cricket grounds by cooking and serving food. These Black male athletes are therefore complicit in systems of domination that subordinate women.

Connell explains that the "constitution of masculinity through bodily performance means that gender is vulnerable when the performance cannot be sustained—for instance, as a result of physical disability" (2005, p. 54). Open derision of men who show age-related physical decline on the pitch reinforced the importance of masculine physicality. On one occasion, spectators engaged in a vituperative exchange over a ball that a fielder attempted to stop with his foot and ended up kicking to the boundary for four runs: "Ah wha' dis 'tall?! [What is this?!] Dis not football, you hear?!" "You noh see he ol'? Looka bandage 'pon de man foot" "Come off de fiel' noh man! You frail, frail, frail!" Flailing arms and pacing accompanied these types of comments, which were shouted from around the boundary to players standing in the field. Speaking in a loud volume, exaggerating disbelief, call-and-response, and repetition to add emphasis are Caribbean vernacular linguistic strategies deployed to discursively construct Caribbean gender identities (see Gadsby, 2006). In this case, Black masculinity is constructed in relation to age and ability.

As Rogers (2001, p. 177) points out, although Black Canadians are less preoccupied with racism than African Americans, due to a lack of long experience with segregation either in the Caribbean or in Canada, this does not mean that Black Canadians are oblivious or indifferent to racial discrimination. Rather, Black Canadians may publicly praise Canadian dominant discourses of tolerance, but choose to share negative racial experiences among friends and family. The space around the boundary at cricket matches is one location where talk of racism occurs. MCSC members recognized the systemic injustices they faced and shared these with their visiting opponents from the Caribbean, England, and the U.S. Their painful stories were typically positioned as "in the past," "in the '70s," and "when I first come." For example, while sitting around the boundary at one game, Douglas, a 58-year-old Jamaican Canadian, told a story of his first job in Canada as a security guard at a small company. His supervisor slowly started asking him to do other menial tasks, such as taking out the garbage and cleaning windows, although these were not part of his job description. Finally, when he was moved from the indoor position for which he was hired to stand outside the building, he had had enough:

> He tink I'm an idiot, like I don't know he's taking advantage. I told him where to go. I told him "fuck off" right to his face and went to *his* supervisor. No way all the White guys gonna sit dere in dey cushy seats while I runnin' all over the place an' standin' outside [in] wintertime like a jackass . . . Dey wouldn't dare treat a Black man so blatant now.

Douglas does not claim that racism has disappeared entirely, but that it is less blatant today. Kaiso, an immigrant from St. Lucia agreed: "We are more multicultural now, so you see things are more fair." Their respective moves from security guard and mechanic to police officer may have something to do with the perception that Canada is less racist.

Police harassment and racial profiling have been regarded as prime examples of racism in Toronto (Wortley & Tanner, 2003; Williams, 2006). In 2002, Toronto's most circulated newspaper, the *Toronto Star*, published a series of articles that revealed Black Torontonians are more likely to be searched, detained, and held in custody for a bail hearing than their White counterparts (Rankin et al., 2002). The police vehemently denied these allegations. Some of the MCSC cricketers and spectators are current or retired Black police officers who at once deny racial profiling, yet suggest that some Black men are "subject to greater levels of criminal justice surveillance than others," which is the very definition of profiling, according to Wortley and Tanner (2003, p. 369). When I asked MCSC club members about racism among the police, one Jamaican MCSC spectator indicated:

> I don't see de problem. If a Black man in a blue car [is] wanted for rape and murder, I *want* de police to pull over every Black man in a blue car til dey fin' him. You tell me what wrong wit dat? Pull *me* over. I didn't do it! (Monty)

Another, from Barbados, insisted:

> I myself am gonna be suspicious if I see a young Jamaican man, say 16, with hip-hop baggy jeans and $1,500 rims on his car. You can call it racism, stereotyping, or what, but I'm thinking to myself how can he afford that? (Jacob)

These racist assumptions of criminality and poverty among Black men, especially youth, are typical of conversations that occur around the boundary at MCSC cricket matches or in pubs after games, where Black men create individual and collective narratives around local political issues, thereby constructing their racial identities (May, 2000). Some club members' representation of the state as (former) police officers who are unable to see their own ideas as racist is representative of Sherene Razack's (2004, pp. 7–8) understanding of how race and racism disappear in the law and national memory: "violence directed against bodies of colour becomes normalized as a necessary part of the civilizing process." Similar to Canadian soldiers in Somalia in Razack's analysis, the Toronto Police—including Black officers—are engaged in "a race war waged by those who constitute themselves as civilized, modern and democratic against those who are constituted as savage, tribal, and immoral" (Razack, 2004, p. 86).

Conversations among Black Caribbean-Canadian and Black American men at cricket games reveal some of the subtle differences between racism in these countries. Players from the U.S. describe ongoing segregation in their cities, such as Atlanta, Georgia. Barney, a Jamaican American who regularly comes north to play cricket, told MCSC members: "When you come down, you just have to know which side of the tracks to stay on," suggesting that violence could befall a Black man who enters the wrong side of Atlanta. Accounts from their American peers "emphasize the notion that racism and discrimination persists as a problem that African-Americans continue to encounter every day" (May, 2000, p. 212). Many of the MCSC players and spectators, in contrast, described racism in Canada as "more so in the past" (Warlie).

In sum, male club members who have "lost [some of] it" use the cricket space to demonstrate that they have "still got it"—that is, markers of Black masculinity: physical skills, quick wit, and women to attend to their culinary desires. Their performance of a Black masculine identity also includes their self-definition as law-abiding, middle-class, *older* Black Canadians who were subjected to racism in the past, but who now enjoy a "more fair" multicultural society. The younger generation of Black Caribbean-Canadian men uses a different sport to perform masculinity in different ways, and is wary of claims of improvements in Canadian racial tolerance.

Challenging White Masculinity and Anti-Black Racism in Canada

Claiming racial space in Canada often involves participation in multicultural festivals where ethnic minorities demonstrate their costumes, cuisine, and corporeal cultures. Eva Mackey (2002) refers to such multicultural festivals as "pedagogies of patriotism" (p. 72) because festivals teach audiences (and participants) to be Canadian though discovery of cultural pluralism and tolerance of ethnic Others. The multicultural festivals Mackey studied are contrasted with unmarked Canada Day celebrations: "the music or dancing of the 'ethnic' groups was often twinned with their nation's name and labels such as 'traditional', 'cultural' and folkloric.' ... [Those] who are different [not White] become located in a distinct conceptual space, as 'other' to that unmarked norm. They are defined by their cultural *difference from* what is simply 'normal'" (p. 106; emphasis in original). During multicultural performances, members of the *capoeira* group, GC, demonstrate their cultural difference as they reject a hegemonic ideal of White masculinity that proscribes singing and dancing. *Capoeira* originated among enslaved African men in Brazil. Players' quests for *liberdade* (freedom) are symbolized through the lyrics of many of the songs that accompany the physical movements—a combination of dancing and fighting—which are performed in a circle of participants called a *roda*.

When they perform *capoeira* and related Afro-Brazilian dances (such as *samba*), GC members display their muscular bodies, move sensuously, complete acrobatic movements, and indicate their difference from the unmarked, White Canadian man. One White English-Canadian participant commented:

> In a lot of ways [*capoeira* is] the antithesis of what [White] North American boys are taught to do. There's singing, there's dancing, there's gymnastics, there's music, and all those things stereotypically are frowned upon for boys to be a part of. (Gigante)

Gigante contrasted dominant Canadian physical activities, such as hockey or lacrosse, in which men learn to move their bodies in aggressive, space-occupying, linear, masculine ways, with the spectacle of *capoeira*, in which the sporting body is objectified and therefore feminized. Black GC capoeiristas' sinewy, naked torsos, superior drumming skills, and rhythmic bodily contortions reinforce assumptions about innate racial difference.

Although they show an outernational affiliation through their performance of authentic Brazilian culture, Black GC members are quick to celebrate the Canadian dimension of their sport. For instance, in a public space such as Queen's Park in Toronto, performing this African-based martial art at the foot of the equestrian statue of King Edward, ruler of the United Kingdom in the early 20th century, metonymically links these Black men to the nation. Though it may be some time before a Black hero is commemorated with a similar statue, *capoeiristas* transform the White space of the park with their music and movements, claiming it as their own. Vão, who was born in Canada to Black Jamaican immigrant parents, explained to me that performing in Queen's Park or for children in schools during Black History Month (February) is important to him as a Canadian. He had very few Black role models as a child, but when he first saw *capoeira*, he felt proud:

> It was a great experience when I first saw it because there — they had an Afro-descendant so it really hit home when I watched it.... I was just amazed how they could use all the instruments and be so aggressive and really it was an expression.... [T]hat's what caught me.

He started training immediately and hopes to inspire another generation of Canadian students or audience members. During 2007, when debates about Africentric schooling as the solution to counter high Black student dropout rates in Toronto filled the media (e.g., see Okonkwo, 2007; Brown, 2007; "Separate" 2007), Vão claimed, "If we can get [*capoeira*] into the schools, we can use it to teach music, drama, history. Yeah guy, Canadian history! ... There was slavery here too!" He continued:

> You have to know your history, especially people that— let's say from African descent—they should know what they're studying [or watching] and even people from non-African descent, it's even better for them to know. It frees their minds even more worldwidely.

Vão is adamant that *all* Canadians improve knowledge of *their* history by learning about *capoeira*, slavery, and Afro-Brazilian culture: "We're multicultural, right? So why not learn about every culture? ... Jamaicans ain't goin' nowhere. Brazilians ain't goin' nowhere. So you know what I'm sayin'? We might as well get to know each other."

Gato Preto, a 1.5 generation Jamaican Canadian, concurred and delivered a speech at the end of one performance to "free their minds" as he asked audience members to shift the focus from the Black Brazilian Other to the Black Canadian Self. He said: "This art is from slave times in Brazil, but it's important today too because the songs are about freedom, liberation. The Black people, all people overcoming adversaries right here in Toronto today." In other words, GC members use festivals to teach Canadian audiences about themselves and the many cultures, and "adversaries" that exist in Canada.

Afrofest, an annual African and Black diaspora cultural festival in Toronto, was the site of one GC performance, which ended with a *samba roda* (dancing *samba* in a circle). I witnessed a group of young Black boys who watched the show in awe approach Sombra, a second-generation Barbadian Canadian to ask how he did the *samba* dance step. He taught the boys his footwork and encouraged them to move their hips. I asked him about the encounter afterwards and Sombra insisted that by seeing men dance in an expressive and sensual way, the audiences at GC shows benefit from alternative strategies for performing manliness. "It's not gay, it's Brazilian—that's totally different. They need to know the difference." Sombra's homophobia is revealed by his desire to distinguish unacceptable "gay" dancing and the "Brazilian" movements he endorses. He makes the limits of alternative masculine performances within GC clear. While young Afro-Caribbean men celebrate alternative (non-White) styles of movement, Alexander (2006, p. 75) notes that due to "the security, power, and attention that come from embodying phallocentric Black masculinity, there is strong resistance by those who have adapted this form to alternative [non-heterosexual] models." Again, Black men who face a range of discriminations are also, at times, perpetrators of discursive violence against other subordinate masculinities.

Most *capoeira* students in GC are aware of stories of Blacks playing *capoeira* in the streets of Brazil despite legal prohibitions, and of using the rhythms of the music to signal the arrival of police. The freedom *capoeira* offered enslaved Africans, and subsequently low- to no-income Black Brazilians, is translated by GC members to mean freedom from racist oppression in Canada. Vão explains his experiences with racism as a youth in the Greater Toronto Area:

> Being Black was tough because teachers would look at you differently, teach you differently. The bus driver would make sure you've got the right change before you enter the bus, women on the train would hold their purse tighter. Yeah, people would get off elevators—it's not even their stop—and people would get off because you're in the elevator ... racism will always be here [in Canada]. (Vão)

In their text entitled *Cool Pose*, Majors and Billson (1992) explain that, when denied access to mainstream avenues of success, Black men in the United States use other strategies to combat racism and create their own voice. Alternative corporeal demonstrations of pride, strength, and control are the hallmarks of a "cool pose," which brings "a dynamic vitality into the Black male's everyday encounters, transforming the mundane into the sublime and making the routine spectacular" (1992, p. 2). The flamboyance, trash-talking, and slam dunk of basketball are examples of how Black males symbolically oppose the dominant White group, bring attention to themselves, and disguise their insecurities through sport (Majors, 1990). *Capoeira* can serve a similar function. Vão explained, "I was never any good at basketball.... Some people draw, sing, ... capoeira is the tool that I use to express myself." The flamboyance expressed in the style of *capoeira* that Vão and his peers perform is called *floreio*. Neither attack nor defence necessarily, the movements are demonstrations of acrobatic explosion and gravity-defying strength and flexibility that symbolize social freedom.

In addition to these symbolic displays of freedom, Black-Canadian *capoeira* players use their sporting spaces to discuss racism. The following short anecdote from my field notes provides an example:

> After class tonight a group of students were chatting outside the academy, and as is typically the case, one student demonstrated an impressive combination of movements, followed by another student's description of a means to counter-attack. One by one we put down our bags, and without music started an informal *capoeira roda*. Sombra, a Black Barbadian-Canadian male student, suddenly took on the persona of a police officer: "Boop, boop!" he cried, imitating the sound of police sirens. He walked directly through the *roda*, halting the action, and approached Curioso, the lone White student. He asked in a snooty voice, "Ah, excuse

me, young man, what's going on here? Is everything ok? Are these hooligans disturbing you? What's this fighting going on?!?" He pretended to search for a walkie-talkie on his belt and said to himself, "I need back up." As Sombra proceeded to feign a frantic hunt for his billy club, the other Black men continued acting out the scene and cursed the police officer in a rant of expletives in Caribbean Patois language before everyone present burst out laughing.

This episode characterized several stereotypes of the Toronto Police's Black racial profiling techniques and negative relationships between young Black men (both in Canada and Brazil) and police officers. Up until the early 20th century, Black male bodies were constructed as threats to White womanhood and, by extension, White civilization. Within this logic, Black men were defined as Other, the antithesis of the friend and neighbour—not White, not innocent, and not civilized (Abdel-Shehid, 2005). The assumption that Black youth who gather in a group are potential criminals is an example of how race is produced and performed in the Greater Toronto Area. Making a joke of the automatic assumption that Curioso was a victim of Black crime provides an example of "reverse humour," which, according to Weaver (2010, pp. 32–33), relies on "an earlier discourse that uses identical signs but which employs these signs for a reverse semantic effect . . . the polysemicity of this humour represents its transformation into 'commonsense' anti-racist critique." Reverse humour is used here to deal with the pain of gendered racism in Toronto. In contrast to the older MCSC, middle-class Caribbean immigrants who have employment and social ties to the police and the nation-state, the young working-class men of GC, most of whom were born in Canada, remain at odds with the nation-state. In real encounters they would not challenge or curse police officers. *Capoeira* is the tool they use to perform resistance and discuss racism, even if only for/among an audience of their peers.

Capoeira spaces are critical sites for Black-Canadian identity formation due to the activity's history as "a black alternative to hegemonic Western, Eurocentric values" (Assunção, 2005, p. 24). The significance of music and dance in the creation of Black diasporic communities and identities cannot be dismissed; they are what Gilroy (1993, p. 75) calls "pre- and anti-discursive constituents of black metacommunication." The worldwide migration of Black cultural forms, from hip hop to jazz, *samba* to *capoeira*, help create a transnational Black identity. An intricately webbed network has developed that leaves Black-Canadian men drawing from (supra)national stocks of knowledge to generate a gender identity. They are connected to Canada, their nation of residence, their ancestral African homeland cultures, and a Brazilian sporting space, putting them both within and outside Gilroy's Black Atlantic.

Gendered Racial Identity in Canadian Sport

Carrington (2010) argues that Canadian class-centric hegemony theorists, such as Richard Gruneau (1999), suggest that sporting practices, particularly at the recreational level, do not challenge the existing social order. However, Carrington (2010, pp. 35–36) points out that their analyses:

> miss out on precisely those forms of sporting resistance to the logics of contemporary commodified sport, that, for example, can often be found within Black recreational sporting spaces through which sports become a modality for self-actualization and the reaffirmation of previously abject identities.

This chapter elucidates the possibilities for understanding how dominant cultures are embraced and resisted via the performances of race, gender, and nation through an examination of non-dominant recreational sport settings.

The two case studies presented here show the complexity of Black masculinities in sport settings. There is no single notion of Black masculinity found among Black-Canadian male athletes; rather, a constellation of masculine rituals, practices, vernacular, and behaviours comprise their identities. Furthermore, age and generation of immigration, significant factors that are often overlooked in discussions of Black masculinity, are shown here to be salient to performances of race and gender. The cricket and *capoeira* players, to borrow Gilroy's (1993, p. 19) words, transcend both the structures of the nation-state and the constraint of national particularity, yet they remain embedded in nation state discourses (for example, multiculturalism) and national particularities (for example, racial profiling). Black Canadians, though welcomed into the polity, have their belonging in Canada constantly questioned (McKittrick, 2006) and therefore often turn to outernational cultural forms, homelands, and ethnic communities for a sense of belonging. Black-Canadian cultural forms of style and communication can be used to signal a Canadian consciousness, yet they rely on diasporic affiliations to the U.S., the U.K., the Caribbean, and Brazil. At the same time, Black-Canadian men may challenge the belonging of women and gays, revealing the disjunctures of diaspora.

It is the deep structure of race in our culture that influences how participants understand themselves and their sporting practices as different. Black men's knowledge of their own subordinated masculinity leads to a performance of a variety of resistance practices, including unique patterns of speech, walk, style, and flair in sport settings. The dominant images of Black athletes, which typically celebrate Black physical superiority, sensuality, and great bodily—but not mental—self-control are, on the one hand, racist one-dimensional images that strip Black athletes of agency, exaggerate their social differences, and reinforce the status quo, as Hartmann (2003) contends. On the other hand, when athletes embrace an ability to move their hips sensually or shout out to their peers and see these acts as resistant to dominant—that is,

White Canadian—ways of being masculine, they use their agency to generate space to challenge dominant gender scripts.

These men advocate seemingly contradictory notions of the nation as multicultural and racist. Indeed, sport, like Canadian culture more broadly, is both of these simultaneously (Mackey, 2002; Thobani, 2007). The cricket and *capoeira* players discussed in this chapter challenge the political balance of Canadian society by putting a Black expressive form in plain sight and emphasizing the histories of their activities despite Canada's desire to silence and erase Blackness from its national narratives, thus making the complexity of Black-Canadian geographies visible (McKittrick, 2006). Sport is productive and not merely receptive of racial discourse, and this discourse has material effects both within sport and beyond (Carrington, 2010). In cricket and *capoeira* settings, race is *made* in Canada.

In conclusion, it is impossible to understand Canadian culture without attending to Black cultures, particularly sport, which challenge the ideological underpinnings of the nation. Alternative sports are settings in which heterosexual Black-Caribbean men construct their identities in opposition and in relation to women, gays, and White men through their understanding and experiences of racism and multiculturalism, and by embracing and challenging stereotypes. In examining these sports, it is integral to inspect the intricate web of cultural and political connections that bind Blacks here to Blacks in other locations. The use of a diaspora lens opens up new ways to study race and gender. Neither is fixed; rather, race and gender are constantly being negotiated, contested, performed, and destabilized in and through national and diasporic discourses.

Questions for Critical Thought

1. Which factors in Black men's lives influence, promote, or prevent their sport participation? How are these factors different from men of other ethnic groups?

2. How might women (wives, girlfriends, daughters, and friends) influence the performances of race and gender depicted in this chapter?
3. Consider the ways in which you have negotiated your own gender and racial identities. How are your performances tied to a range of national contexts?

References

Abdel-Shehid, G. (2005). *Who da man? Black masculinities and sporting cultures*. Toronto: Canadian Scholars' Press Inc.

Alexander, B.K. (2006). *Performing Black masculinity: Race, culture, and queer identity*. Lanham: AltaMira.

Anthias, F. (1998). Evaluating "diaspora": Beyond ethnicity. *Sociology*, 32, 557.

Assunção, M.R. (2005). *Capoeira: A history of an Afro-Brazilian martial art*. New York: Taylor and Francis.

Brown, L. (2007, November 10). Black only but don't use the 'S' word. *Toronto Star*, retrieved November 18, 2007 from www.thestar.com/news/ideas/article/274911

Burton, R.D.E. (1995). Cricket, carnival, and street culture in the Caribbean. In H. Beckles & B. Stoddart (Eds.), *Liberation cricket: Windies cricket culture* (pp. 89–106). New York: Manchester University Press.

Butler, J.P. (1990). *Gender trouble: Feminism and the subversion of identity*. New York: Routledge.

Carby, H. (1982). White woman listen! Black feminism and the boundaries of sisterhood. In Centre for Contemporary Cultural Studies (Ed.), *The empire strikes back: Race and racism in 70's Britain* (pp. 211–234). London: Hutchinson & Co.

Carrington, B. (2010). *Race, sport, and politics: The sporting Black diaspora*. Thousand Oaks: Sage.

Connell, R.W. (2005). *Masculinities* (2nd ed.). Cambridge: Polity Press.

Crenshaw, K. (1989). Demarginalizing the intersection of race and sex: A Black feminist critique of anti-discrimination doctrine, feminist theory, and antiracist politics. *University of Chicago Legal Forum,* 1989, 139–167.

Edwards, B.H. (2001). The uses of diaspora. *Social Text, 19,* 45–73.

Gadsby, M.M. (2006). *Sucking salt: Caribbean women writers, migration, and survival.* Columbia: University of Missouri Press.

Gilroy, P. (1993). *The Black Atlantic: Modernity and double consciousness.* Cambridge: Harvard University Press.

Gruneau, R. (1999). *Class, sport, and social development.* Champaign: Human Kinetics.

Hall, M.A. (2002). *The girl and the game: A history of women's sport in Canada.* Toronto: University of Toronto Press.

Hall, S. (2006). New ethnicities. In B. Ashcroft, G. Griffiths & H. Tiffin (Eds.), *The postcolonial studies reader* (2nd ed., pp. 199–202). New York: Routledge. (Original work published 1989.)

Hartmann, D. (2003). What can we learn from sport if we take sport seriously as a racial force? Lessons from C.L.R. James's *Beyond a boundary. Ethnic and Racial Studies, 26*(3), 451–483.

Jackson, S.J. (1998). A twist of race: Ben Johnson and the Canadian Crisis of racial and national identity. *Sociology of Sport Journal, 15*(1), 21–40.

Jackson, S.J. (2004). Exorcizing the ghost: Donovan Bailey, Ben Johnson, and the politics of Canadian identity. *Media, Culture & Society, 26*(1), 121–141.

James, C. (2005). I feel like a Trini: Narrative of a generation-and-a-half Canadian. In V. Agnew (Ed.), *Diaspora, memory, and identity: A search for home* (pp. 3–18). Toronto: University of Toronto Press.

James, C.L.R. (1963). *Beyond a boundary.* London: Stanley Paul and Co.

Levitt, P. & Waters, M.C. (2002). *The changing face of home: The transnational lives of the second generation.* New York: Russell Sage Foundation.

Mackey, E. (2002). *The house of difference: Cultural politics and national belonging in Canada.* New York: Routledge.

Majors, R. (1990). Cool pose: Black masculinity and sports. In M. Messner & D. Sabo (Eds.), *Sport, men, and the gender order: Critical feminist perspectives* (pp. 109–114). Champaign: Human Kinetics.

Majors, R. & Billson, J. (1992). *Cool pose: The dilemmas of Black manhood.* New York: Lexington Books.

May, R.B. (2000). Race talk and local collective memory among African American men in a neighborhood tavern. *Qualitative Sociology,* 23(2), 201–214.

McKay, J., Messner, M.A. & Sabo, D. (2000). Studying sport, men, and masculinities from feminist standpoints. In. J. McKay, M.A. Messner & D. Sabo (Eds.), *Masculinities, gender relations, and sport* (pp. 1–11). Thousand Oaks: Sage.

McKittrick, K. (2006). *Demonic grounds: Black women and the cartographies of struggle.* Minneapolis: University of Minnesota Press.

McNeil, D. (2009). Lennox Lewis and Black Atlantic politics: The hard sell. *Journal of Sport and Social Issues, 33,* 25–38.

Okonkwo, C. (2007, November 13). Diversity, not separation, in schools. *Toronto Star,* AA6.

Park, K. (1999) "I really do feel I'm 1.5!": The construction of self and community by young Korean Americans. *Amerasia Journal, 25,* 139–163.

Portes, A. & Rumbaut, R.G. (2001). *Legacies: The story of the immigrant second generation.* Berkeley: University of California Press.

Rankin, J., Quinn, J., Shephard, M., Simmie, S. & Duncanson, J. (2002). Police target Black drivers. *Toronto Star* (October 20), A1.

Razack, S. (2004). *Dark threats and White knights: The Somalia affair, peacekeeping, and the new imperialism.* Toronto: University of Toronto Press.

Rogers, R. (2001). Black like who? Afro-Caribbean immigrants, African Americans, and the politics of group identity. In N. Foner (Ed.), *Islands in the city: West Indian migration to New York* (pp. 163–192). Los Angeles: University of California Press.

Ross, M. (1998). In search of Black men's masculinities. *Feminist Studies,* 24(3), 547–626.

Seecharan, C. (2006). *Muscular learning: Cricket and education in the making of the British West Indies at the end of the 19th century.* Kingston: Ian Randle Publishers.

Separate but equal again? (2007, November 8). *Toronto Star,* AA5.

Talmon-Chvaicer, M. (2008). *The hidden history of capoeira: A collision of cultures in the Brazilian battle dance.* Austin: University of Texas Press.

Thobani, S. (2007). *Exalted subjects: Studies in the making of race and nation in Canada.* Toronto: University of Toronto Press.

Weaver, S. (2010). The "Other" laughs back: Humour and resistance in anti-racist comedy. *Sociology, 44*(1), 31–48.

Williams, C.J. (2006). Obscurantism in action: How the Ontario Human Rights Commission frames racial profiling. *Canadian Ethnic Studies, 38*(2), 1–18.

Wortley, S. & Tanner, J. (2003). Data, denials, and confusion: The racial profiling debate in Toronto. *Canadian Journal of Criminology and Criminal Justice, 45*(3), 367–389.

Yelvington, K.A. (1995). Cricket, colonialism, and the culture of Caribbean politics. In M. Malec (Ed.), *The social roles of sport in Caribbean societies* (pp. 13–51). Amsterdam: Gordon and Breach.

CHAPTER 10

Athletic Aspirations: NCAA Scholarships and Canadian Athletes

SANDY WELLS

Introduction

There is a popular myth that National Collegiate Athletic Association (NCAA) scholarships provide a means for underprivileged and racially marginalized youth to access social structures of upward mobility, or that scholarships provide poor but talented student-athletes a way out of poverty and its associated stigmas and hardships.[1] In Canada, this trope circulates through sport media, high school sport culture, and popular culture in general, often personified in stories of athletes whose athletic talent secures a scholarship to an American university, a professional sport career, and other future rewards. These rags-to-riches stories both fuel and feed off of the aspirations of youth from racialized and poor or working-class families looking for a life that is different from that of their parents or peers, though the effects of these discourses rarely receive close scrutiny.

An exception is offered by Carl James (2003, 2005), who reports that young Black males in the basketball subculture of Greater Toronto Area (GTA) high schools come to view U.S. athletic scholarships as "the primary means by which they can expect to achieve their educational, occupational and career goals" (James, 2005, p. 102). Combined with the pervasive cultural image of tall Black men as natural athletes, as opposed to good students, James argues that discourses regarding U.S. athletic scholarships perpetuate a social order in which young, working-class, Black students understand their future success as dependent on sport. The troubling reality is, however, that the number of poor, racialized, sport-minded youth far exceeds the opportunities available through the NCAA scholarship system.

According to an NCAA report, less than 10 percent of U.S. high school athletes go on to compete in the NCAA, and even fewer receive some form of athletic financial aid (National Collegiate Athletic Association [NCAA], 2007). Coakley and Donnelly (2009) estimate that out of more than 200,000 NCAA Division I or II athletes, only 4.7 percent receive full athletic scholarships and most athletes (65 percent) receive no athletic aid (p. 328). For young Black students from poor or working-class U.S. schools hoping to play basketball in the NCAA, the situation is even less optimistic: it is estimated that about 1 percent of them "win the basketball lottery" and receive a scholarship to play and study (Sperber, 1995, p. 59). With this kind of competition for NCAA funding within the U.S., it is about twice as difficult for Canadian student-athletes to receive a scholarship to a U.S. university (Higgins, 2003, cited in James, 2005, p. 85).

Even this cursory analysis shows that social mobility through athletic scholarships is an unlikely outcome of sport involvement for poor and racialized youth. That this myth perpetuates in Canadian society has led scholars to argue that sport scholarships both rely on race- and class-based social inequalities for their intelligibility *and* solidify inequality by obscuring the need to attend to the structural social and institutional processes that perpetuate marginalization (Eitle & Eitle, 2002; James, 2003, 2005). What is more, the good-news scholarship stories also lead us to believe that they are exclusively about and for Black people from poor or working-class backgrounds who seek fame and fortune in the National Basketball Association (NBA), implying that White or middle-upper-class student-athletes in Canada, or those who do not aspire to lucrative professional sport careers, do not play a role in the classed and raced scholarship narrative. This chapter begins to address this oversight. Drawing on the theory of social distinction (Bourdieu, 1984), the work of Carl James (2003, 2005), and the interviews I conducted with former NCAA scholarship track-and-field athletes, this chapter makes two related arguments: first, that social class and race are fluid and relational concepts that influence the way student-athletes make sense of their athletic scholarship aspirations; and, second, that athletic scholarships help to reproduce and secure the classed and raced positions of relative privilege in Canadian society.

Scholarships and Social Distinction

To date, sociological discussions of athletic scholarships have been rare. Most accounts of NCAA sport have elaborated on the exploitative nature of high-profile, revenue-generating sport such as men's football and basketball, the primarily negative effects of such sport on most student-athletes, and on higher education in the U.S. in general (see, for example, Adler & Adler, 1991; Bryers & Hammer, 1995; Stack & Staurowsky, 1998; Sperber, 2000). In Canadian Interuniversity Sport (CIS), where commercial pressures are far less prevalent, more attention has been paid to the experiences of student-athletes (in psychology, see Miller & Kerr, 2002).[2] However, attempts to examine the experiences of Canadian student-athletes in the NCAA have only recently begun (in anthropology, see Dyck, 2010). The general dearth of scholarly work on the topic suggests that some thinking tools and strategies are required to help make sense of the roles sport scholarships play in the lives of Canadian youth. The theory of social distinction, developed by Pierre Bourdieu, is appropriate here because it provides concepts for understanding the forces that govern social action. These concepts—*field, habitus,* and *capital*—link the structural history of a particular context to the social history of a particular actor or group of actors in a given context. Thus, the theory of distinction helps us to think about the ways in which one's social history—class, race, education, gender, family organization, ability, age, etc.—interacts with the norms, discourses, and organizational apparatus that structure elite junior sport in Canada to shape which meanings, preferences, and practices are available to student-athletes.

We can think of the context as the *field,* or the social space, which helps to structure social action (Laberge, 1995). In this case, high school and elite sport cultures constitute the field in which student-athletes move and act. The rules, norms, and conventions of the field help to define how student-athletes come to understand what they want from school and sport, what is possible for them, and how to achieve it. But the field of elite junior athletics does not *definitively* structure all possibilities for meaning and action related to athletic scholarships. How student-athletes take up their position in the field of possibilities can both reproduce the social structures of a given field and challenge them, which opens the possibility for change.

The concept of *habitus* refers to an individual's propensity toward certain behaviours and tastes, which are acquired mainly from the social field(s) one inhabits. It can be thought of as the *style* with which one navigates social life, understands one's place within it, and pursues one's interests. Habitus is best understood, therefore, as "a model that makes social comportment intelligible" rather than as a causal explanation of it (Brown, 2006, p. 169). I use the concept of a scholarship habitus as a shorthand to denote a whole constellation of social beliefs, experiences, and attitudes, informed by the positions one occupies in Canadian society, that helps to explain how the same phenomenon—Canadians seeking U.S. athletic scholarships—can carry different meanings and implications according to the racialized and classed backgrounds of student-athletes.

Finally, the concept of *capital* denotes any material or symbolic good that presents itself as rare and worthy of being sought after in a particular cultural field. Bourdieu identifies different forms of capital that can be used by social actors: economic, cultural, social, and symbolic. Economic capital refers generally to money and wealth, cultural to accumulated knowledge from different upbringings and education, social to connections to influential people and institutions, and symbolic to reputation (Tomlinson, 2004). Capital helps to create the conditions that make any action more or less possible in a given field. Athletic ability, for example, is a salient form of capital within the field of high-level junior athletics in Canada because it confers on the holder a range of future possibilities (such as athletic scholarships) not available to all Canadian high school students. As we will see, class and race can also be seen as salient forms of capital that can give meaning to NCAA scholarships.

With these concepts in mind, I now turn to an examination of the field of elite junior track and field in Canada, the scholarship habitus of Canadian track athletes, and the ways in which these athletes' economic and social capital produces intersecting codes of class and race in and through their scholarship aspirations.

Reading NCAA Scholarships through Class and Race in Canada

As the introduction to this volume suggests, the official Canadian policy of multiculturalism can obscure or distract from the ways in which Whiteness, as the dominant racial category in Canada, is privileged in everyday life. Multicultural narratives promote the idea that people in Canada have equal opportunities for education, advancement, and success, regardless of their colour, ethnicity, religion, or citizenship/immigration status (James, 2005) when, in fact, markers of non-Whiteness and Whiteness continue to stratify Canadian society, keeping the promise of multicultural equality out of reach. I mentioned earlier that athletic scholarship narratives often centre on poor or working-class, non-White youth, typified in James's discussion of Black working-class student-athletes in the GTA. In comparison, Whiteness is not often highlighted as central to the choices made by White people. Whiteness is assumed to be incidental to, and not the explanation for, the actions, priorities, and motivations of White people. The invisibility of White privilege—and the hypervisibility of non-White status—affect how student-athletes understand their futures within the sport and school systems. This is what allows us to think of athletic scholarships as the primary tool, instead of scholastic achievement, for marginalized students to navigate the Canadian educational system.

However, an analysis of racial discourses in scholarship seeking is incomplete without a simultaneous understanding of class privilege. Ample evidence in the sociology of Canadian sport suggests that higher social class standing is associated with more and varied sport participation (White & McTeer, 1990; White & Wilson, 1999; Wilson, 2002). Canadian data also indicates that higher educational attainment and higher family income is correlated with higher rates of sport participation (Ifedi, 2008). In other words, a person's tendency to play sport, and the choice of which sport one plays, depends on cultural (education, occupation) and economic (income) capital. For example, the costs of junior-level sport climb as participation becomes more elite, making athletic development more difficult for young athletes whose families cannot afford the costs of this kind of sport participation, which can include club membership or coaching fees, specialized equipment, travel to tournaments and training camps, uniforms, and competition costs, among others. There are also demands on the time of parents or guardians to take young athletes to practices, competitions, or camps, and to do supplemental work such as fundraising, chaperoning, or serving on committees in the sport club organization. These demands require flexibility in the parents' work schedule and/or enough leisure time to make these tasks possible. As we will see, there is also significant benefit to having social networks that include skilled coaches or other influential "insiders." Thus, elite junior sport participation in Canada is structured to favour those with a significant amount of economic capital (to pay the costs of training and competition) and social capital (to know influential people in the sport development system).

In the discussion above, class and race in sport are treated as separate and self-evident reflections of family income/wealth or skin colour/ethnicity, but, in fact, class and race are complexly interrelated constructs invested with power according to how others perceive and relate to them. If we understand Whiteness and class respectability to be forms of power at the top of a social hierarchy, it becomes possible to understand them as connected and therefore to see how access to one form of power facilitates identification with the other, blurring the line between race and class (Roediger, 1999). For example, Gans (2005) shows how race operates as a marker of class in the U.S. by tracing how European immigrants effectively became White following their achievement of middle-class status. The Industrial Revolution in the U.S. required a large, low-wage workforce, which was filled largely by peasants from Europe. When they arrived, these very poor people were at the bottom of the class hierarchy and were categorized as non-White races: Italians, Irish, eastern Europeans, and southern Europeans. After the descendants of these immigrants became visibly middle class, the perception of their race changed as well: "The biological skin color of the second and third generations had not changed, but it was socially blanched or Whitened.... [They] became known as White ethnics" (Gans, 2005, p. 19). The privilege of racial invisibility—of Whiteness—is not merely a consequence of ethnic origin or skin colour or citizenship status, although these are important factors. Rather, Gans explains that Whiteness is also generated through the adoption of middle-class status, values, and lifestyles. Thus, disentangling considerations of class and race in social hierarchies is not a simple or particularly useful endeavour as they are inextricably connected to each other and are created simultaneously.

In sport specifically, race intersects with class to differently structure the social perceptions of, and opportunities for, student-athletes, as well as the cultural meanings invested in their sport participation. This makes NCAA athletic scholarships a compelling context for exploring the intersections of class and race that produce and secure positions of relative privilege among Canadian youth. The following section compares the NCAA scholarship narratives of two groups of former student-athletes in the GTA: the working-class Black basketball players described by James (2003, 2005); and the predominantly White, middle-class, track-and-field athletes I interviewed. Although both groups of student-athletes were committed throughout high school to obtaining an athletic scholarship to an NCAA university, the motivations and meanings for this pursuit differ according to the social status of the student-athlete. The working-class Black youth in James's study invested aspirational meaning in their basketball scholarships, seeing them as a way to achieve social status in a culture and school system that marginalizes them and their contributions (2003, 2005), while the White, middle-class student-athletes I interviewed understood athletic scholarships as a right-of-passage for talented youth like themselves. Rather than aspirational, athletic scholarships for these student-athletes were confirmatory, securing the social position they understood as natural to, and for, them.

Privilege at Play

In *Race in Play*, Carl James explores the idea that sport provides opportunities for socially and economically marginalized youth to climb socio-economic ladders. He interviews Toronto-area Black/African high school basketball players from working-class backgrounds who aspired to obtain athletic scholarships to NCAA universities.[3] James asked these players about their relationships to school and sport, and found that these student-athletes believed that basketball, rather than schooling, would provide them with the opportunities they would need to get ahead in life, such as winning the respect of others and getting into university. They were not as confident in their abilities to achieve the grades required to qualify for athletic financial aid in Canada (a B average is usually required to be eligible for athletic financial aid at a Canadian university), and they worried about carrying burdensome student-loan debt into their adult years. Consequently, playing basketball was prioritized over schooling, and their plans to obtain athletic scholarships became the focus of their school lives.

James (2005) argues that these attitudes toward schooling in Canada and U.S. athletic scholarships are telling. He contends that these perceptions are connected to "the marginalization, racialization, and assimilative structure of schools and society" in which non-White, non-middle-class traits, values, or preferences are defined as external to "Canadian culture" and therefore objects for assimilation or exclusion (2005, p. 101). In this context, James argues, non-White, working-class student-athletes (especially boys/men) do not see their own traits, values, and preferences reflected in the priorities and activities of their high schools and they therefore cannot see their futures as being connected to mainstream schooling. As a result, these young men construct alternative visions for themselves based on cultural images of successful Black men. In a culture that readily takes up the "mythical narrative" of Black masculinity (James, 2005, p. 98), which represents Black boys as natural athletes rather than capable students, NCAA athletic scholarships can seem like the best opportunity for racialized, working-class youth to exercise agency in their present and future school lives.

However, while essentially confirming the narrative of sport as the most likely gateway to prosperity for young, working-class Black men, James's respondents also described difficulties in accessing the structures needed to achieve athletic success, such as winning teams and influential coaches, and so devised strategies to improve their odds of attracting basketball scholarship opportunities, some of which compromised their ability to perform well scholastically. For example, as exposure and visibility to U.S. scouts was seen as the best method for attracting scholarships, the student-athletes reported transferring high schools several times in the hopes of finding a team and/or coach that would bring U.S. scouts and coaches to them (p. 89). According to research, the high mobility of these student-athletes increases their likelihood to feel disenfranchised at school, obtain lower grades, or even drop out (Rumberger & Larson, 1998). These student-athletes also tried to attract U.S. interest by attending training camps, sending out profile sheets, and networking with the coaches of other teams to build their reputations. However, they noted that the elite camps they desired to attend were both geographically and financially unreachable for them, and that the number of other high school basketball prospects in Canada and the U.S. would most likely limit the effectiveness of their written overtures (James, 2005, p. 93).

In Bourdieusian terms, the analysis summarized here shows that the *field* in which James's respondents live and act is structured, in part, by discourses that position high school-aged Black boys/men primarily as athletes. Athletic ability is therefore seen as the most salient form of cultural capital that young Black men can use to achieve future success. Given the perceived constraints to using this capital in Canada and the social construction of non-White, non-middle-class people as less than fully Canadian (James, 2005), leaving Canada for NCAA scholarships comes to be seen as the most relevant avenue for advancement, both athletically and academically. The analysis also shows how other forms of capital, aside from athleticism, are also required to access the brightly imagined future.

Contrast this narrative of naturalized marginalization with the following reading of the scholarship aspirations of White, middle-class athletes. In 2004–2005, I interviewed 12 former NCAA track-and-field athletes for a broader study of Canadian athletes in the

NCAA. As a former scholarship athlete and national-level track competitor, I was familiar with many Canadians who pursued an NCAA career in the sport.[4] Through my connections with athletes, coaches, and officials, I was able to contact other former NCAA student-athletes and ask them to talk about their scholarship journey. All interviews were conducted in person or over the telephone within one year of the athletes' graduation from university. Topics discussed during the interviews that are relevant to this analysis included the athletes' entrance into elite junior competition, the experience of track clubs and training during high school, beliefs about high school sport and academics, and their thoughts on NCAA scholarships as they moved through junior competition to high school graduation. I interviewed eight women and four men for this project, only two of whom identified as non-White (one person described himself as "Indo-Canadian" and one woman identified as "Black"). Most of the student-athletes competed in running events (11), while one was a field event competitor. All of the interviewees had university-educated parents, and all of them reported being able to afford a university education in Canada.

Due to their relative privilege, the narrative of sport as a vehicle for upward social mobility seemed inappropriate for these student-athletes. Nevertheless, these former student-athletes were as committed to obtaining an NCAA scholarship as those interviewed by James. In fact, athletic scholarships were routinely constructed as the *only* post-secondary option considered by the student-athletes I interviewed. As L.P. recalled,

> It wasn't even a question whether I was going to go to the States or not on a scholarship.... [I]f you're a [club] runner and you're good, you go to the States on a full scholarship. That's it. I mean that was it.

Another respondent told me, "You know, I just had it in my head for so long that that was my goal—you know, to get a scholarship at an American university—I didn't really consider not going"

(P.B.). Most participants I spoke with could not even recall making the decision to seek a scholarship; the idea of receiving an athletic scholarship to a U.S. university was so seamlessly integrated into junior track culture that it presented itself as a natural part of the athletic experience. More than simply desirable, these awards appeared guaranteed or, in J.G.'s words, "It's almost like you cross the finish line and they go, 'Here's your scholarship.'"

Obviously, given the high stakes and low odds that structure NCAA scholarship opportunities, scholarships are not distributed so easily to Canadian runners. Therefore, two important questions can be asked here: How did these athletes come to see athletic scholarships as inevitable? Why was the NCAA scholarship central to athletes who could afford a university education almost anywhere? In answering these questions, I refer back to the three concepts that comprise Bourdieu's theory of social distinction (field, habitus, and capital) to discuss how the privileges of class and race within the field of elite junior athletics in Canada inform the scholarship aspirations of Canadian student-athletes. I then compare this reading of scholarship aspirations to that presented by James (2005) to illustrate how their shared objective—obtaining an athletic scholarship—serves their different priorities and interests, and reinforces existing social hierarchies in Canadian society.

A central point of comparison concerns the sporting context described by James's respondents and the student-athletes with whom I spoke for this project. While the student-athletes in James's study described their difficulties in finding teams or coaches that would attract positive attention from U.S. scouts, the same was not true for the athletes in my study. A major reason for this seems to relate to the predominance of the club system of track-and-field athlete development. In Canada, high school track teams are generally not the places where future Canadian scholarship runners develop. Instead, high school coaches, teachers, and peers who are already members of club teams often direct talented athletes to track clubs, where professional coaches and better training facilities are available, and where high-level athletes from different high schools train and compete together. While not all club athletes will seek or obtain an NCAA scholarship, all of the former NCAA student-athletes I interviewed came out of the Canadian club system.

Directing young athletes to the club system is not simply an organizational convenience, although it does help to identify and develop potential elite track and field athletes. It also allows the student-athletes to begin to see and understand themselves as distinctively athletic compared to high schoolers who only compete on high school track teams.

> When we had to run in gym class, I was just better at it than everyone, so I've always been known for that. And in the club, here were a bunch of other girls that were like that too, all running together. (E.M.)

Track clubs foster the notion that members consist of the cream of the high school crop; those who compete only on high school teams are understood to be less elite. L.P. noted that her club was "where the fast girls were.... You don't train with slower people if you want to run fast." According to these student-athletes, effective athletic development and success existed apart from the high school system, creating a hierarchy of athleticism with club athletes at the apex and "regular" high school competitors beneath.

This hierarchy is elaborated through consistent exposure to U.S. competitions, which few high school teams can pursue. The popularity of high school sport in the U.S. is such that track-and-field meets are far more frequent, and attended in higher numbers, than in Canada. Canadian junior track clubs access this high-calibre competition early and often, bringing their best student-athletes to the more frequent and better-attended track meets south of the border. For the student-athletes, the U.S. exposure helped to normalize the U.S. option:

> Mostly the running that I was doing was with the [club] track team and we were pretty good about travelling, especially to the U.S. for different competitions, so I had actually experienced running in the United States at a bunch of the U.S. junior meets. If they [the club coaches] hadn't have done that, I probably would never have gotten a scholarship. (Y.T.)

> In high school it was just about, like, we'd go to these big meets [in the U.S.] and I just felt ... I just thought that's where the big meets were. That's just where you went, you know? (M.R.)

But the U.S. competitions were not always the first, or only, exposure the respondents in this project had to the NCAA. Several student-athletes had parents who were National team athletes, or former scholarship holders themselves, as well as other personal connections to the NCAA:

> Well, my best friend at the time went to [State U] and, of course, BK [a well-known Canadian runner] went to [State U] and these were the people I really admired and they ran the same kind of events I did, so that kind of influenced me wanting to go there. (L.P.)

> I had friends who were already attending [other Midwest universities] and I got responses from both of those schools because I had contacts there. (T.V.)

Recruiters and coaches underscored such Canadian connections in their pitches to high school recruits, explicitly connecting the highly competitive and prestigious NCAA to Canadian high schoolers:

> He talked up, you know, stories of the Canadian runners

that had been there and the successes they had, and basically told me that "If you come here, you're going to be just like them. They were just like you coming out of high school, you're going to do the same thing." (L.P.)

Taken together, the Canadian track club system and the social and athletic histories of the athletes I interviewed helped to naturalize their NCAA scholarship expectations. My respondents described being filtered into an enhanced training environment, exposed to higher calibre competition in the U.S., and encouraged to think of themselves as the next generation of NCAA scholarship recipients. Unlike the student-athletes interviewed by James, the athletes in this study also clearly benefited from a development system and a social network geared toward their success. In Bourdieusian terms, we can say that this field of elite junior athletics, centred in private track clubs, helps to create the conditions wherein Canadian high school student-athletes can imagine themselves, and position themselves, primarily as future NCAA scholarship athletes.

While clearly talented and committed student-athletes, these narratives of naturalized privilege described above depend on more than athletic talent and hard work to materialize. When a former scholarship athlete in my study, J.G., said "It's almost like you cross the finish line and they go, 'Here's your scholarship,'" he was expressing a confidence not only in his athletic ability, but also in his position in the cultural landscape of Canada. This confidence is an artifact of his privilege as a member of Canada's mainstream culture, a culture that takes Whiteness as the norm toward which diverse "Others" are encouraged to assimilate. It also comes from the financial security that ensured J.G. and the other interviewees would be able to attend university regardless of their scholarship status. Being within the mainstream means that J.G. and the other former student-athletes I interviewed could see their own privilege as natural, since their values and interests are constructed as normal in Canadian society.

In turn, understanding one's claim to an athletic scholarship as "natural" is an expression of the privilege of class respectability, which marks some as members of the dominant culture just as those who rely on scholarships to get a university education and to move into the mainstream from a racially or economically marginal positions are marked as Others. In fact, not needing the scholarship to go to university was *part of the appeal* for White, middle-class athletes. Free from cultural or financial constraints to their university admission, the respondents discussed NCAA scholarships as opportunities for personal growth, adventure, and elitism through NCAA competition. For example, when asked about what they wanted from an athletic scholarship to the NCAA, since studying and competing at a university in Canada was within their means, the respondents described their thrill at being contacted and recruited by university coaches from faraway places or prestigious institutions, going on expenses-paid trips to visit a university, touring the impressive athletic facilities and campuses, competing in hugely popular events that might even be televised, and moving to another country (sometimes thousands of miles away). E.M. put it this way:

> I was going for kind of an adventure and so I wanted to be somewhere where I would feel like that's the experience I wanted. One of the things I was looking for was a whole university experience that I was going to enjoy. It wasn't so much about ... you know, I wanted to run fast, I wanted to be competitive, I wanted to be in a good program, but I wanted to experience something different too.

E.M. captures the idea that for student-athletes whose futures and positions within the dominant culture are more secure, NCAA scholarships become meaningful as adventures and opportunities for personal growth. This is certainly an important aspect to the university experience, but it becomes salient only for student-athletes for whom the more instrumental goals of attending an

NCAA university are fulfilled—student-athletes predominantly drawn from middle- or upper-class communities.

In addition to adventure and personal growth, NCAA scholarships also represented elitism and exclusivity to the student-athletes I interviewed. The promise of elite status is frequently used to appeal to recruits during campus visits. Y.T. describes his impressions of attending a high-profile track meet during his recruiting trip to [Home U]:

> Yeah, at the home meet, the thing that differentiates athletes at [Home U] is the fact that the infield is reserved for the, like, Nike professional athletes running in the meet and [Home U] athletes. No one else is allowed in there. So you're in this mini-microcosm of all these professional athletes like Gail Devers, all these people you see on TV all the time, and then the [Home U] hosts it, so we get to hang out in the middle.

In this case, to "hang out in the middle" meant to be associated with famous professional athletes, and to access a space restricted to others. Such spaces are common on NCAA campuses and are not limited to special events. The former NCAA athletes in my study described varsity-only spaces for working out, studying, and living. Having access to exclusive spaces appealed to my interviewees, and enhanced the sense that attending an NCAA university would mark them as members of an elite class. This principle held for the non-athletic reputation of the university as well.

The student-athletes I spoke with sought the symbolic capital of a university of renown:

> [Elite U] is fairly well known, at least in the United States and in Canada. If you have heard of [Elite U], you don't think it is a public school. People have a tendency to think it's a private school or an Ivy League school. So the name, although superficial, is part of the reason I went there. (K.G.)

> It's not like you're just going to some little community college in the middle of nowhere. It [a degree from this school] would be recognized. (E.M.)

> [Renown U] is, you know, "The Ivy League of the South," it's a very good academic university. (T.V.)

Given that all of the respondents had economic and social capital necessary to easily enrol in a Canadian university, the scholarship opportunity was useful for reasons other than accessing a higher education. Of course, this is not to say that the academic reputation of a university should not be used as a criterion for post-secondary-bound athletes. But by seeking U.S. universities with particular reputations, facilities, and privileges for athletes, these student-athletes were able to establish and confirm an elite social status through the athletic scholarship opportunity.

Considering Race, Class, and Privilege

Considering the scholarship narratives discussed above, some observations regarding racial and class privilege can be made. Importantly, for people firmly positioned in the mainstream of Canadian society, the scholarship reflected and secured their privilege. For those outside of the cultural and economic centre, the NCAA scholarship narrative reflects this marginal social position, and helps to reconstruct non-White students as Others. As James (2005) explains:

> This subculture [of high school sport] ... conveys a cultural image of Black people as good athletes (and tall Black males as basketball players), and more generally as "Other" Canadians—people who are "outsiders." The resulting "outer-national political identification" (Walcott, 1997) of Blacks helps to socialize them into thinking that their

means of attaining their goals exists elsewhere. In this case, their aspirations are directed toward winning U.S. athletic scholarships and moving to the United States. (p. 102)

Here, James summarizes the role that race plays in defining the conditions by which non-White student-athletes expect to find or receive respect or acknowledgement in Canada. Because of the readiness with which they are viewed as athletes, NCAA scholarships (and sport more generally) are meaningful for Black student-athletes in ways that differ from the former student-athletes in my study. However, this difference in meaning is not reducible to an analysis of race alone. An important factor in the scholarship narratives of the White, middle-class student-athletes is that they were already privileged in many ways *before* they obtained an athletic scholarship.

In addition to the talent and hard work of the student-athletes (i.e., their *athletic capital*), their middle-class backgrounds not only decreased the economic barriers to joining private track clubs and travelling often to U.S. meets, but it also provided social connections to other people who have or have had similar opportunities. Thus, these former student-athletes also had personal knowledge of and connections to high-level coaches and other athletes who had gone before them into the NCAA. These former student-athletes were also often inheriting an expectation of university attendance, wherein concerns over student loans, minimum averages, and tuition fees were not seen as obstacles. Here, we can see class and race combine to create different meaning systems based around athletic scholarships to the NCAA. While they shared a goal of NCAA scholarship success, those athletes with more money and connections were assisted in pursuing them—materially and socially—by their class standing.

In addition, the recognition, reward, and validation available through athletic scholarships took on different dimensions for the Black, working-class basketball players versus the predominantly White, middle-class runners. Whereas the relatively privileged track-and-field athletes sought scholarships to access adventure and elitism, the less privileged basketball players were attracted to NCAA scholarships primarily as a means to "gain respect, prestige, and acknowledgement," and to understand themselves as valuable individuals in Canadian society (James, 2005). The White, middle-class student-athletes in this study did not see their U.S. scholarship hopes as "hope" at all, but as a normal and natural progression in their scholastic and athletic careers—and therefore unconnected to notions of race, class, or gender that differently frame the experiences of Canadians. Their social privileges allowed and enabled the student-athletes I interviewed to understand scholarships as a natural a part of their future, rather than a result of social structures that enhanced their opportunities. For student-athletes with the privileges afforded by class and Whiteness, then, athletic scholarships helped to *secure* their social status and privilege, naturalized through a legacy of middle-class Whiteness and reinforced in the field of elite junior track and field in Canada. The aspirational nature of athletic scholarships reveals itself only for those student-athletes in positions of relative marginality, such as the young Black athletes with working-class backgrounds interviewed by James (2003, 2005). Both the privileges of the White middle class and the marginality of the non-White working class are secured through NCAA scholarship experiences. That is, athletic scholarships operate as symbols of *distinction* (Bourdieu, 1984).

Final Thoughts

In describing the ways in which athletic scholarships articulate the classed and racialized positions of student-athletes, this study supports the notion that sport often takes up, mobilizes, and reinforces social hierarchies of class and race. The popular NCAA scholarship narrative tends both to overemphasize individuals' capacity to navigate educational and social structures, and to obscure the ways in which the stratification of society defines these narratives. According to Bourdieu, this conflation of the personal and the social is central to the process of distinction, which operates through institutions such as schools and sport to "grade, label, track, and credential each of us with the force of universal authority which recognizes socially structured abilities and dispositions as personally achieved knowledge and abilities" (Stempel, 2005, pp. 412–413).

This has implications for both Black, working-class student-athletes and White, middle-class student-athletes, all of whom participate in and take up circulating discourses of class and race "as personally achieved knowledge and abilities" to construct their scholarship narratives. In order to intervene in the narrative of athletic scholarships that merely reflects the unequal social positions of student-athletes in Canadian society, both schools and sport organizations must do more to reveal the hidden machinations of class and race that differently structure the possibilities available through sport. If they are to participate in creating a more equal society, both school and school sport must also do more to expand the athletic and academic repertoires of those students marginalized by class and race, so that a more diverse range of opportunities can be envisioned by the students whose futures are the least secure.

Questions for Critical Thought

1. Given the ways that class and race shape the meanings given to sport experiences of Canadian youth (and their ideas about what is possible for them through sport), how do you think sport can contribute to racial/class equity in Canada?
2. How might an understanding of the influences of class and race inform sport policy in Canadian schools?
3. Stories of professional athletes who come from poor or working-class backgrounds are standard ways of reporting

and understanding the power of sport to positively influence lives. Given the argument presented here, should we interpret these stories differently? Why? Why not? What might a new interpretation look like?
4. This chapter is primarily concerned with class and race in youth sport. What do you think an analysis of the ways in which gender influences athletic scholarship aspirations would contribute to the issue?

Notes

1. National Collegiate Athletic Association, the governing body for interuniversity sport in the U.S.
2. I use "high school student-athlete" interchangeably with "high school athlete" and "junior athlete" to avoid tedious repetition in the text. These terms refer to experiences of respondents in high school sport. The unmodified term "student-athlete" refers to respondents' college- or university-level sporting experiences.
3. James reports findings from his inquiry into the socio-cultural world of student-athletes in James (2003) and James (2005), but my discussion here is drawn primarily from the latter, which is the more extensive treatment.
4. I spoke with a purposive sample: namely, student-athletes who went to a U.S. university on a full athletic scholarship. A limitation of this sampling method is that questions regarding why some club athletes do not choose to seek an athletic scholarship, or what happens to those athletes who seek a scholarship and do not receive an offer, cannot be addressed in this study. Future research with a broader range of scholarship-seeking Canadian student-athletes may contribute to answering these questions.

References

Adler, P. & Adler, P. (1991). *Backboards and blackboards: College athletes and role engulfment*. New York: Columbia University Press.

Bourdieu, P. (1984). *Distinction: A social critique of the judgment of taste*. Cambridge: Harvard University Press.

Brown, D. (2006). Pierre Bourdieu's "masculine domination" thesis and the gendered physical body in sport and physical culture. *Sociology of Sport Journal, 23*(2), 162–188.

Bryers, W. & Hammer, C. (1995). *Unsportsmanlike conduct: Exploiting College Athletes*. Ann Arbor: University of Michigan Press.

Coakley, J. & Donnelly, P. (2009). *Sports in society: Issues and controversies* (2nd ed.). Toronto: McGraw-Hill Ryerson.

Dolby, N. (2000). The shifting ground of race: The role of taste in youth's production of identities. *Race, Ethnicity, and Education, 3*(1), 7–23.

Dyck, N. (2010). Going south: Canadians' engagement with American athletic scholarships. *Anthropology in Action, 17*(1), 41–54.

Eitle, T.M. & Eitle, D.J. (2002). Race, cultural capital, and the educational effects of participation in sports. *Sociology of Education, 75*(2), 123–147.

Gans, H. (2005). *Race as class*. Contexts, 4(4), 17–21.

Ifedi, F. (2008). Sport participation in Canada. Ottawa: Statistics Canada. Retrieved from http://www.statcan.gc.ca/pub/81-595-m/81-595-m2008060-eng.pdf

James, C.E. (2003). Schooling, basketball, and U.S. scholarship aspirations of Canadian student-athletes. *Race, Ethnicity, and Education, 6*(2), 123–144.

James, C.E. (2005). *Race in play: Understanding the socio-cultural worlds of student athletes*. Toronto: Canadian Scholars' Press Inc.

Laberge, S. (1995). Toward an integration of gender into Bourdieu's concept of cultural capital. *Sociology of Sport Journal, 12*(2), 132–146.

Miller, P. & Kerr, G. (2002). The athletic, academic, and social experiences of intercollegiate student-athletes. *Journal of Sport Behavior, 25*(4), 346–268.

National Collegiate Athletic Association (NCAA). (2007). Estimated probability of competing in athletics beyond the high school interscholastic level. Retrieved from Academics+and+Athletes/Education+and+Research/Probability+of+Competing/Methodology+-+Prob+of+Competing

Roediger, D.R. (1999). *Wages of Whiteness: Race and the making of the American working class.* New York: Verso.

Rumberger R.W. & Larson, K.A. (1998) Student mobility and the increased risk of dropout. *American Journal of Education, 107,* 1–12.

Sperber, M. (1995). Affirmative action for athletes. *Education Digest, 61*(December), 57–59.

Sperber, M. (2000). *Beer and circus: How big-time college sports has crippled undergraduate education.* New York: Henry Holt.

Sack, A. & Staurowsky, E. (1998). *College athletes for hire: The evolution and legacy of the NCAA's amateur myth.* Westport, CT: Praeger.

Stempel, C. (2006). Adult participation sports as cultural capital: A test of Bourdieu's theory of the field of sports. *International Review for the Sociology of Sport, 40*(4), 411–432.

Taras, D. (2000). Swimming against the current: American mass entertainment and Canadian identity. In D. Thomas (Ed.), *Canada and the United States: Differences that count* (2nd ed., pp. 192–210). Peterborough: Broadview Press.

Tomlinson, A. (2004). Pierre Bourdieu and the sociology of sport. In R. Giulianotti (Ed.), *Sport and modern social theorists* (pp. 161–172). New York: Palgrave Macmillan.

Veenstra, G. (2007). Social space, social class, and Bourdieu: Health inequalities in British Columbia, Canada. *Health and Place, 13*(1), 14–31.

White, P. & McTeer, W.G. (1990). Sport as a component of cultural capital: Survey findings on the impact of participation in different types of sports on educational attainment in Ontario high schools. *Physical Education Review, 13,* 66–71.

White, P. & Wilson, B. (1999). Distinctions in the stands: An investigation of Bourdieu's "habitus," socioeconomic status, and sport spectatorship in Canada. *International Review for the Sociology of Sport,* 34(3), 245–264.

Wilson, T. (2002). The paradox of social class and sports involvement: The roles of cultural and economic capital. *International Review for the Sociology of Sport,* 37(1), 5–16.

CONTRIBUTORS

Simon Darnell completed a PhD at the University of Toronto and a SSHRC postdoctoral fellowship at Dalhousie University in Halifax, Nova Scotia. He is currently a lecturer in sport within the School of Applied Social Sciences at Durham University, UK. His research focuses on the social and political dimensions of mobilizing sport to meet international development goals. He is the author of *Sport for Development and Peace: A Critical Sociology* (2012), and his research has been published in the *Sociology of Sport Journal*, *Development in Practice*, and the *Journal of Global Citizenship and Equity Education*.

Russell Field is an assistant professor in the Faculty of Kinesiology and Recreation Management at the University of Manitoba, where he teaches courses on Canadian sport history, and sport and film. His doctoral dissertation, a historical examination of hockey spectators at Toronto's Maple Leaf Gardens and New York's Madison Square Garden in the 1930s, is the subject of a forthcoming monograph. His current research explores international sporting events as sites of protests and resistance.

Wendy Frisby is a professor in the School of Kinesiology and the former chair of Women's and Gender Studies at the University of British Columbia. She has written extensively on poverty, feminist participatory action research, and leisure services. Her most recent project is analyzing a newcomer health and wellness project from the perspectives of recent immigrant women, local recreation staff, and various community partners. She is a past editor of the *Journal of Sport Management* and has received numerous awards for her scholarly contributions.

Xin Huang received her PhD in Women's and Gender Studies from the University of British Columbia. She is a visiting assistant professor at the University of Wisconsin in Milwaukee. Her areas of research include gender issues in contemporary China and Chinese women in a transnational context, the Maoist gender construction and its legacy, feminist theories of gender and sexuality, the representation of gender in oral narrative and visual forms, gender and popular culture, narrative studies, and issues related to conducting feminist research across cultural and linguistic boundaries.

Janelle Joseph currently holds a Banting Postdoctoral Fellowship hosted by the University of Ontario Institute of Technology. She completed a postdoctoral fellowship at the University of Otago in New Zealand/Aotearoa after earning a doctorate at the University of Toronto. Her research within physical cultural studies focuses on how members of diasporas use physical activity to express their cultures and maintain their heritage, social networks, and identities. She draws connections between sport or kinetics, aesthetics, and politics in her work published in *Ethnic and Racial Studies*, *Global Networks*, and the *Sociology of Sport Journal*.

Andreas Krebs received his doctorate in political science from the University of Ottawa, specializing in the production of colonial subjectivity in contemporary Canada. He is the editor of the political satire section at Rabble.ca and co-founder of Wildrun Productions, a web-based communications company focusing on silly entertainment and sneaky education. He lives in Toronto.

Lori A. Livingston completed a master's degree at Queen's University and a PhD at the University of Calgary, and is a full professor and the dean of the Faculty of Health and Behavioural Sciences at Lakehead University. A physical educator, biomechanist, and statistician by training, her research has spanned a broad range of topics, including clinical biomechanics, injury prevention, physical activity, coaching, and sports officiating. She has served as an assistant coach with the Canadian women's senior field lacrosse team, chair of the Women's Sector of the Canadian Lacrosse Association, and as an officer of the International Federation of Women's Lacrosse Associations.

Yuka Nakamura completed her PhD in the Faculty of Physical Education and Health at the University of Toronto and a postdoctoral Fellowship at the York Institute for Health Research. She is currently an assistant professor in the School of Kinesiology and Health Science at York University. Her area of research focuses on how unequal power relations, enacted through social categories like race, gender, and class, shape lives, identities, and opportunities to participate in sport and physical activity. In doing so, she hopes to identify strategies to resist social inequity.

Lucie Thibault is a professor of Sport Management at Brock University. She studies the Canadian sport system, government involvement in sport, sport policy, interorganizational relationships in public and nonprofit sport, strategy and organizational change; athlete involvement in the governance of sport organizations, and global issues in sport management.

Susan Tirone received her PhD from the University of Waterloo. She currently researches and teaches in the School of Health and

Human Performance at Dalhousie University. She is interested in leisure as it intersects with multiculturalism, youth, poverty, and people with disabilities.

John Valentine has taught at Grant MacEwan University in Edmonton since 1998, serving as the chair of the Physical Education program since 2002. He has earned degrees from McGill University, King's University College, the University of Alberta, and Carleton University. John enjoys teaching and researching in the areas of sociology of sport, the history of sport in Canada, and ethics of physical activity

Rinaldo Walcott is associate professor and chair of the Department of Humanities, Social Sciences, and Social Justice Education at the Ontario Institute for Studies in Education, University of Toronto. His research and teaching are in the area of Black diaspora cultural studies with an emphasis on queer sexualities, masculinity, cultural politics, and popular culture. A secondary research area is multicultural and transnational debates with an emphasis on nation, citizenship, and coloniality. As an interdisciplinary scholar, Rinaldo has published on music, literature, film, and theatre, among other topics. He is the author of *Black Like Who: Writing Black Canada* (1997; revised edition, 2003) and the co-editor of *Counselling Across and Beyond Cultures: Exploring the Work of Clemment Vontress in Clinical Practice* (2010).

Sandy Wells is a PhD student in the School of Kinesiology at the University of British Columbia. She uses sport to think about the role of the body in mediating the relationship between biology and society. Her work on sex testing and fairness in sport is forthcoming in the *Sociology of Sport Journal* and in an edited collection entitled *Sport, Games, and Play: Bodies of Practice, Communities of Desire*.

INDEX

A
Abdel-Shehid, G., 11–12, 19, 59–61, 63, 69, 75, 240, 242, 256, 260
Aboriginal athletes, 110–11, 115–16, 129
Aboriginal hockey players, 14, 107, 111–12, 117–18, 120, 125–6, 128–9
Aboriginal peoples, 83, 92, 108, 110, 116–17, 127–8, 130, 161
 in Canada, 3, 107–8, 116
 and colonialism, 84, 117
 segregation of, 111
 and sport, 110
acculturation, 34, 37–9, 49
Africa, 31, 82, 175, 187, 191, 194, 196–7
agency, 30, 126, 129, 239, 258–9
American culture, 21, 55, 73

anti-racism, 22, 202, 208
Atlantic Canada, 15, 167, 172, 178, 183

B
Bannerji, H., 2, 6–8, 19
baseball, xiii, 29, 35, 37–40, 48, 51–6, 61, 77, 114
basketball, 12, 35, 48, 55, 156, 173, 233, 255, 266–7, 273, 287
 and gender, 157, 230
 and identities, 10
 and performance, 255
Black athletes, 11–12, 16, 18, 20, 26, 59, 67, 86, 113, 130, 258
Black Atlantic, 238, 241, 257, 261–2
Black Canadians, xii, 5, 23, 51, 60, 74, 242–3, 248, 250, 258
Black diasporas, 238, 241–2, 253, 260

Black masculinities, 16, 19, 26, 75, 237, 243, 248, 250, 254, 258, 260–1
   and agency, 239, 245
   as natural, 242, 273
   and performance, 242
Black quarterbacks, 57, 69–71
Blackness, 13, 57, 59–61, 64–5, 69, 75, 86
bodies, xi, 1, 10, 82, 86, 126, 155, 157, 162, 166, 175, 250, 252, 286
Bourdieu, 228, 233, 267, 269, 284–5, 287–8
Brazil, 238, 245, 251, 253–4, 256, 258

C

Canada
   modern, 54, 148
   multicultural, xii, 20
   nineteenth-century, 130, 135
Canada Broadcasting Corporation (CBC), 86, 101, 134
Canadian cities, 29, 32, 49, 68, 212
Canadian culture, 1, 8, 59–60, 69, 75, 90, 209, 259, 273
Canadian football, 13, 57, 59, 61–3, 65, 68, 70, 72, 75–6, 79
Canadian Football League, 77–8
Canadian Multiculturalism Act, 20
capoeira, 18, 238, 240, 244–5, 251–3, 255–7, 260, 263
Caribbean, 31, 191, 194, 238, 242, 244, 246, 248, 258, 260
Carrington, B., 9–10, 20, 237, 241–2, 257, 259–60

China, ix, 15, 145–6, 150–1, 156, 158–9, 162, 218, 224, 227
   immigration from, 31, 140–1, 148, 150, 218
   physical activity in, 154
   women in, 154, 157
Chinatown, viii, 16, 213–25, 227, 229–33, 235
Chinese Canadians, 12, 142, 162
Chineseness, 157, 216–18, 220, 222–3, 235
citizenship, xi–xii, 1, 3, 25, 83, 147, 214, 221–2, 224, 228–32, 234
colonialism, vii, x, xii, 12, 14, 81, 83–5, 87–9, 91, 96, 98, 100, 117, 263
   and capitalism, 191
Commonwealth Games Canada, 15, 188, 207
cricket, xiii, 10, 82, 101, 114, 133, 238, 244–6, 258–60, 262–3
   in 19th century, 239
   in the Caribbean, 244, 246, 250
   in England, 81

D

diaspora, 16, 210, 233, 237, 240–1, 243, 258, 260–1
discrimination, 48, 51, 65–7, 74, 125, 128–9, 250, 254
   against immigrants, 148, 216–17, 220
   in Canada, 7, 65–6, 73
   and racism, 69
   in the United States, 68

dominance, 8, 61, 68, 75, 82, 188–9, 201, 203, 205, 210, 239

E

Edmonton, 19, 23, 59, 64, 67, 77–8, 130
education, ix, 22, 24–5, 35, 52, 79, 205, 212, 234–5, 262, 268, 287–8
    and Asians, 225
    and capital, 269–70
    and employment, 160
    and gender, 142, 148, 159
    and immigration, 141, 155
    and race, 269
    and social mobility, 108
ethnicity, 1, 49, 88, 114, 141, 173, 210, 243, 245, 269
    and culture, 60
    and diaspora, 240
    and privilege, 2
    and segregation, 61
    and sport, 33, 37

F

football, vii, xiii, 10, 13, 48–9, 57–9, 61, 63, 65–7, 69, 71, 73–5, 77, 81–2, 114
    professional, 61, 63, 67, 75, 77
French Canadians, 12, 31

G

gender, viii, 19, 22, 24, 26, 75, 78, 100–2, 139–40, 143, 157, 163, 239, 246–7, 258–60
    and intersections, 1, 8, 10, 12, 16, 49, 81, 99, 129, 141, 191, 241, 243, 257, 284
    and multiculturalism, 15, 139
    and physical activity, 144
    and race, 240
    and Whiteness, 188
Globe and Mail, 3, 25, 76, 79, 108, 113, 130–1, 133, 135
Government of Canada, iv, 45
Grey Cup, 67, 70–1, 77

H

habitus, 268, 276, 288
Henry, F., 5, 21, 58, 76, 109–10, 113, 127, 131–2, 135
high schools, 71, 85, 108, 228, 265, 268, 272–5, 278–9, 288
hockey, vii, xiii, 4, 12, 14, 19, 50, 81–91, 93–7, 99–105, 112–13, 116–17, 127–8, 130–1, 133–5
    in Canada, 14, 18, 98, 128
    and colonialism, 81, 96, 98
    and Don Cherry, 90
    and gender, 89
    and girls, 94
    and national belonging, 3
    and nationalism, 85
    and racism, 4, 14, 61
    as resistance, 126
    and stacking, 116
    and violence, 95, 117
hockey enforcers, 14, 107–8, 112, 116–28, 130
Hong Kong, 139, 141, 147, 149, 156, 163–4
Hylton, K., 1, 7, 10, 22, 184

I

Icelandic Canadians, 46, 52
immigrant communities, 29, 37–8, 49–50
immigrant experience, 25, 29
immigrant women, 142, 144, 148–54, 156, 159–60
immigration, viii, 30–1, 45, 54, 139, 141–9, 151, 153, 155, 157, 159, 161–3, 184, 238
inequalities, 2, 6, 9, 115, 190, 200, 207–8
international development, 187–8, 190–1, 203, 208–11
intersectional analyses, xi, 4, 10, 237–8, 240–1

J

Jackson, S., 6, 12, 22, 61, 71, 77, 118, 130, 243, 261
James, C., 265, 267, 272
Jews, 31–2, 40–1, 43, 55–6
Johnson, Ben, xi, 6, 22, 77, 233, 243, 261

K

Kidd, B., 44, 54–5, 103, 187, 211

L

lacrosse, 48, 92, 104, 110–11, 252
league, 119

M

Mainland China, 139, 141, 145, 148–9, 151–2, 154, 156
masculinity, 10, 83, 91, 95, 100, 144, 155, 159, 239, 247, 251
   and Aboriginal culture, 110
   and agression, 9
   and the body, 247
   dominant and subordinate, 245
   and hockey, 99
   and intersections, 14, 83, 88, 240
   and race, 89, 91
   and space, 96
   and violence, 98
   and Whiteness, 85, 239
media coverage, 12, 14, 20, 115, 127
Montreal, xii, 18, 31–2, 42, 59, 62, 85, 213
multiculturalism, xi, 15, 19–20, 22, 25, 75, 83, 134, 139, 143, 156, 161–2, 203, 209, 215
   as difference, 6
   and equity, 6
   as failure, xi
   and gender, 139
   as ideology, 7
   and immigration, 160
   vs. interculturalism, 159
   and nation, 258
   and nationalism, 83, 85
   as policy, 269
   and racism, 259
   and sport, 11, 155
   vs. Whiteness, 5

N

nation, x–xii, 3, 6, 8, 16, 18–19, 81–2, 86–7, 202–3, 212–13, 219–22, 229, 231–3, 257, 259

National Basketball Association (NBA), 23, 267
nationalism, 10, 14, 19, 81, 83, 85, 241, 243
NCAA scholarships, viii, 269, 275–7, 280–4
National Hockey League (NHL), 3, 14, 88, 90, 95, 107, 112–13, 117–21, 123–9, 131, 133, 135
and francophones, 89–90
history of, 14, 117
and violence, 89
NSOs (national sport organizations), 168–9, 175, 178–80, 182–3

O
Ottawa, 62, 67–8

P
Paraschak, V., 12, 24, 82, 101, 104, 110, 134, 183
performances of race, 257–8, 260
physical education, 18, 25, 55, 164, 194, 209, 225, 229, 231, 234–5
Pitter, R., 19, 55, 165, 167, 170, 177, 183
politics, cultural, 23, 25, 53, 103–4, 130–1, 234, 261
privilege, 98, 189, 193, 197, 201–2, 204–9, 224, 272, 279, 282, 284
and class, 280
and inequality, 2
and race, 1
and scholarships, 282
trading on, 205
and volunteer interns, 197–8, 200
and Whiteness, 7–8, 11, 17, 89, 188–9, 201, 206, 271, 284

R
race
intersections of, 13, 188, 200
intractability of, 3, 5, 7, 9, 11, 13, 15, 17, 19, 21, 23, 25
social construction of, 190, 239
racial hierarchies, 2, 11, 16, 75, 86, 89, 109, 189–90, 199–200, 203, 207–8, 221
racial privilege, 4, 15, 188, 202
racism
new, 109–11, 113, 115, 117, 119, 121, 123, 125, 127–31, 133, 135
overt, 40, 65
positive, 206–7
Razack, S., 3, 7–9, 22, 24–6, 72, 78, 95–6, 98, 104, 190–2, 196, 203, 208, 210–11, 235
Robidoux, M., 92, 96, 98, 104, 110, 117, 126, 134

S
Sport for Development and Peace (SDP), 15–16, 187–9, 191–3, 196, 199–200, 202, 204, 206–9
sexuality, 1, 8, 22, 83, 93, 188, 191, 209, 212
space, 16, 19, 24, 49, 81, 83, 96–8, 100, 192, 196–7, 207–9, 211, 217, 219, 281

Sport Canada, 169, 171, 176
Sports Illustrated, 69, 77, 79, 113, 132–3, 135
stacking, vii, 14, 107, 114, 116, 125, 128–9, 131–3
Statistics Canada, 56, 84, 105, 141–2, 163–4, 183, 287
stereotypes, 88, 90, 109, 111, 125–7, 129, 155, 157, 201–2, 216, 220, 225–8, 256, 259
student-athletes, 267–8, 270, 272–86
subject positions, 81–2, 188, 195, 205–6, 208, 238

T

Tator, C., 21, 58, 76, 109–10, 113, 127, 131–2, 135
Thobani, S., 1, 3, 7–8, 22, 25–6, 83, 105, 189, 203, 210–12, 259, 263
Toronto, 18, 31–2, 40–1, 44, 97, 141, 187, 213–14, 216, 219–21, 223, 249, 252–3, 256
Toronto Star, 23, 40, 249, 260, 262

U

United States, 2, 13, 25, 42, 57–65, 71–2, 74–5, 78, 86, 184, 238, 241–2, 245, 255, 278

V

Vancouver, 18, 32, 39, 141, 145, 161, 213, 217, 219
Vancouver's Chinatown, 52, 217–19

violence, xi, 9, 11, 83, 88–90, 93–6, 98, 100, 104, 108–10, 133, 250
volleyball, 225, 227–8, 234

W

Walcott, 5–6, 19, 26, 58–9, 69, 78–9, 282
Whiteness, xi, xiii, 4–5, 7–8, 11, 16–17, 21–3, 83, 85, 188–95, 198–211, 239, 269–71, 279
and class, 284
construction of, 189, 191
management of, 194, 202, 205
normativity of, 13, 60–1, 203
Whitestream, 14, 83, 86, 88, 90, 93, 98
wicked problems, 15, 167, 171–3, 181–2, 184
Wilson, B., 12, 18, 23, 26, 60, 79, 235, 270, 288
Winnipeg, 31–2, 45, 47–8, 62, 68, 98, 224

Y

Young Men's Christian Association (YMCA), 35–6, 43, 227